The Ultimate Writer's Workbook For Books And Scripts

By Serita Deborah Stevens

Motivational Press®
LEADERS IN GLOBAL PUBLISHING

Published by Motivational Press, Inc.
2360 Corporate Circle
Suite 400
Henderson, NV 89074
www.MotivationalPress.com

Manufactured in the United States of America.

ISBN: 978-1-62865-100-3

Contents

FORWARD.....v
THE START.....1
CHARACTERS COME ALIVE.....22
POINTING THE WAY—THE PLOT.....47
BEGIN NOT AT THE BEGINNING.....68
SEEING THE WORLD THROUGH ROSE'S GLASSES.....78
TALK IS CHEAP: DIALOGUE.....88
RESEARCHING THE HISTORICAL, SCIENCE FICTION OR FANTASY.....99
FLASHBACKS, FORESHADOWING, AND TRANSITIONS.....108
THOSE TORRID SCENES: SEX AND VIOLENCE.....114
METAPHORICALLY SPEAKING.....119
MAINSTREAM AND GENRE WRITING.....125
KILLER ENDINGS.....162
FINISHING TOUCHES: THE TITLE.....164
POLISHING THE ROUGH STONE: REWRITING.....166
PROCRASTINATION.....174
QUERIES AND SYNOPSIS: YOUR SELLING TOOLS.....176
THE NON FICTION BOOK PROPOSAL.....187
AGENTS: KEY TO SUCCESS.....188
CONTRACTS: THE FINAL STEPS.....195
PROFESSIONAL SURVIVAL.....204
DEALING WITH WRITER'S BLOCK.....208
THE JOYS OF PUBLICITY: OR JIMMY FALLON HERE I COME.....214
DEALING WITH REJECTION.....221
SELF–PUBLISHING.....227
WRITING FOR THE YOUNG ADULT MARKET.....231
WRITING SHORT STORIES.....236
NOVELIZATIONS, SCREENPLAYS, AND BEYOND.....239
WHAT MAKES A WRITER?.....258
NON–FICTION, MEMOIRS AND BLOGS.....259
REFERENCES.....308
SELF-PUBLISHING RESOURCES.....310
APPENDIX.....312
TRAITS TO PICK.....312

FORWARD

LEARNING is a repetitive process. We repeat what we are doing until it goes from a strained, awkward action to a smooth flowing one. Seldom does someone get an action right the very first time. Don't despair.

For that reason, I have also repeatedly stressed issues of importance. The more you hear something, the more you do it, the more natural it will become.

Imagination, like our other muscles, must be exercised, stretched, and stimulated in all possible ways. For that reason, many of the exercises in different chapters will seem to be the same. The words may be the same, but what they produce will be different, since each time you do that exercise you'll be stretching your mind muscle to the limit. Yes, it might take you some moments to limber up, but once you've started, there will (I hope) be no stopping you.

If you go over this book again next year, you'll come up with different answers than the first time. This workbook is meant to be used over and over again.

Many of my students have succeeded in selling their books based on reading and doing what this workbook suggests. You can too, if you work at it.

I love to hear from readers of this workbook and readers of my books. If you have comments or questions, please contact me through my website at:

www. seritastevens.com
sstevenstarlow@gmail.com

PRESS ON!Nothing in the world can take the place of persistence. Talent will not; nothing is more common than unsuccessful men and women with talent. Genius will not: unrewarded genius is almost a proverb. Education alone will not: the world is full of educated derelicts.

PERSISTENCE AND DETERMINATION ALONE ARE OMNIPOTENT. (unknown)

THE START

"We want to heighten our awareness of life. We write to taste life twice in the moment and in the retrospective. We want to transcend our life, to move beyond it, to teach ourselves to speak to others, to record journeys into the constricted and the lonely. When I don't write, I feel my world shrinking. I feel I lose my fire and my color."

Anais Nin

This book is a result of over thirty–five years of teaching writing at major universities in Chicago and Los Angeles. It came about because there was so much information to get across in my classes that I often found myself extending the class, and extending and extending. There was so much to get across that the only way we could work on our manuscripts and get the basics across was for me to have outlines for the exercises written up prior to class.

Then several of my students wanted to buy copies of the notes I had used for lecture and finally, these notes were formed into this. It would be helpful if you thought of this not as a book, but as a class. That means, in the class you must do your homework and exercises assigned. I suggest you keep a notebook at your side while reading this text. I'd be happy to take a look at work done by those of you in this "class" and give you suggestions for improvement.

Like Anais Nin, I, too, lose my fire and my color when I don't write, and so I dedicate myself to my writing —doing it whenever and wherever I can, even sometimes to the exclusion of other parts of my life.

Writing is a lonely and sometimes sad profession, but if it's in your blood, you can't give up—even if you want to. I know. Many times when things weren't going well for me, and I admit that even now— with all my books out—things don't always go the way I want. Sometimes it's a matter of my not reading the market right. Other times, it's a matter of learning to reshift my gears and realizing that success doesn't always come on the first try. (One book was submitted twenty–two times to the same publisher until the editor thought the market was right.)

Writing is 98% perspiration and discipline, sometimes with only 2% talent. When I was studying in London, England, in the Antioch program, there were many very talented writers with me. Most of them were what I call "belly button" writers. That is, they only wrote what they felt in their gut, when the muse called to them.

Since they spent most of their time pubbing (going to the bars), they spent very little time writing, and the muse ignored them.

The muse, however, is like a pet, which needs to be tamed. If you don't tame it, it runs wild and you can't catch it. If you do tame it, it will purr in your lap as your fingers fly over the keyboard. Because I learned how to tame my muse, I am probably the only graduate of my class of twenty who is still writing and making a decent living at it.

One way to tame the muse is to have a daily schedule set up for writing—even if it's only fifteen minutes a day. Get used to writing—anything, even grocery lists, journals, or letters to friends—at that time of day.

Writing by free association will sometimes stimulate and give you some good ideas. Take a word, such as babies, and then draw arrows to words, which seem to connect to that word.

For example:

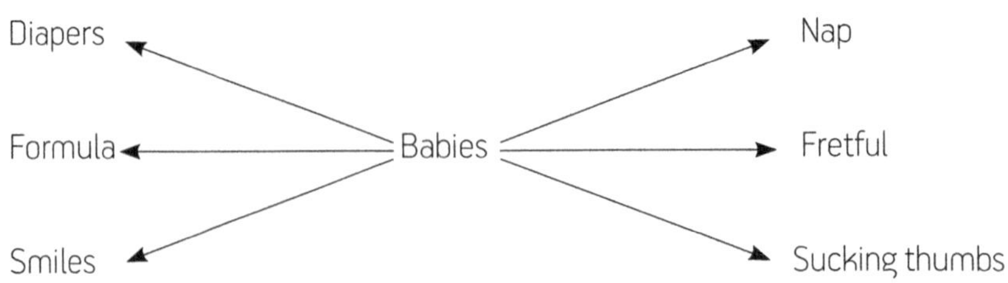

Pretty soon, the muse will come rubbing your ankle when you call her, and you'll be able to really write.

Another muse–tamer is to have a personal deadline of one to ten pages a day. (I, myself, try to get in thirty to forty pages a day, but I write full–time.) Even if what you're writing seems like garbage, write it anyway.

You can always change your writing, but you can't rewrite something you haven't written. Despite what you hear about people selling their first draft, rewriting is a must—even if it's only proofreading what comes out of the typewriter or computer—and making sure it says what you want it to say.

I, myself, fell into the category of thinking the computer was infallible and that once I put it through my spell checker, grammar checker, etc. , everything would be fine and I could ship it off.

Well, I soon learned that the computer made mistakes just like I did. You must recheck EVERYTHING that comes out of your printer! It's just as important to have friends with knowledge of the genre you're writing in to read over your material. Often others proofreading can catch things that you and your machine might not have. Joining a writing group helps with this a lot.

Even reading out loud–a good way to catch mistakes–isn't infallible. We often read what we think we wrote and not what's on the page.

WHAT CONSTITUTES WRITING POPULAR FICTION

Before you decide to start writing, you need to ask yourself what it is that you most like to read? Don't worry about what's being bought today. What do you read? Sweet romances, westerns, historical, regencies, fantasy, sci–fi, sexy romances, mystery, or mainstream? Whatever YOU like to read is what you should be writing–at least for your first attempt.

Too many people think that because one area—such as romances—might be selling well, they should write that and make lots of money. The fact is if you don't enjoy reading romances, you won't be able to write one effectively because you won't be able to empathize with the characters. You won't have the necessary beats in your story. And if you are looking down your nose upon the people who read the type of book you are trying to write, you'll soon be found out.

This goes for any category—and the fact is that the romance boom is over. Only those who really care about romances, and only those who are willing to expand their scope to include the growing area of multi–genre romances, will be able to succeed.

Now, what constitutes popular fiction?

By definition, it's what is popular or what the masses are reading. That's how we get the term "mass market paperback."

There is no shame in being published in paper—even in mass–market paper. In fact, with the costs of books today, very few novels get into hardback. Think for yourself. When was the last time you paid twenty–five dollars for a hardcover novel?

It may be hard to believe, but Dickens, Thackery, Austin, the Brontes—all of whose works we now revere as classics—were once considered "popular pulp." "They wrote for the people, using the emotions of the people, and gave the people what they wanted to read. Their works were published in serials–or penny pulps–or in newspapers of the day.

This isn't to say that everything being published today will be a classic in the next century, but good writing will last—whether you're in paper or in hardback.

Popular fiction covers many areas. In romance alone there are at least six categories.

The sweet romance was started by Mills and Boon in London and then came over here as Harlequin (just recently bought by Rupert Murdoch). The sweet romance still flourishes along with its sister, the inspirational romance done by Christian publishers.

The short, sexy book, started by Vivian Stephens at Dell, were called the

Candlelight Ecstasy books. She also heralded the first integrated romances. Dell, however, has since been sold to Bantam (part of Random House) and does not have a romance line anymore, just books that are romantic, but stand alone.)

Harlequin expanded their lines to Silhouette Desire, Temptation (Harlequin), and Loveswept.

The larger books that include sex are Harlequin Superromance, Silhouette Intimate Moments, Supreme, and Harlequin American.

In the shorter books mentioned above, the whole story centers on the lovers and their problems with the romance. There is very little subplot. The longer books work in more externals.

The romantic suspense, another longer book, combines elements of romance and mystery. Usually it has about 50–50, in a contemporary setting. Harlequin Intrigue is one of the lines, but the other larger publishers also are willing to look at suspenseful romances. (My western romantic suspense was published by Leisure–a now defunct house.) The Harlequin Intrigue asks for what amounts to a straight mystery with only 25% romance, if that. Sex is not necessary unless it fits in with the story.

The Gothic, which was started by Horace Walpoles' ***CASTLE ONTARTO*** and Ann Radcliffe's ***THE ITALIAN, OR THE CONFESSIONAL OF THE BLACK PENITENTS*** and ***MYSTERIES OF UDOLPHO***, has come a along way. The setting remains isolated and moody, the heroine continues to be very much alone, and in a dangerous situation. Often she must choose between two men—one who is the villain and one who is the hero. These were down for a while and are now on an upswing again—witness my own two gothics from Zebra (***THE SHRIEKING SHADOWS OF PENPORTH ISLAND*** and ***BLOODSTONE INHERITANCE***). NAL started a gothic line, but like the Zebra gothics, these were longer (100,000 words) and sexy. Because mood is all–important here, first person is often used the best.

Romantic suspense has taken over where the Gothics left off.

Historicals are divided into three categories. The "bodice rippers" made

Rosemary Rogers famous are in the first group, but these are no longer selling. (They were called that because the heroine was raped by the hero and then preceded to fall in love with him! At some point in the rape her bodice was ripped open. Hence the name. Most of the story was a series of costumed erotica. That's not to say they weren't good tales, but the fact of the rape has turned many people against them.)

Historical romance, like my book, ***TAME THE WILD HEART,*** is the second type of historical. In this, a particular time period is used along with real events from the past and real people. All of this is background for the romance between your hero and heroine who might be the only fictional people in the book.

Historical mainstream takes a period of history—as I am doing now for a book—***MARK OF THE DRAGON***–and develops the characters that lived in that time. It might have a romance in it, but neither that nor a happy ending is a necessary requirement. The ending must, of course, be satisfactory with no loose ends. Fictional characters are all right for your protagonists and antagonists, but you'll want to make references to the real events often—without your research showing.

Both of these latter books are built around major events in history and show how they affect the lives of ordinary people of that period. They are not merely set in a background of the past. In researching the past (or things that I am not familiar with, such as certain scientific discoveries), I often go to the children's section of the library since those books will be written for the novice to understand. Once you glean the terminology and necessary knowledge from them, you can progress to the intermediate book level and beyond.

The Regency novel, popularized by Georgette Heyer, is also a historical romance and takes place in England and France during the time of 1780–1815, when George 4th was Regent of England because his father, George 3rd, was ill. Often these are comedy of manners books similar to Jane Austen's books. However, several other publishers have now expanded the category to make sexier regencies.

There is actually a fourth category in the historical, and that is the straight historical or the fictionalized biography. Because access to actual dialogue, letters, and contemporary accounts are often limited, the author can only surmise, based on what she has learned about her character, what the hero or heroine would actually say. A good example of this is Norah Lofts, Victoria Holt, or Philippa Carr books on Queens of England and Europe.

Westerns are also historical novels since you must research the West before you can write about it. Many western writers today are combining other elements such as romance and mystery to make the genre more entertaining for everyone, as my ***DECEPTIVE DESIRES*** (now a script called Logan's Land.) Francine Rivers and Janet Dailey are writers known for their romantic westerns.

Science fiction is, in its own way, a historical since you must research not the past but the future and develop a whole new world, much as you must do when writing a historical. These, too, are being combined with other genres. A good example of this is the movie, ***STAR WARS***. An offshoot, but increasingly popular section here, is the fantasy. ***LORD OF THE RINGS*** by Tolkien is a superb example.

If you choose to do a historical, you had best be enchanted with that time period, because you'll be living with it for some time. If you're bored, then your reader will be too.

The last of the romance categories is the young adult—of which there are two types. The young adult problem novel is where the teen must come to terms with herself and deal with problems such as her parents' divorce, death, abortion, anorexia nervosa, or other modern problems as my novel, ***AGAINST HER WILL***.

The young adult romance is a sweet romance with a high school setting and only kisses.

To do either, you must know your high school kids well.

All of the major publishing houses have guidelines, which you can write for. Each has its own requirements. I won't call them formulas because most of the old formulas have gone. What you do need to know when reading the guidelines is how long do they want the book, the age of the hero/heroine, how sexy, and if they have a preference for location or time periods. Or if they tell you they've had too many of one time period. The Civil War and Revolutionary War are the most overused times, but a good writer can overcome that with great characters.

Many smaller publishers have also gotten on the romance bandwagon now, including omnificpublishing.com, which did the recent NY Times Bestsellers—Gabriel's Inferno series. For a nearly complete list of current publishers of romance and their guidelines, check out http://www. killerbookmarketing. com/passionate-pen-romance-publishers-list/.

Of course you can mix any of the categories with mainstream.

Mainstream is a word that often confuses people, and I confess the definition eludes me since it seems to change for everyone.

What mainstream means to me is a larger-than-life book, where you might have romance, but where you'll have several other subplots as well, all being tied into one major story line. The longer books come in two forms: the journey through time, of which Dickens' ***THE PICKWICK PAPERS*** is a prime example, since the character grows as he experiences his adventures, and the episodic, as ***TOM JONES*** or ***SMART WOMEN***, where the lives of several characters develop.

Robert Ludlum, who wrote spy novels, that were sometimes classed as mainstream. Perhaps that's because not only does the hero get to point X before the world is blown up and does the hero get the heroine, but other issues, as well. Danielle Steele is considered to be mainstream even though she writes romances, because her stories encompass a larger scope than just the two people. Sometimes her work is generational.

Whatever type of writing you do, you have to make the reader feel what your heroine/hero is feeling. You do this by using your senses.

EXERCISE:

TAKE AN EMOTION NOW: (hate, greed, envy, lust, love, frightened, crabby, defeated, startled, happy, jealousy, frustration, inadequate, puzzled, hurt, wistful, annoyed, embarrassed, tense, revolted, anxious—to name a few) AND WRITE FOR TEN MINUTES DESCRIBING YOUR CHARACTER EXPERIENCING THIS SENSATION.

DO THIS BEFORE YOU READ FURTHER. WRITE YOUR RESPONSE IN YOUR NOTEBOOK .

WRITING ABOUT EMOTIONS

What you come up with should have a lot of physical attributes. Think about what happens when you feel fearful: your heart may pound, your mouth might go dry, you might sweat, or feel your palms grow damp, your stomach might tighten. What happens when you see someone you love: you might feel a warm glow, tingle or (if a man) get hard, flush or stammer, or get nervy and bold.

Other physical responses might be: groin aching, head throbbing, shaking, trembling, neck aching, throat closing, hands getting cold, shortness of breath, heaviness in arms and legs, dizziness. Using all the senses—seeing, touching, hearing, tasting, and smelling—we are able to make our writing sensual. All emotions can be reduced to the body's senses.

How you react to these emotions is how your character might very well react. Of course, everyone is different. Your character might clench her fist when angry, while another might feel her head pound. But these are things which the reader identifies with. You want to be careful about using clichés like throat tightened, and warm flushed her face, as well as others, which are overused in the romances. The facts and the action must match the emotion or your reader will think the character is a teary–eyed wimp.

These are experiences that you are feeling now. Body sensations, feelings, body posture, and facial expression are all part of universal body sensations. They combine with emotion, attitudes, opinion, and images of the past to make our characters and us unique.

In order for us to be in tune with the character and her plight, even though the predicament might be far removed from our daily life, we must be able to identify with her, see that she has the same feelings we do, and that she responds in a way, which we might.

This is especially important when we are describing a foreign land or alien planet. The readers must be able to see that while the main characters' physical shape—color of skin, hair, or eyes might not be like ours—their emotions are.

Through time, manners and morals might have changed; the emotions of people remained the same.

You've probably often heard that one should show and not tell. Using all your senses is a way to show and not tell things. Sometimes when writing your first draft, it's important to relate things chronologically—EVERYTHING that has happened to the character before you can decide what needs to stay for readability and what can go.

While it's important to know your characters before you write, often the writer forgets that the reader doesn't know these characters as well. And what seems (to you the writer) an obvious motive for an action is often confusing for the reader. Cutting is always easier than adding.

If you have trouble with this, think of "Show and Tell Days" from school. If Jane told you about her pet snake, you were bored. But if she brought the snake to class and dropped it into your lap, you would feel its papery skin, see its length, smell it, hear it hiss, and perhaps taste the fear in your mouth!

Other good examples of this might be: It was a dark and stormy night translates into "Icy rain stung her face as she stumbled across the dark courtyard, gripping her fur cape across her breast and leaning into the wind. "

Katya's blonde hair was beautiful. Her shoulders were smooth. This translates into: "The long golden silk of Katya's hair brushed the cream of her shoulders. "

Rafe was angry. Translates to: "He slammed his coffee mug down, glaring across the table at her." You see this SHOWS his anger.

Or—She could see the lightning and thunder outside can equal–"Lightning knifed across the silver curtain of rain while thunder rattled the window." The same holds true for historical. While the costume and the manners might be different, the emotions and needs will remain the same. While you might (I hope) never been raped, you can easily envision what your heroine is feeling when this happens because you will be feeling her emotions.

EXERCISE:

WRITE A SCENIC DESCRIPTION—USING THE SENSES. SOME IDEAS MIGHT BE: BEING FOLLOWED ON A DARK NIGHT, STAYING WITH A DYING RELATIVE, BEING ALONE IN A HOUSE DURING A STORM, A FEELING OF BEING WATCHED, A TEMPESTUOUS LOVE SCENE. ANY OTHER SENSUAL SCENE IS FINE. (That is, any scene using the senses.)

The descriptive setting should balance with your character so that it acts almost like another character. How the character interacts with a scene is what makes it crucial.

WHAT EMOTIONS ARE YOU TRYING TO PORTRAY IN YOUR STORY? HOW WILL YOU SHOW THEM? WHAT IS THE EMOTIONAL TONE OF YOUR STORY?

Giving your people emotions creates verisimilitude. It makes your story realistic. A reader wants to be entertained and wants to escape with these books. You must have them care about your characters. If you don't care and don't show emotions, the reader won't care either.

CHARACTERIZATION

QUESTION:

WHO WAS THE HEROINE OF THACKERY'S NOVEL, VANITY FAIR?

Many of you will say Becky Sharp, but she wasn't. She was considered the villainess then, because the heroine was a goody–good girl named Amelia who never did anything wrong. It's Becky we love and remember; however, because she had spunk. She went after what she wanted. She wasn't an insipid creature—as many of the old heroines were.

Character is what makes your book count. Character is memorable. Character is conflict and the facing of jeopardy. Even if you have the same plot as someone else, it's how the characters relate to one another which is important.

There are several schools of thought when it comes to writing. Some say characters come first; others say plot. I say that you cannot plot well until you know who your characters are. Therefore, characters are the most important part of your story.

You are creating a world that you want the reader to share. You do this through the people in your story and through the everyday things they share. Have them get angry about the toothpaste cap being left off, or the toilet seat up. Then when they run into real trouble, we identify with them much more.

THINK STRESS — Change, pressure, conflict, disagreement, and forcing of issues; think death defying; think what is at stake for these characters.

It's the people you remember first and foremost: real, living, breathing people with thoughts, emotions, and impaired understanding. Perfect heroines who never get a run in their pantyhose don't exist. Be sure your characters are balanced with both good and bad.

As a reader, I want to be surprised, distracted, and astonished, but I want to be able to see everything happening from the character's viewpoint. For this reason, we'll be dealing with characterization next, and I'll be referring to it several times during the course of this book.

If you were not familiar with the genre in which you wish to write, I would recommend you read at least thirty books in that area to gain a good idea of what's required. Know, too, that you are passionate about this idea. You'll be working with it at between six months to a year or more.

Remember to have faith in yourself. If your story is good, it will sell. If you are meant to be a writer, then you must write—no matter what the odds.

ANALYSIS EXERCISE:

TAKE A BOOK SIMILAR TO WHAT YOU WANT TO WRITE;

WRITE A ONE LINE SENTENCE TO SUM UP THAT BOOK. (Pretend it's going to be a movie of the week and you have to write something for the T. V. guide. Make it snappy.)

WRITE A COUPLE OF SENTENCES SUMMING UP EACH CHAPTER. What were the two or three major events in each chapter? List them in an outline.

WRITE THUMBNAIL SKETCHES OF THE MAJOR CHARACTERS: only one or two paragraphs. Who they are and why they are what they are. What motives do they have for being where they are and for trying to get what they're going after?

THINK LOCATION AND TIME. A woman telling her finance that she won't marry him will create stress for the character, but what if she tells him just before the wedding as they are waiting in the church hallway? How much more stress and conflict does that create?

NOW ANSWER THESE:

IS THE MAIN CHARACTER SOMEONE YOU CAN IDENTIFY WITH? WHY OR WHY NOT?

IS THE MAIN CHARACTER SOMEONE YOU COULD (if you were correct sex) FALL IN LOVE WITH?

FROM WHOSE VIEWPOINT IS THE STORY WRITTEN? IS S/HE THE MAIN CHARACTER? IF NOT, WHY WAS THIS VIEWPOINT CHOSEN? DOES IT WORK FOR THE BOOK? (Viewpoint character is usually the main character. It's usually to him or her that the events happen and s/he that causes things to happen.)

- IS THE SITUATION BELIEVABLE?
- ARE YOU ABLE TO SUSPEND DISBELIEF IN YOUR READING? OR ARE THERE

TOO MANY COINCIDENCES?

- IF THIS IS A ROMANCE OR HAS ROMANTIC ELEMENTS—HOW MANY OBSTACLES MUST THE COUPLE GO THROUGH BEFORE DECLARING LOVE— IF THEY DO?
- HOW ARE THE CONFLICTS ESTABLISHED?
- WHAT CAUSES THEM?
- DO THE MAIN CHARACTERS HAVE SEX?
- HOW SOON?
- HOW MANY CHAPTERS INTO THE STORY?
- HOW OFTEN DO THEY REPEAT?
- HOW DETAILED IS THE SEX?
- DOES IT FEEL NATURAL FOR THE STORY OR IS IT FORCED?
- WHAT IS/ARE THE SUBPLOT (S)? HOW DO THEY RELATE—COMPLEMENT OR CONTRAST THE MAIN STORY?
- DID THE OPENING HOOK YOU?
- HOW MUCH DID YOU HAVE TO READ BEFORE YOU WERE INTO THE MOOD OF THE BOOK AND TIME PERIOD?
- HOW SOON WAS THE MAIN CHARACTER'S PROBLEM ESTABLISHED?
- DID THE ENDING SATISFY YOU? WERE ALL THE LOSE ENDS TIED UP?
- DID THE RESEARCH SHOW? WHERE? HOW? IF THIS SCENE DIDN'T WORK FOR YOU, HOW WOULD YOU HAVE REWRITTEN THAT SCENE? WAS THE MATERIAL THE AUTHOR PUT IN NECESSARY TO THE STORY LINE? IF NOT, DID IT SERVE SOME OTHER VITAL PURPOSE? WHAT WAS THAT PURPOSE?
- WHAT COMPELLED YOU TO READ ON? (The fact that this is an assignment is not a good answer!)
- WHAT DID YOU LIKE AND DISLIKE ABOUT THIS BOOK?
- IS IT HISTORICALLY OR SCIENTIFICALLY ACCURATE? (Nothing is more irritating than a novel, that is inaccurate!)
- DID YOU CRY WHEN THE CHARACTERS CRIED? OR LAUGH WHEN THEY LAUGHED?

DO THIS FOR SEVERAL BOOKS.

According to Lee Wyndham, the Writer's Ten Commandments are:

1. Love thy Subject.
2. Love thy Reader.
3. Thou shalt not Begin without Prior Meditation.
4. Thou shalt Know thy Characters as well as thou knowest thyself—even better!
5. Thou shalt not Begin until thou Knowest Whither Thou Goest, or have a well—thought—out Plan for the Journey.
6. Thou shalt stop when thy story is finished.
7. Thou shalt not Worship thy Words as Images Graven in precious Marble.
8. Thou shalt make a Clear, dark copy of thy Work and never use poor quality printers.
9. Thou shalt Study the Markets diligently (or preferably query thy intended publisher or magazine) and Only Then send thy manuscript into the world.
10. Thou shalt not brood upon its fate, but set about the Workings of thy Next Project, with good will and high heart.

WARM UPS

Just like the body has to be warmed up, the mind and imagination must be as well.

DO THESE EXERCISES:

FIND NEW WORDS TO END—As angry as, as soft as, as silent as, as red as, as curved as, as frightening as, as funny as, as bright as, as inspiring as . . .

USE YOUR MEMORY—Write a scene special from your childhood, write about a private moment, write about a frightening moment as a child.

CHANGE LOCALE—If you weren't here, where would you be? What would you be doing? See the locale. What would you hear, see, taste, and feel? Where would it be?

LETTERS—Write a letter to your character asking questions? Let the character answer in her own voice. (This might take a few days to get.)

LET YOUR SUBCONSCIOUS WORK—Ask a question of the right brain and then let yourself jog, exercise, garden, take a bath, or do housework.

DO CLUSTER—As the exercise indicated in the chapter before.

DO WHAT IF: Take a story from the news and twist it, bend it. What are the characters motives? Why did they do what they did? Write the back–story—what would have happened just before this incident, which led up to the news story?

DEFINITIONS

A LIST: These are stars or celebrities who, by their very name being attached to a story, can sell the script to a producer or a studio and that fans will flock (the studio hopes) to see them. Stars go in and out of popularity, however, and you have to know the right ones to ask. Some current A list stars are George Clooney, Sandra Bullock, Jennifer Lawrence–but these change often. They are only as popular as their last successful film.

A TICKING CLOCK: Increases the suspense. The hero/ine must reach or receive something crucial by a certain time or else bad things will happen.

ADVANCE: Money paid upon signing of contract. Usually 1/2 is paid now and 1/2 upon satisfactory completion of book. Can be recalled if you do not finish book, or if not earned out. Must be earned out before you receive a royalty check.

AGENT: The person who sells your book to the publisher and takes 10–15% of the advance and royalties for his work. He knows what the publishers want and which editor is looking for what. Unless you are dealing with a small independent publisher, you need an agent to sell your book or screenplay. Many agents will not take on new authors until they have proven themselves. There are differences between book agents and script agents so make sure that the person you are talking to is capable of doing the function that you need.

BACKSTORY: The events that happened to your character before the start of the story. This might include her wound or flaw. This does not come out as a full story in your work but often appears as bits and pieces and will often foreshadow a character's abilities. (Ie., If later in the book you have her balancing a bar between two buildings, you must show earlier that she has gymnastic abilities.)

BEAT: A section of a scene and sometimes confused with a scene. It can also be a pause or moment of time.

BIBLE: No. This is not the Old Testament. This is a history of the TV show you are trying to write. It includes the major characters, the arena, it's premise and logline, a synopsis of the pilot, and samples of other epi-sodes in the series.

BIOGRAPHY: Can be totally factual (and usually drier) or can be factualized—combination of fact and fiction—to make it more readable, but still must be as true to fact as is possible.

CATEGORY ROMANCE: Usually associated with brand name marketing and written to a publishing house's slant, such as Harlequin, Zebra, etc.

CHARACTER ARC: How the character changes—or doesn't—throughout the story. If the main character doesn't change, than one of the subordinate characters will change to fit in with your theme.

CONTEMPORARY ROMANCE: Generally not written to formula requirements, longer than category, usually marketed as a single title release.

COVERAGE: A short document that summarizes a script and provides an overall "pass," "consider," or "recommend." It does not include feedback or recommendations for fixing the script's problems. It often focuses on why that script may not be acceptable for a specific production company and it is directed toward production companies, studios, and agency execs. It is done by the readers to judge the level of the script, and if the writer is to be considered for future assignments.

DEVELOPMENT NOTES: This is an extensive report with detailed notes on premise, structure, pacing, dialogue, etc. It includes feedback and recommendations on improving the script and how it can be strengthened and made more marketable. This is directed toward the writer of the script.

GOTHIC/SUSPENSE ROMANCE: Gothics contain a strong element of mystery, possibly overtones of supernatural. Suspense leads to adventure. In both, the heroine is in danger. First is moodier, second more action.

HISTORICAL NOVEL: Truer to history, still fictionalized, always a single release and does not require a happy ending, only a satisfactory one, but one that is true to the historical period. Real characters are used here more than in the romance.

HISTORICAL ROMANCE: Uses historical setting as background, may be marketed as category (such as Tapestry), or more frequently, as a single title.

INCITING INCIDENT: This happens anywhere from ten pages or perhaps two chapters into your story where things begin changing for the main character. His life, as he knew it before, is now on a different path. An example of this would be when the Hobbit is taken out of his comfortable home and told he is going on an adventure.

INSPIRATIONAL ROMANCE: Romance built around "Christian" ideals. No sex scenes. Amish Romances are a new version of this, as well.

MAINSTREAM NOVEL: Books that transcend a genre, not category. Marketed as a single title and have broad general appeal.

MANAGER: Book authors don't usually need a manager, but screenwriters often do. The manager will help guide their career and find them work. While they are not agents, and are not supposed to negotiate, they often do. They take 15–20% of the writer's income and will often help in finding a correct agent. It's often easier to find a manager to take you on than it is an agent, but, as managers, they are not regulated like agents are. Managers often seek to produce their writers' works, in addition to being managers.

MIDPOINT: As you would guess it happens around the middle of the book or screenplay, (middle second act), but it also serves as a turning point where the hero thinks that he has conquered the situation, only to find it getting worse or visa versa.

MYSTERY: Action oriented, may have some romance but not thc key issue.

OUTLINE: Often confused with the word synopsis. Outlines or table of contents go for non–fiction books. Outlines are also used to guide the writer while writing the book. Some can be as short as a page or as long as forty pages.

PREMISE or LOGLINE: One or two sentences hooking your audience into reading your novel or script. It must have something of the main characters' conflict and obstacles, as well as the character arc–how the character changes.

PROPOSAL: Your synopsis and the first three chapters of your book with a brief cover letter. For historicals and longer contemporaries, usually the first one hundred pages instead of first three chapters.

QUERY: A pre–approach, brief (usually one page) description of your book and a request to submit. Enclose SASE (self addressed stamped envelope large enough for return letter/or return manuscript). Usually only three chapters and a synopsis are sent.

REGENCY: A historical novel of manners set in 1780–1815. Sex is seldom mentioned in these.

ROYALTY: Paid usually twice yearly, a percent of book's cover price. Varies anywhere from 2–15%, depending on who your publisher is, your own selling track record and of course the contract that your agent has negotiated.

SHOWRUNNER: The executive producer and head writer of a television show. Needed if you want to sell a TV pilot.

SIZZLE REEL: A taped sample of your story—perhaps a few scenes. Needed if you want to sell a reality series, showing how the series will proceed and who the protagonists are.

SPEC SCRIPT: A story or script written without pay. Most writers create many spec stories before their first are produced or published.

STRUCTURE: How your story is outlined with the beats alluded to and developed.

SUBTEXT: When words are meant, but not said. The hidden meaning of the dialogue. This is used especially in screenwriting, and often expressed in visuals not in dialogue. A person might say "Please stay," but visuals show the character turning away and really saying the very opposite.

SWEET/SENSUOUS ROMANCES: Sweets have no sex scenes. Sensuous have one with most of the tension being sexual tension. Spicy tends to have several sex scenes.

SYNOPSIS: A short narrative tale of your book (no more than two to ten pages) or written as a chapter–by–chapter narrative of what happens in each chapter. They must be included in every proposal you send—even when sending whole a manuscript. Synopsis always has the ending written in. Never say "read the book to find out the ending."

THEME: The essence of the story. Usually you will find your theme after you finish your first draft. Themes vary, and something like justice will be served, or love will survive. The story and subplots intermingle the theme without force feeding it to the reader. Theme is different than premise.

TREATMENT: A beat by beat of your story, usually used in reference to screenplays, it is a more detailed synopsis or outline used to give the producers. It can be twenty to forty pages. Usually done for scripts, but can be asked for in novels, as well.

TURNING POINT: When things turn around for the main character and get worse or better. This is usually at the act breaks or about three chapters after the inciting incident.

YOUNG ADULT PROBLEM NOVEL: Teens are still the focus, but issues dealt with are more realistic, like divorce of parents, abortion, drugs, and mental health.

YOUNG ADULT ROMANCE: Light romances. Hero is seventeen to eighteen years of age, Heroine is fifteen to sixteen years of age. Concerns are typically does she go to prom with him, does she get the new boy, etc. No sex. Nothing beyond a kiss. No drugs.

NOTES

CHARACTERS COME ALIVE

Characters are the basis of your story. Stories fail when we don't know them well enough or when their motives aren't clear to us.

According to traditional sources, there are only thirty-six central plots. (There are actually more, but that is another chapter.)It is how and why your character acts and reacts to the situation that causes the reader to identify and care for your hero. ***This is your whole story***.

It's frustrating when characters remain wooden. Everyone in your book—be they good guys or bad, main or minor–must have clearly established goals and motives.

How we, as writers and readers, feel towards a character tells a lot about that character as well. How we write that character affects how the reader feels toward him.

One student had a prostitute for her main character and as she was reading about this girl rolling a John, I said, "I don't like this girl very much. "

"Neither do I," said the student.

She changed her viewpoint character.

The fact is, if you don't like your character then your reader probably won't either.

Is there anything about the character that he or she is trying to change about him or herself or someone else? Often the character is unaware of his need to change, but might have an unconscious block, fear, or limitation that he cannot express, which by the end of the story he will not only be able to face, but will overcome. The story will contain different phases of emotional struggle and inner conflict for your character. These will add to the depth of your story.

Is there anything the character truly cares about—above and beyond anything else? (i.e., I would go to the ends of the earth to protect my daughter and I would go pretty far to protect my religion, my country, and many of my friends.) What and who is important to your character?

As a writer of fiction, your primary interest is to manipulate the reader's vicarious feelings by the use of the character.

Your main consideration should be how to draw life—like characters and involve them in plausible circumstances. Even when the situation is "farfetched and melodramatic," it must sound like a plausible combination of characters and circumstances. Only when you make the reader actually live the stories you are setting down and have extorted the maximum empathy will you achieve your goal.

Your hero (with whom we identify) leaves his/her normal world, and with reservations, must enter a new world. He is sucked into something over which he has no control. The hero usually, but not always, has an emotional fear, limitation, block, or wound. If the hero doesn't, then usually one or more of the other characters in the story must. ***Ask yourself what your hero's flaw and fears are***?

In this new world, the hero's past makes him unprepared for what he must do. (But it does give him skills that he can use. You don't want to have your heroine jump over tall buildings, unless you've previously shown us—that she is a world class gymnast.)

In most cases, the hero would rather not do what is called for. However, he must take his step because something is at stake. (Something bad or undesirable will happen if the hero doesn't move forward. The stakes have to be high in his world—it can be as simple as he won't get a date, that he will die, or that the world will die. The higher the stakes, the more tension and the more the reader wants to read on.)

What is your hero's motivation for going on his journey? (This can change throughout the story as the stakes get higher. For example, in my story, ***THE UNBORN WITNESS***, the heroine, at first, just wants to find her mother. Then as she learns her mother has been murdered, wants to find the killer, and finally, it's to save herself.)

The hero usually has an effect on this new world or even becomes pivotal within it . . . if not right off the bat, and then as the story progresses his effect grows.

A story is about a person who enters a new world. Once there, he goes through physical and/or emotional ordeals and comes to the "Oh No!" factor. These ordeals are composed of obstacles, accidents, complications, and/or the work of enemies. Ordeals can be serious or comedic, physical or emotional.

Frequently these ordeals get worse as the story moves forward, right up until the dire end when we worry if he will actually accomplish his goal of saving himself or saving the world.

As an example, if we were in a store and my daughter was kidnapped by some baby racket who wanted to sell her. I try to tell the police, but they don't believe me. Maybe they think I did something to her myself, maybe evidence of my adopting my daughter has disappeared so that I cannot prove I am the mother; maybe they just don't seem to be doing much. Whatever the reason, I am forced into a situation I might not normally have considered . . . going after the kidnappers myself and uncovering the scheme. One of my ***Oh No's*** might be that the officer or detective I thought was helping me was really aligned with the crooks; another might be that I have the capability to take revenge in a way I never thought possible. Could I an "ordinary" mom, actually shoot someone?

Another good example is a movie with Sally Field, where her daughter is murdered. The police refused to do anything even though she has tracked down the killer . . . and so she must set herself up as a target and kill a man . . . something she never thought she had the ability or strength to do.

Much of the suspense and sometimes conflict arises as the hero either tries to figure out, prepares to face, actually faces the ordeals, or when we see the ordeal coming before the hero does. This is suspense that heightens the story for the reader.

Being able to predict stories, sections of stories, or scenes is bad. You don't want to telegraph what is going to happen or you will lose the reader. Let the hero do something out of the ordinary but still within reason for his skill set. If your reader does not identify with your character, you won't get anywhere with the reader.

As the story progresses, the hero often undergoes scenes, which force him to grow (or causes another character to grow) through his emotional fear, limit, block, or wound. The hero (or person growing) resists the process every step of the way, but the growth is important for him to accomplish his final goal.

Let's say that your character, we've established early on, has a fear of water, and yet when push comes to shove and her friend is drowning, she barely hesitates before jumping in to save the friend, because at that point she realizes that the friendship is worth saving.

Another writer put it well when he said that you are like a personnel director, hiring the people you need for an exacting job. You need to know what qualifications the job requires and what you should be looking for in the candidates for that position.

Your main character, your view point character, must want something—desperately, (As I want to find my daughter and Sally wants justice for her daughter.) so desperately that he is willing to risk his whole future on the outcome.

As the main character, s/he is going to provide the forward movement for your story. Even if they only want things to remain the same—which they never do—their feelings as they fight this are impetus for the story to move on.

In a romance, especially when the story is about two characters and how they interact with each other, the drawing of life-like characters is of prime importance. They are the plots and anything else is side material.

Think for a moment on how you plot. Usually, you plot by determining what the character wants, what obstacles s/he'll encounter, and what his/her high and low points (turning points) are.

We need to know what the character's intention is, the initial barrier: why s/he goes on after encountering the barrier, (We have to be convinced that the goal s/he's seeking is so important it would overcome any barrier.) What gives him/her some hope when things don't seem to be going his/her way; what's the high point—where we think s/he almost gets what s/he wants.) the start of the fall, the final catastrophe when it seems as if s/he will never achieve his/her goal, and then the final (sometimes ironic) achievement of his/her intention?

"W" Diagram of dramatic writing–skeletal suspense device

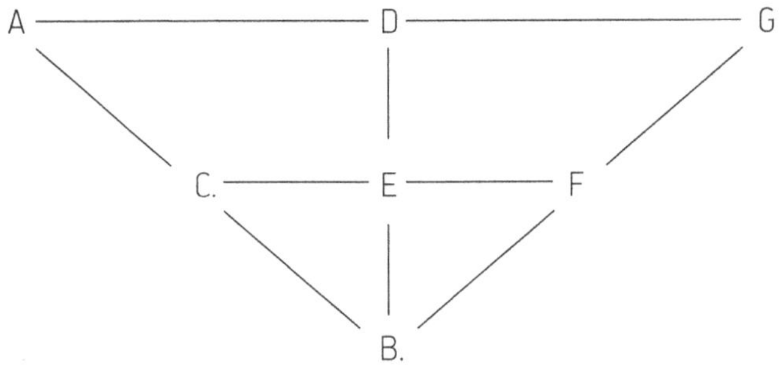

AG Intention of the character (premise of story)

AB Initial barrier

BC Barrier reversal

CD High point (Character almost gets what he wants.)

DE Rug pulling

EF Catastrophe

FG Character achieves his intention—sometimes ironically.

EXERCISE:

MAKE A "W" CHART FOR EACH CHARACTER—SHOWING THE BARRIERS THEY GO THROUGH AND THE HIGH POINTS.

Blanche DuBois in ***STREETCAR NAMED DESIRE*** wanted a safe place (AG). Her initial barrier is being forced to leave her home; the barrier reversal is finding a home with her sister and Stan. Her high point is thinking she's found someone to marry her; the rug is pulled when Stan tells her friend her true story. The catastrophe is Stan's rape, and ironically she has her safe place when she's committed to an asylum.

Minor characters also need to have some depth to them— but you don't want to have too many people cluttering up a story. It's exasperating to read a book, which introduces more and more characters in each chapter—pulling them out of a hat. Limit the number of the minor characters and leave the "cast of thousands" for the movies. (Even then, due to budget considerations, you don't want a lot of characters or you'll never sell that script.)

Don't allow the minor characters to outshine the main ones. If you find yourself getting carried away with a minor character, then you aren't writing the story you thought, and you need to rethink your plot. If you want to keep the plot, then the minor character needs to be re-thought—perhaps by giving him some nasty traits so that the heroine won't prefer him to the hero.

You have to be succinct in your writing since, especially with the shorter books of 60,000, you don't have much time to develop characters that aren't your main focus. The minor characters should add color, but not dominate the scene. And you should keep away from the stereotypical ones found in many old romances or old mysteries such as Scottish or black housekeeper, the old family friend, etc. Use your own creativity in perhaps developing the heroine's parents as minor characters. Her relationship with them will tell us more about her—as well as liven your book.

If your heroine has a friend as a sidekick, she shouldn't be a mirror of the heroine, but a person in her own right. Through their relationship, we can see more about the heroine. Your hero and heroine aren't going to hang around with cruel or depressed people. If they do, we want to know why—and what that tells us about them.

The fact is you cannot have a good plot unless you have believable characters. They push the plot along and make the story vibrate. It is their emotions we are feeling on the pages.

People do not spring full–blown out of the womb, nor do they spring full blown on page ten. We must take time to get to know them. By the end of your character study, you should know them better than you know your best friend, and perhaps better than you know yourself.

The reader also must take time to know the character. You aren't going to tell his whole life history on the first few pages. A hint there, a hint here is all you need to keep the reader interested. LATER, you can fill in details. In fact, like any form of research, most of your character study will not show on the page, but it will show in your knowledge of the person, and how he reacts in a situation.

It's important that each character develop his own voice and own way of handling things. Voice is not just what he says, but how he talks: tone, texture, and feel of words.

EXERCISE:

ROLE–PLAY WITH ANOTHER PERSON (or with yourself pretending to be a second person). You can also tape this and replay it for yourself with your eyes closed.

CLOSE YOUR EYES. IMAGINE YOU ARE WALKING DOWN A LONG HALL AND YOU SEE A DOOR AT THE END OF THE TUNNEL. WHAT TYPE OF DOOR IS IT? WOOD, METAL, THICK, THIN, HOLLOW? DO YOU HEAR ANYTHING AS IT OPENS OR IS IT WELL OILED?

WHAT DOES THE ROOM LOOK LIKE? RUSTIC? ORNATE? PICTURES ON THE WALL? FURNITURE? AS YOU LOOK OUT OF THE WINDOW, WHAT DO YOU SEE?

ARE THEIR BOOKS IN THE ROOM? WHAT BOOKS ARE THEY? WHAT SMELLS? LOOK FOR A TITLE THAT TELLS US ABOUT YOUR CHARACTER.

SOMEONE COMES INTO THE ROOM. IT'S ONE OF YOUR CHARACTERS. WHAT DOES HE WEAR? WHAT DOES HE DO? LISTEN TO HIM AS ANOTHER CHARACTER COMES INTO THE ROOM.

HAVE TWO CHARACTERS ASKING QUESTIONS OF ONE ANOTHER. HOW DOES EACH CHARACTER'S VOICE DIFFER? LISTEN.

WALK IN THE WOODS NEAR THE HOUSE? WHAT BIRDS DO YOU SEE? WHAT DO YOU HEAR? WHAT DO YOU FEEL? WHAT DO YOU SMELL?

Be specific.

Characters must do what is typical and natural to their own personalities. The plot should flow from them so that there is no implausibility. Everything must relate to everything else.

In order for them to come alive, we need to know not only major things about them (their need and how they change), but also minor things (like their hobbies, how they relate to their families). We need to know what they like to read, what shows they like to watch, what brand beer or soft drink they favor, and what type of pictures hang on their walls. I emphasize minor because these things are not minor at all. It's the small things, which makes the characters real for us.

How they handle their emotions also makes them real for us, since everyone handles anger and upset in different ways.

For example, in the Cagney and Lacey book I was hired by the studio to write as a prequel to the series, Cagney has difficulty expressing emotion, would rather laugh than cry, thinks of herself as being very liberated, loves her father, but hates any woman he's with, wants to be like Dad's son rather than his daughter, and did not come home for her mother's funeral. Even though Chris Cagney does not like children or animals, she can be likeable, but it's hard.

Lacey, on the other hand, is Earth Mother embodied—warm, talkative, friendly, always expressing her feelings, caring very much for the underdog, and for people's rights. She loves her family to extremes, and when she's upset, she bakes bread or cleans the kitchen.

A key to having your reader care about your characters is to make them vulnerable. Give them a secret (like Victoria in ***SHRIEKING SHADOWS***); have them help the underdog, love children, or animals. Give them some fault as well, to make them human. Quick temper, pride, and guilt are good examples.

The character's dramatic need is what he needs to accomplish, or wants. What he is seeking or perhaps hiding—and why? Know why he makes the choices he does. Is there a deeper reason than what he is telling you? Ask your character again. Your character has his own voice; if you let him speak to you, he will tell you.

There must be a strong reason why he does something—so strong that you would believe he would risk any danger to accomplish his goal. Motives must be totally convincing and should be well grounded in his past. Love, hate, greed, fear, yearning for security, power, desires for revenge—all of these are solid motives. For more possible motives, you might want to check a psychology text for Maslow's hierarchy of needs.

Show the pain they're in. Show us how they cope with emotional and physical pain. This creates sympathy for them. (Of course, you don't want to overdo the pain. Too much of a good thing will destroy what we want to create rather than develop it. You do, however, want the hero to suffer.)

As a main character, s/he is drawn into a situation by chance (fate or circumstance, if you want to call it that), in which only sheer doggedness and courage brings him/her out on top. It is a sense of justice, and an inflexible code of ethics, which motivates the hero/ine to seek the truth (or item) s/he is seeking. (Victoria in ***SHRIEKING SHADOWS*** is motivated only by the desire to see justice done to her sister's killer.)

You must make it clear that even though she might find herself in a situation where she is ordered by a superior to betray someone or something, her values can never be impinged upon. (Roxanna in ***TAME THE WILD HEART*** refused at the end to betray Sebastian and her uncle, because her heart had become her first priority then.)

It is this code of ethics and sense of justice that makes the character what s/he is to your reader.

Characters show themselves through what they think, say, and do. ACTION IS CHARACTER. It's not enough to spend five or six pages describing her golden tresses, the willow–wand figure, or her deep violet eyes. It's not how she walks, talks, and looks; it's what she loves, hates, fears, and dislikes. It's how she reacts to situations. If her baby is crying for her and she's not there, that will tell you more about her than her "inner beauty."

NAMING YOUR CHARACTER

WHY DID YOU CHOOSE THE NAME YOU DID? WHAT SIGNIFICANCE DOES IT HAVE? IS IT CORRECT FOR THAT TIME PERIOD? FOR THE PERSON YOU HAVE? DOES IT FEEL RIGHT? (If you've checked with the book YOU ARE YOUR FIRST NAME, you'll get another view of the character and his/her name.)

YOUR CHARACTER'S CHARACTER

In writing your character history, you might also want to use astrology and numerology. I use Linda Goodman's Sun Signs for a basic sense of sign and then I sometimes do up a chart for my characters. I also use a book called ***YOU ARE***

YOUR FIRST NAME, by Ellin Dodge Young, Long Shadow Press. (The book is available on Amazon and in the libraries.)

For example; in the book, under ***ROXANNA***, you find ability to incorporate originality, aristocratic tastes, and love of beauty into career. She is reserved, charming, and independent and has discretion, artistic interest, and an analytic approach. The bearer of the name combines imagination, research, and progressive ideas. Some jobs for that name might be designer, secret service agent, and lawyer. She often feels restless, is pleasure seeking, and resourceful. She desires beauty, joy, and romance and attracts diversification and needs to concentrate. They are most comfortable dividing their interests.

From that description, I determined (though I had partly guessed already) that Roxanna was going to be an Aries. Linda Goodman says of Aries women: "When told someone is in love with them, their response is often—I don't know whether to congratulate you or sympathize with you." Roxanna uses those exact words to Sebastian; the Aries woman is looking for the hero of her dreams, believes in romance and miracles, as well as leprechauns. On page 168, Sebastian confronts Roxanna about her dreams, and her response is, "Why can't my dreams come true? Why can't I believe in miracles?"

Often the Aries woman may irritate more than soothe you. Sebastian will tell you, however, no matter how much Roxanna irked him, he couldn't live without her.

A man who resists the Aries woman always intrigues her. She will gather every available man in the room, but her eyes always go towards the man she can't have. In the ballroom scene, it's very obvious that Roxanna is upset because Sebastian is not paying attention to her, and yet, every other man in the room, including the king, is falling at her feet.

An Aries woman has a strong desire to control and yet be controlled. Her conflicting feelings about marriage to Sebastian and being with him are seen in her jealous explosion on page 251 of ***TAME THE WILD HEART***.

Since the Aries woman rarely complains of illness or fatigue, and is, as a patient, hard to take care of, the scene where she becomes ill and where he has to watch over her and keep her from becoming more ill follows naturally.

Then, of course, the Aries woman will want to open her own doors and hire her own taxi. Roxanna, rather than standing aside and letting James II ruin her country, does something about it. She also takes the lead in her relationship with Sebastian.

THE ANTAGONIST

It's possible for the "villain" or major obstacle to be something other than human: the land in the story of a western couple trying to make it as with Janet Dailey's Calder series, and the houses in many gothics are villains in themselves, since they are fighting the characters getting what they want. Of course, you'll have human villains too.

Once you decide on the main character's qualities and the way she sees the world (perhaps she's a vegetarian, or pro–choice), then the villains can have the opposite qualities. This will create conflict for your story, since much of the empathy the reader experiences for the main character comes from the despicable actions of the villains.

Just as our hero/ine is prompted by ethics, courage, and a determined desire to succeed, so, too, must our villain have the same conviction that he is right and should succeed. For the story to be dramatic, the antagonist must appear to have an equal chance at success. Therefore, we must know his desires, needs, and wants the same as we know the hero/ine's. His ability must be equal to our heroine's — if not the battle is unequal. You can't have an insipid good heroine and a totally evil villain —otherwise it would be too easy for the villain to walk all over the heroine.

Of course, not all your villains will be obvious and obnoxious. Some will be quite charming. (Take Percy in ***SHRIEKING SHADOWS***, as an example. Not until the very end did he show his true colors.) If you are doing a mystery, romantic suspense, or gothic, you will, of course, want the villain to have many of the same traits as the hero. That will make the heroine's choice harder and therefore create more conflict.

We all know that not everyone in the world is nice—but sometimes we forget this when we are writing. We people our books with wonderful strong characters that can do no wrong. In fact, a little evil makes things more interesting. Look at Alexis on *Dynasty*. What she does is almost more interesting to us than Krystle. I confess, I, myself, am guilty of sometimes wanting all my characters to be good, noble people, but the fact is that I, myself, am not good and noble in all instances. There are times when, like my characters, I will fight for what I want—even if it means a little lying and a little cheating. Your characters are like this too.

With the villains, we want to understand them as well as we understand the hero. Child abusers are a good example. They were usually abused as children themselves. Another way to make the villain more human is to give him an endearing trait or two, as I did with Percy in ***SHRIEKING SHADOWS***.

The villain must be as well developed as your main character. What he wants, the hero is trying to prevent or visa versa.

Truly, as much as we must love our hero/ines, there must be a little of the sadist in us. We must ask ourselves—how can s/he suffer more? What more terrible things can we heap on her/him just as s/he thinks s/he is getting what s/he is seeking? Like you did with the hero, interview your villain on the therapist sofa or TV talk show.

TIME CHARTS

Emotions are crucial in any book, but especially in romances. We need to know how characters feel about each other at all points in the story. To help me with this, I draw out a time chart for my characters, detailing not only what world events are affecting them, but also how they are changing in their feelings (if at all) towards the other characters. (At first, Victoria hates Julian and likes Percy in ***SHRIEKING SHADOWS***, but midway through she starts to believe that Julian might not be so bad. Not until the very end, however, does she come to realize she loves Julian and dislikes Percy.) In a book I am working on now, I gave the hero's mother cancer and no money to pay for the operations, causing him to participate in a major robbery.

Time charts are also important, since the world is seen through the eyes of your character. You can't throw in dates of events for background if what happened then doesn't directly affect the character's life.

The same applies for doing historical research. While it's all right to use real people, be sure you are accurate and that your hero is in the correct time and place to be affected by this character. Having your hero dance with Queen Elizabeth in 1504, when she died in 1502, will not endear you to your readers.

This can be divided according to days, weeks, years, or even hours depending on the time span of your story.

While the 1670 date is not in my novel's first chapters, it is part of the pre–story and the history of the characters and who they are. Therefore, it's a necessary part to plot out. This information will be filtered through in bits and pieces during the story.

EXERCISE:

1. MAKE A LIST OF ALL YOUR CHARACTERS. WHO ARE THEY? HOW DO THEY RELATE TO ONE ANOTHER? HOW DO THEY FEEL ABOUT EACH OTHER? HOW IS THE READER SUPPOSED TO FEEL ABOUT THEM?

2. DO A TIME CHART—BREAKING DOWN BY CHAPTER; HOW DO FEELINGS IN THE CHARACTERS CHANGE TOWARD EACH OTHER? INDICATE SPECIFIC SCENES IF POSSIBLE. INDICATE, ALSO, WHAT WORLD EVENTS ARE HAPPENING WHICH AFFECT THE CHARACTER.

CHARACTERS CHANGE

You might want to make notes to yourself, not only on how the character changes (or doesn't change when he has a choice), but also in what scenes the change will be shown and how.

Changes must be plausible for who your character is. If you have a Walter Mitty type, having him suddenly break out with a gun and start shooting people or suddenly able to save someone, isn't going to work for the reader—not unless you effectively build up to the change. For instance, if his wife has just left him, his kid is on drugs, his car was stolen, and then he gets to work and finds a younger man is taking his job—well, he might have provocation enough to start killing. Remember that action tells all. You want the scene to show the change and not to tell it. Let your reader know the feelings and thoughts of your character. Get them involved with his life. (Of course, in writing screenplays, you cannot tell the feelings and thoughts. Everything must be visual and must be shown. Sometimes, it can be shown through another character, but it must be visual.)

Characters should never be puppets being put through their paces, and they shouldn't be too similar to you or people you know. In one instance, I was trying to do a contemporary romance about a travel writer down in St. Maarten who fell in love with an American boat captain there. I was a travel writer and I was down in St. Maarten, and I did have an infatuation for a handsome American boat captain there.

Every time I tried to write a love scene, however, I got stuck because I kept thinking, "What would Bruce think if he read this?" As a result, my characters were never able to come to life. I was inhibited. Then, too, people have been sued over using characters too similar to people they knew. You need to identify with your heroines (as I identified with Roxanna's rebelliousness), but you also need to have some distance.

FIRST IMPRESSIONS

First impressions are important. You might want to describe the character as he walks into a strange room and how he relates to that room. What he sees first tells not only about him, but also about the person who has that room. Think about minor characters, too. Even they can have character arcs.

What are other character's first impressions of him? Does the character have any unusual physical features? Are they aware of it? Ashamed of it? (Of course, in writing screenplays, you cannot tell the feelings and thoughts. Everything must be visual and must be shown. Sometimes, it can be shown through another character, but it must be visual.)

First impressions, how the character is introduced, is crucial in the screenplay as that can be the turning point of having an A list star attach themselves or not. (Stars reading material want to know that their characters will not only be unique but will stand out.)

EXERCISE:

1. WHAT IS THE FIRST IMPRESSION YOU HAVE OF THIS CHARACTER? WHAT DO YOU NOTICE ABOUT THIS CHARACTER AS HE WALKS INTO A ROOM?

2. DESCRIBE CHARACTER'S HOME FROM HIS POINT OF VIEW. (POV) Take "Better Homes and Gardens" or "Good Housekeeping" and look at homes.

3. DESCRIBE A FRIEND'S HOME FROM CHARACTER'S P. O. V. (This process should tell us not only about him, but about the people he chooses as friends and what's important to him.) DESCRIBE THE SCENE SO VIVIDLY THAT IT FUNCTIONS AS ANOTHER CHARACTER.

4. WRITE A CHARACTER HISTORY BASED ON THE CHARACTER CHART (which follows in the appendix). Personality and warmth doesn't come in twenty-five words or less. Be prepared to write several pages of history for your character.

5. IMAGINE HOW YOU WOULD ACT IN A GIVEN SET OF CIRCUMSTANCES IF YOU WERE THE CHARACTER, THINK OF FACIAL EXPRESSION, WALK, TONE OF VOICE, SPEECH PATTERNS, AS WELL AS ACTION.

Characters (people) reveal themselves in a million different ways—some minor and some major. How does he act with servants or cab drivers? How does he act with equals? (When I go out with a man, I notice not only how he treats me, but how he treats the waitress and how big a tip he leaves.) Notice, too, how he acts with superiors. What flaws and imperfections does he have? If he were told to do something—like swim the length of a pool—and he didn't know how, would he pretend he did and make a fool of himself, admit he didn't, or flub through and say he was trying for the first time? Would he curse? You don't want to use real people's ways of dealing with things, since we take ambiguity for granted in every day life; our characters have to be clearly drawn. Just because Aunt Sophie would rattle her keys when she was upset, doesn't mean your character should—unless you've already indicated that that is a trait.

EVOKING SYMPATHY IN THE READER

If we are to be sympathetic to a character, that sympathy must be held through the story. Again, motives have a good place in keeping this emotion. We might not like them lying and cheating, but if it's for a good cause (like Roxanna or Victoria) then, because we identify with the motive, we have sympathy for them. Before we have our character doing something that is essentially negative, we should check the emotional reaction it produces.

EXERCISE:

Choose goals for the character from the goal sheet in the appendix. (Stars reading material want to know that their characters will not only be unique, but will stand out. They need to know more than the physical description of the character; they need to know the attitude and their tone. What is the subtext and action in that first scene where they are introduced?)

CREATE A SCENE WHERE THE CHARACTER IS IN DANGER, AND HAVE US CARE ABOUT THE CHARACTER (but without giving a lot of details about the character.) Let his personality come through by his reaction to the scene. If you have trouble with this, read the Bible. Notice that we seldom get physical descriptions of the characters. What we do get is action and dialogue to make the characters come alive. In the story of Jacob, Esau, and Isaac—we have little narrative. Only that Jacob agrees to his mother's idea to fool their father, and that one brother has smooth skin, the other hairy. Read this passage if you can. There's good example of subtext (meaning below the words) here too.

In the romances, even though the couple isn't willing to admit their love early on, the sexual tension should be there from the first chapter. They should yearn to be together and be stopped with obstacles.

THE HERO

Our male in romances is no longer the silent, John Wayne—type, but the more devil–may–care, Harrison Ford–type. He's appealing, assertive, athletic, attractive, and aware of her feelings, caring, dynamic, masculine, sensitive, sexy, strong, successful, witty, and willing to cry. But remember beauty is in the eyes of the beholder. He doesn't have to be Robert Redford. He no longer lets misunderstandings stand in the way of his relationship—and neither does she. If he is arrogant, I want to know why. If he has a bad temper, why? Does he come from a broken home? Why does he feel the way he does about women? Just one breakup isn't enough to make someone sour. What's his past?

THE HEROINE

While the females, especially in romance, are spirited, independent, and probably have a career, they also have a lack of self–esteem when it comes to love. Sexual liberation depends on the book you are writing and who your audience is, but the truly helpless female is out.

The new heroine is vivacious, goes after what she wants, is capable, experienced, independent, mature, resourceful, sensitive, successful, and attractive. She's no longer the fragile flower who passively waits for the hero to come to her. Though she can still be prideful and vulnerable at times, she won't let that keep her from the hero.

Both must be fully developed, especially since the male viewpoint is being encouraged more and more. We must know his thoughts as much as we know hers. They are both yearning for that love and are vulnerable when it comes to love. (Again, know thoughts when you are writing a screenplay. Know them, but show them, don't tell them.)

EMOTIONAL CORE

The secret to successful series, be they TV or novels, is the characters. How much do we care about them? We continue to come back to them because we want to see what happens to them. Caring + conflict = hope + worry = reader/viewer engagement. You have to hope and worry about the character and the end has to be unpredictable. You can't know if he really reaches his goal until the very end. I especially like Janet Evanovich's Stephanie Plum character who has a choice between two hunky men, loves peanut butter, and has a hamster as a pet.

To relate to readers, minor characters must have human traits, even if they are not. (animation bears, fish, planes or cars, etc.)

How a character succeeds at his relationships and emotions give us the emotional core.

Some traits that we need to consider for our characters are undeserved misfortune, injustice, bad luck, being bullied, a tragedy, physical or mental handicap, being humiliated, lonely, neglected, or otherwise defenseless. Other good points are when a character cares deeply for someone else such as a child or an animal, even a plant. In addition, there is the risking of our lives for another person, self sacrifice, or dying for the cause.

In ***FINDING NEMO***, the father is attacked by the shark, and his children, all except Nemo, and his wife are gone. So he has undeserved misfortune and cares deeply for his son. Whereas in ***SHARK TALE***, there was no pity or empathy for the Will Smith character who is supposed to be the hero of the story..

You can show the human traits in a private moment. Maybe they pet the dog. In ***SHRIEKING SHADOWS***, Julian takes care of the dying seal when he thinks no one else is looking.

We also care for characters that we admire. They are leaders, have charisma, courage, stand up for freedom or someone else, are witty and clever and have a sense of self. If they are loved by others, we might care for them even if we don't like them.

All your characters have to be actively seeking their goals and not just passively waiting for things to happen.

We also care about characters that have a worthy motive. Ask what would happen if they fail to achieve their goal? A good ending would be death (physical or emotional). There must be something at stake to cause us to care about the character.

Some worthy motivations are taken from Maslow's Hierarchy, and those include safety and survival at the top. Love, duty, honor, patriotism, dignity, redemption, and doing something for another fellow.

IF YOU ARE STILL HAVING PROBLEMS WITH DEVELOPING CHARACTER, TAKE SOME MAGAZINES AND LOOK THROUGH THEM UNTIL YOU FIND ONE MODEL THAT LOOKS LIKE YOUR CHARACTER—THEN GIVE HER SOME FLAWS. YOU MIGHT ALSO WANT TO DESCRIBE WHAT SHE LOOKS LIKE, WHAT SHE'S WEARING, AND WHAT SHE LIKES TO WEAR.

If your reader feels her problem is too easy, or that he's too strong, then the reader will have trouble caring for him at the worst moments and won't be able to worry about him. We might KNOW they will get together in the end or that they will survive, but as readers we can't be allowed to see it too easily. Have them show some basic flaws.

GABRIEL'S INFERNO is a good example. While being handsome, rich and worldly, he has a problem with alcohol and sexual addictions. The heroine is brilliant, but lacks self–esteem, especially when it comes to love because of her past experiences.

Characters should not be killed off in the end, unless they are truly unredeemable. But even then, their death must serve a purpose. Evil characters, though, are often kept alive for possible sequels, and of course, family sagas need villains to be kept alive. All romances, of course, must have a happy ending—even if there is death in the story.

Characters are not always easy to control. What they do or say sometimes takes over as the story progresses. You know you're doing it right when they speak to you. Let them have their way. The story will be the better for it.

Above all, always meditate and ask your characters why they are doing something and why this and why that. Then maybe you'll find out why they decided to come live with you and why it's so important to write their stories.

EXERCISE:

Write down:

What is my hero's need or longing? What changes are they making to pursue it?

What is their motivation to continue toward the goal?

What is the hero's flaw? What is their wound? (It could have just happened, or maybe it happened many years ago. Having been abandoned by her mother, my heroine feels everyone else will abandon her.)

What is their belief? If they believe that no one will ever love them, then they are pushing people away (Shrek). How does that belief change through the story?

What skills do they have that will help them pursue their goal? They can't just pick up a sword to fight if we haven't seen that they have that skill before. (It's called set up and pay off.)

What is the hero's identity? If they come across as a secretary, that is who they are seen as that is until they let their essence come through.

What is their essence? What do they really want to be? (Tess, in *Working Girl* really wanted to be a broker, but she came across as a secretary.)

Who are the other characters involved? What are their relationships to the protagonist?

Lastly, what is the villain's goal and how far are they willing to go to see it accomplished? Why does the antagonist want the protagonist to fail so badly?

According to writer Ron Bass, "Stories are what happens between people."

Minor characters are important and each should have their own goals and motivations throughout the story. Their stories should resonate with your theme (perhaps show a different side of it), and/or expand on, or give us information about, the hero's problem. Too many of us writers crowd our stories with characters that are not crucial for the plot. Be sure that everyone has a need in your story and serves a purpose.

EXERCISE:

Go into your meditative space. Be that minor character for just a moment and allow yourself to write, as that character, how you are going to advance the story–either helping the protagonist or (knowingly or not) assisting the antagonist.

Location is also crucial and can affect a story just as much as any character might. Remember to use your senses when writing the settings–smell the baking bread or the scent of the ocean, hear the clash of swords or the cry of the hawks, feel the pain as the knights joust or the fear of the Egyptian army chasing you, watch as someone is hung for treason or beheaded. Think about where you are setting your story and how it touches the lives of your people.

A BRIEF ASTROLOGICAL PICTURE TO HELP YOU CHOOSE YOUR CHARACTER'S SUN SIGN.

ARIES: "I AM." Color: red. Energy high. Initiative, ego, creative, aggressive. Rules head, eyes ears. Impulsive, natural leader desires to excel and be first in nearly every undertaking. Sometimes headstrong. Has to learn to think before acting.

TAURUS: "I HAVE/I POSSESS." Color: yellow. Passionate. Obstinate, slow but sure. Patient and thoughtful. Trouble with communicating desire to others. Loves beauty and harmony, pleasure. Dislikes disruption of order. Steadfast. Has trouble with neck tension.

GEMINI: "I THINK." Color: lite–violet. Intellectual. Versatile, restless, loves a debate, enjoys switching sides and playing "devil's advocate." Talkative, quick. Changeable and flexible. Must learn concentration. Very mental and creative. Lungs and joints are a problem.

CANCER: "I FEEL" or "I think this is so." Color: green. Uses instinct. Timid, emotional, easy to change. If hurt, will withdraw and give you silent treatment. Very sensitive. Fearful. Shy with strangers. Nurturing and wants to take care of all she comes in contact with. Often faced with sad partings because she clings tenaciously to relationships. Stomach problems.

LEO: "I WILL." Color: orange. Gets cold easily. Chill. Males very child–like. Females are the stronger of the two. Arrogant, self–willed. Very proud but loyal. Optimism abounds. Natural confidence. A born leader. Creative but tends to be overindulgent. Dislikes change. Lacks discrimination in personal involvements. Problems in lower back and heart.

VIRGO: "I ANALYZE." Color: dark–violet. Tough as nails on outside but sensitive, critical, witty as well. Discriminating. Quiet, studious, reserved and very practical. Exacting and likes to be organized. Once he makes a decision, he often looks back and wonders if it was right. Often worries about health. A hypochondriac. Problems with the intestines.

LIBRA: "I BALANCE." Color: lite yellow. Very fair. Has trouble making decisions. Vacillates and wants peace at "any cost." Humanitarian, impossible to argue with. Problems with bladder and kidney.

SCORPIO: "I DESIRE, I WANT." Color: dark red. Intense, passionate. Great lover. Sensual, stubborn. Endurance, courage, deep sense of revenge. Holds grudges. Powerful desire. Loyal friend and vengeful enemy. Loves mysteries and puts a lot of energy into solving them. Always looking for others motives. Their stinging words can be deadly—once they decide you are not their friend. But will go to end of earth for you if you are. Problems with reproduction and glands.

SAGITTARIUS: "I SEE OR FORESEE." Color: light purple. Know five years from now but not what's now. Future minded. Athletic. The Bachelor sign. Marries late. Best gift is a set of luggage, they love to travel. See the world through rose glasses. Strong sense of integrity and honor. Always looking for new horizons. Impetuous and has flashes of inspiration. Lower back and legs affected.

CAPRICORN: "I USE/I UTILIZE." Color: dark blue. Serious, materialistic, organized, ambitious, willpower, good memory, hard working. Methodical. Usually get what they want. Distrust things, which can't be scientifically proven. Also a romantic at heart, but will seldom admit this. Problems with hips and bad knees.

AQUARIUS: "I KNOW." Color: light blue. Unique, inventive, inspiration, humanity comes first, idealistic, but dispassionate. Rarely allows emotion to influence judgement. Often years ahead of others in thinking. Seldom feels understood. Politically astute. Problems with legs and ankles.

PISCES: "I BELIEVE/I HAVE FAITH." Color: dark purple. Spiritual. Kind, sensitive, gentle soul. Usually helping people and often psychic. Radiates an inner beauty. Timid, fearful. Absorbs problems of others. Compassionate. Problems with feet.

NOTES

POINTING THE WAY—THE PLOT

If you remove the characters, and nothing happens, then you don't need them in the story.

Plot isn't just an interesting rock that the characters picnic on, or a tricky maze that they walk through. It's the consequences of their actions, the ripples that spread from those actions and strike other characters, who move with or against or not at all, and cause more ripples and reflections.

If the characters are really characters, and not just conveniences of the puzzle, then the ripples they cause will be individual, not generic. Just as you and I did different things this morning, causing different consequences in our different lives, two well–realized characters will do different things in the same situation, causing different ripples that interact with others in different ways.

To use E.M. Forster's famous example, "The king died, and then the queen died." This is a series of events, but it is not a plot.

"The king died, and then the queen died of grief" is a plot.

The difference is causality; plot is about "what," but it is more pointedly about "why."

Forster's reason for bringing this up was to point out the difference between plot and series of events. My reason for quoting it is different: I would point out that "why" comes from characters.

This very lean little plot only works if the queen loves the king. If she hates him, "the king died, and then the queen died of grief" doesn't work.

Why? Character and plot are the meshing. To try to separate them is like trying to separate reason and memory. Without memory, there's nothing for you to reason about, and without reason, memory is meaningless. They're really just aspects of one thing: consciousness.

It's said that Georgette Heyer, the queen of Regency romances and Barbara Cartland, a queen of romances, used to plug characters in to the same basic plot.

Yes, they were successful because they made a lot of money selling their books, but can you recall any of their characters. Did any of them stand out?

If a plot works just as well with any old character plugged into it, that's formula. If I say there are "a lot of formulaic mysteries," that's what I mean. Someone's come up with a clever or interesting idea, painstakingly constructed a foundation and roof for it, and is marching characters through on a schedule. To your left is the dead body; please stay with the group, do not dawdle, and do not pass the velvet ropes; we have a lot of ground to cover in the next sixty thousand words.

Plot and character are essentially the same thing. One must feed into the other. I suppose I should amend my thesis statement to say: plot and character are the same thing . . . only in really good books.

Each plot line should have its own ordeals to face. The plot lines finish in order of least importance. These ordeals (or impending ordeals) are interrupted by periodic, short moments when the ordeals lessen or seem to be over, but even as the characters come up for air and make their choices, something else has to be coming along the track to derail them.

Plotting, a necessary skill is probably one of the most elusive. Both new and established writers have problems in shaping the direction of their book and keeping the momentum going. I still have problems, at times. (And that's why I outline, but more about that later.)

Why do books sell? Two good reasons are pacing and the giving of information that people don't know about. A good example of the latter is ***CLAN OF THE CAVE BEAR***.

In 500 B.C., Aristotle defined plot as a cause and effect pattern where events flow to one and from another, where each event causes something else to happen. Cause and effect/ or action–reaction means you must have a plausible reason for everything that happens. The story, outline, research, and situations are all integral parts of plotting, which one must master.

The story is a sequence of events, not necessarily in chronological order, but arranged to reach the desired conclusion based on the overall theme. The plot carries out the action of these events. However, in order to know how to shape the story, we must know first what we want to put into the story—that's research, and situation.

Situations come from events, characters, and from the interaction of the two. Situations are—or should be—unique to that character at that time. They are a factor or set of factors that pit a man and women against each other in a unique environment. (If there is still a formula for the romance, then this is it.)

The plot necessitates an outline.

The outline of the plot is rather like the road map. It will direct us, tell us where to stop and rest, tell us where to detour, and will—in general—keep us from rambling on and getting lost. The outline, the most basic part of the plot, is a harmonic designing of the story events. It's the framework, structure, or skeletal system upon which everything must properly hang.

If your story line wanders it's because you haven't any direction, and often you haven't direction because the main character doesn't have a strong enough motivation, or things aren't difficult enough for him/her.

When I come to a problem in plot, I always go back to the characters and see where I have gone off the track of what they want. Notice I say they and not I, the writer. Sometimes, it's a matter of setting up an incident that will happen later. (In one script, I almost forget to set up the gum wrapper that would later give the heroine a clue as to the killer. So I had to go back and put that in.)

Failing to do this framework is rather like telling a long joke. Before you get to the punch line, you've forgotten what the story is. Writers who don't pre–plot their books often find they start off with a bang and end with a whimper somewhere along the mid–point, just when the tension needs to be kept strong.

We will be going into the creation of a synopsis and outline at a later point.

Each plot (and subplot within your plot) should have a proper beginning, middle, and end. And each of these points needs to build up, bit by bit, to the final crisis and climax. At each point, we think things will culminate—but they don't.

There are two basic ways to plot. One is by character and letting the story flow from who the character is and what he wants, and the other is from story—making sure the characters fit into the story you want to tell. Because we are told that there are only thirty-six basic plots in the universe, I prefer the first, since it ensures lifelike characters that are memorable. But even if you chose the latter, plot demands that you know who your character is, what he wants, and that he attempts to get what he wants.

Since I work from character, I find asking what my character wants—or thinks he wants, or thinks will make him happy (though in fact it might make him miserable) is the key to the story. This is where the "W" form comes in. The hero should achieve the goal through his own work. No one should step in and give the hero what he wants. He should be strong and courageous enough to achieve what he wants—unlike in the movie ***ARTHUR.*** In the story, which you can rent from Netflix, the character is given everything by his late aunt. Arthur is a weak character—until the end, when he proved he could go after what he really wanted.

Plot, for me, always seems closely aligned to character motivation.

WHAT ARE SOME STRONG MOTIVES?

What would cause you to lie, cheat, steal, or murder? Think of some things now. List them.

If your character dies in the end, you have to feel the pain and it must be believable. It can only be believable if your situation is believable, and if you've done your research so that the reader identifies with the hero/ine and the problem s/he's in.

At the catastrophe, the character must confront death, or the final choice where it seems s/he won't get what he wants (in the romance this is where the couple parts seemingly, never to get back together). Your hero/ine must wrestle the crisis as Jacob (in the Bible) does and achieve something of value—either what s/he thought s/he wanted in the beginning or something far more valuable. If outside forces must come in to rescue your character, that's a weak plot. The Greeks called it ending by machine of the Gods or Deus Ex Machina. (The recent movie, ***RETURN OF THE MUMMY***, had this exact thing in it where the archeologists are rescued by a flying ship.)

Integrity and tension in your story depend on the character's goal—how necessary is it? If the character doesn't want anything, that's okay, but make sure this is truly the case. What s/he really may want is for things to stay the same—which they never do.

VIEWPOINT AND TIME

Before you start writing, you need to know who is telling the story.

The viewpoint of the story is always told from the person who is most affected. Who wants the goal? Who achieves it? That's what your story is about. If the protagonist doesn't do anything toward the goal, then he isn't the protagonist. S/he must work towards solving his own problem.

Take the example of the Dreamworks animation ***SHARK TALE***. They show the Will Smith character as being the protagonist, but in reality, the story was about Lenny, the shark. It was he who should have been telling the story.

Stories which seem confusing, usually are, since the writer hasn't yet decided who's story this is, or perhaps hasn't yet centered on a way to focus the narrative. The only way to handle this is to go back and review each character.

I meet many new screenwriters and novelists who want to do an ensemble piece. They believe that each character can carry the show. In reality, only one character truly leads. The rest of the stories are subplots that enhance the theme. Ensemble stories are hard to carry out and only established writers can do them well.

In novels, it's a bit easier, because each character can carry their own chapter. Nevertheless, you need someone to be the leader of the pack.

Go over your character list. Who is necessary and who isn't? If you can reduce the number of characters and combine some of them, now is the time to do it. But remember we must care about the character you're focusing on, or the story will seem pointless.

If you're writing something, which really happened, you must be aware of collapsed time.

Many people have told me they think I lead an exciting life and that I should write my own story—but if I were to tell everything I do on a daily basis it would be boring! Only if I take certain events then magnify them, and embellish them—perhaps making them seem even worse or better than they were—will I have a story worth telling.

FIRST DRAFTS

Despite what new writers think, plots are not carved in stone. Merely because you've typed it out and it looks great on that white paper, with no typos, doesn't mean it's perfect. A first draft is just that. You must learn to listen to your character and follow what s/he wants. It's the security of knowing whom your characters are which keeps your plot moving. (It's 10 p.m. Do you know where your characters are?)

The short romance books of 60,000 words might look simple, but there is more to the plot than he loves her and she loves him.

Ask: ***What is the time frame of your story?***

A story, which takes places in six days, differs only slightly from one that takes place over several years, but the urgency in a story occurring in six days will enhance the tension you feel. This is where the ticking clock comes in. Who are the other characters involved? How do they affect the feelings of each of these main characters toward the other?

I use the paradigm, which Syd Field (a screen writing teacher—author of

WRITING THE SCREENPLAY—Dell) developed. It works well for the shorter books, though for the longer books you might want to have one paradigm for each subplot as well.

Briefly, your beginning must indicate some type of problem. (In the manuscript, the tip of the problem—enough to hook the reader—should appear no later than page 7.) Someone has to want something and someone or something else stands in the way.

Often the beginning starts with the main character's normal life and then quickly goes into the problem. It doesn't have to be the main problem, but something that will keep the audience going for a while.

Fear builds tension, and leads to action, which leads to more action—but if they fear something in chapter one, don't wait until chapter three (or the end of Act 1)for the culmination of that fear.

In the first chapter of ***SHRIEKING SHADOWS*** (one of my romantic suspense books), she fears that Percy knows who she is and will expose her. She forgets about him until we see him at the house, and then we learn who he really is—and her fear is magnified. Something should happen quickly so that the fear grows—in a different direction.

By the end of the first chapter(or somewhere about page 20), something unexpected happens to turn the story so that what the character thought would happen is obviously changing. This would be the inciting incident that we speak of in screenwriting. It is something which propels your story in another direction?

In ***SHRIEKING SHADOWS,*** she finds out that she is expected to wed the Lord of the manor the following day.

In ***TAME THE WILD HEART,*** my Tapestry Historical—I give the clue of her problem and show how her desire for Sebastian and fear of him spins us into the middle of the story.

To create more tension, many authors—with longer books—will start their subplots here. The reader, however, will become frustrated if left hanging too long.

Harmony and flow combining action with contemplative moments are needed, since too much excitement can also cause boredom.

The movie, ***INDIANA JONES II—TEMPLE OF DOOM,*** is a good example of this. There was so much action, you couldn't catch your breath and enjoy the story.

Whatever happens must grow out of the character and the inevitable so that the reader will be satisfied.

After you've passed the first point (foreshadowing of the middle), you can fill in some of the background material on the characters—but don't overdo. A series of small points, which Syd calls pitches, keeps the tension tight and foreshadows the events of the mid–point or the end.

The middle is how the hero thinks he's solving the problem. Like a bell curve, it's the high point where tension is keenest and just before the drastic drop—and it's where more new authors fail. The event, which has been foreshadowed at the end of the first chapter, will occur here. The character will quickly realize that this is not what they really want or need and the rest of the story goes toward that new goal.

Open a well–constructed book to the exact middle. You should find something of importance happening within those few pages. Halfway to the end, you will discover another turning point where the story will once more twist in a direction that the character does not expect.

This is a calculated scene, the end of Act 2 in screenwriting, which will foreshadow the climax. Just before the end is the catastrophe where the hero is as low as he can go and still live. It's where your hero thinks he has been beaten, but then gets his last wind as he sees the villain about to rape his girlfriend.

The end will be the success, ironic success, or failure of the hero's mission, or when the couple gets together.

Knowing when to end the book, when to tie up all the strings, is something new writers also forget. They tend to ramble and philosophize, boring the reader as they do in the beginning, where they should have started with action and didn't. They overwrite. This is why it is so important for the writer to know and understand their ending before they begin. It helps to know where to plan the clues and payoffs.

During the course of the story, the protagonist must have a recognition scene and must understand something about himself, which he didn't acknowledge before. This is his arc. Each character has a character arc which shows how he grows during the story. As the story unravels, he discovers his own weakness or strength—and becomes better because of it. The discovery might even be what is standing between the hero and heroine is as simple as pride. (Jane Austin's ***PRIDE AND PREJUDICE*** is an excellent example.)

BODY HEAT is also a good example of paradigm plotting. You start by seeing a man who doesn't seem too successful at his profession. By the first point, he meets Mattie. The tension is so great they throw things about the house and make passionate love.

The crucial point, which foreshadows the middle, is when Mattie says how nice it would be if her husband was dead. If your character had been established as a hard worker, you'd know he wouldn't go along with it, but our hero here has already been seen to be someone who is rather lazy and likes things the easy way. At the midpoint, they kill her husband.

The end is foreshadowed with two points—one where the character calls him saying a woman called asking for another bomb.

Our hero isn't smart enough to understand that this is Mattie, but we know. In fact, at one point in the movie, she says, "You're not too smart, are you? I like that."

Our final spin comes when she doesn't answer his phone calls. We know she's not going to keep her end of the bargain and Ned ends up in jail.

Our darkest point always comes after the high—the midpoint when everything seemed so wonderful, and then from the depths of despair, it climbs higher and higher so that life is even better than it was at the beginning.

In ***FATAL ATTRACTION***, it's where Michael thinks he has gotten away with the affair and is sure that the woman, Glen Close, is off his case. His life with his wife is wonderful—until his mistress decides that she will fight for his affection.

There are no accidents in a good book—everything must flow from everything else. You want to be careful of having too many coincidences or luck. Everything must be cause and effect. You don't want an escaping con to "just happen to find" a car with the keys dangling. Luck like that doesn't happen in real life and shouldn't happen in your story. If you are going to use a scene like that, it has to be set up prior. Maybe a mother drops her son off at daycare and runs into the school for a moment, stupidly leaving the keys there. Even that's a bit far-fetched. Everything should be set up so that there can be a pay off. If you find you have a coincidence or "accidental luck," you need to go back and set it up so that it doesn't appear contrived.

As writers, we secretly play with our characters, but we don't want this to appear obvious or forced. The plot must appear to be natural to who the characters are and their history. Everything should happen for a reason. We don't want two characters to be "accidentally" getting into the elevator at the same time and have a cute meet there unless we have set it up ahead of time. Maybe they are both at the same conference.

Bad luck or bad coincidences can create comedy, but you want to be careful of having too many of those. Using coincidences are a sign of lazy writing. Take what you have and twist it around to something not expected.

Outlining helps you develop the cliffhangers and the end of each chapter. These are necessary because they keep the reader turning the pages.

THE PARADIGM

From Syd Field's book—WRITING THE SCREENPLAY—Dell)

Syd's paradigmapplies to both novels and screenplays, though, of course, the page numbers differ.

Pages 1–10 SET UP THE SITUATION. THE NORMAL LIFE OF THE HERO. DON'T USE THE WHOLE PAST OR YOU'LL SUFFOCATE THE READER. FORESHADOW WHAT WILL HAPPEN. HINT AT THE PROBLEM.

AROUND PAGE 10–12 THE INCITING INCIDENT HAPPENS WHEN WE REALIZE THAT THE NORMAL LIFE IS ABOUT THE CHANGE.

END FIRST CHAPTER—OR about pages 27–30 IN LONGER BOOKS—PLOT POINT 1—THE STORY SPINS AROUND TO SOMETHING YOU DON'T SUSPECT.

MID WAY TO MID POINT IS A PINCH (rather like the tuck a dressmaker does in a skirt to tighten it and make it fit), WHICH FORESHADOWS THE MID POINT. (If she's going to sleep with the hero at the midpoint then this could be as simple as a sentence indicating that she thinks he's handsome enough for her to throw away her scruples.)

MID POINT—SOMETHING EXCITING HAPPENS. THE HIGH POINT OF THE BOOK—THIS CAN BE SEXUAL. (SYD says page 60—since that's about the center of a screenplay, though these days screenplays have gotten shorter and may be as short as ninety-five pages. Therefore, you have to calculate accordingly.)

2nd PINCH—(ABOUT PAGE 75 IN THE SCRIPT) FORESHADOWS THE DARK MOMENT.

PLOT POINT#2—(90–97) THE DARKEST MOMENT AND THE STRUGGLE WHERE THE BOOK SPINS AROUND AND THE STORY ENDS—USUALLY HAPPIER OR BETTER THAN THEY WERE AT THE BEGINNING.

RESOLUTION—from plot point 2 UNTIL END OF BOOK (95–120 pages in a screen play, 240 in a short book).

This is only a very brief discussion of Syd's method and I suggest you read his book on screenplay writing if you need further information.

EXERCISE:

TAKE A BOOK AND BREAK IT DOWN ON THE PARADIGM.

DO YOUR OWN BOOK ON THE PARADIGM.

SCENES

When doing the plotting, you have between three and five scenes in each chapter. If you have several subplots, or if you're doing a romantic suspense—two of those scenes will forward the romance, another scene will forward the mystery.

A scene is any place where you've made a major change in time, location, viewpoint, or character. A scene can last as long as twenty pages (in a book) or as short as half a page. Scenes are mini–short stories. They have their own beginning, middle, and end. Scenes together make up a chapter, which makes up a book. Like a puzzle, they all fit.

EXERCISE:

TAKE YOUR OWN BOOK, OR ONE YOU ARE BREAKING DOWN, AND SEE HOW MANY SCENES PER CHAPTER. SEE HOW MANY SCENES IN EACH CHAPTER ARE DEVOTED TO THE MAIN PLOT, TO THE SUBPLOTS.

STARTING TO OUTLINE

If you're doing a historical, then you already have a skeleton on which to hang the flesh of your story, but even then, for every movement of the hero, there must be a movement of the villain. The villain must be a worthy opponent for the hero and have every reason to expect success, himself. He wants what the hero wants just as badly.

Remember to use the emotions. We as writers have to manipulate the emotions of the characters so that the audience feels our hero's pain when he is injured and joy when he is happy. Things must seem realistic, too.

As an example, think of when Jason Bourne's leg is injured. He must limp around for part of the book. That means, when he's trying to get away on a foot chase, he can stumble and fall so that we fear the villain will catch up with him.

EXERCISE:

WRITE A NARRATIVE OUTLINE FOR YOUR STORY—SCENE BY SCENE—AND IF BASED ON HISTORICAL FACT, BE PREPARED TO DETAIL THIS, SHOWING HOW THE HISTORY AFFECTS THE CHARACTERS.

ENDINGS

Those writers who don't pre–plot often come to the end and find that things just aren't making sense. They'll grab an answer out of the air—usually one that's weak, illogical, and really doesn't fit in with the plot, but has what the author thinks s/he wants. Readers are disappointed, and so are the editors.

To know how to begin, you must know where you want to end. You must have an idea of the tone you want to set in the story and how you want it resolved.

EXERCISE:

If you don't have your story fully in your head, then answer this for the story you are breaking down. When you are ready to write and plot your own story, go back and answer these questions.

KNOW WHERE YOUR CHARACTERS ARE GOING. KNOW HOW THEIR STORY WILL END.

DID YOU PLAN FOR THE ENDING TO BE THIS WAY, OR DID IT JUST SURPRISE YOU?

HAVE YOU FORESHADOWED ALL THE CLUES THAT LEAD TO THE END?

DOES THE END COME FROM THE EMOTION AND BACKGROUND OF ONE OF THE CHARACTER'S?

DOES IT FLOW WITH THEIR STORY AND THEIR MOTIVES?

OR IS THE ENDING OBVIOUSLY A QUICK WAY TO GET OUT OF THE STORY?

"WHAT IF"

Those who have trouble plotting can go back to their characters and do a "what if."

What if the little girl crying on the corner was kidnapped?

What if she was trying to get back to her parents?

What if you helped her and got entangled in the problem, yourself?

PUBLISHERS GUIDELINES

While I said there are no more formulas for genre books, there are, nevertheless, certain guidelines you must follow. There are general ones—as with romance—you must have a happy ending, a minimum of death and violence, no rape*, etc. Then there are specific ones for each publishing house, which you must follow—like location (some editors like foreign locales, some prefer USA), ages of characters, marital status, etc.

*(The older romances used to use rape as a means to get the hero and heroine together, but it was never popular with the readers.)

If you are trying to write for a line, as with the romances, then you should read books by that publisher to see what special things they want and how they like the situation approached.

Publishing houses for the other genres don't usually give guidelines, but it is a good idea to read books, which that house has produced. Romance houses, as Harlequin, often have listed guidelines that include the items they want to see in a book. (See earlier section on romantic lines and guidelines.)

The "what if" can also help you when you're stuck and asking your characters—well, what happens next? Listen to your characters and to your inner voice—and visualize the story on a board before you. If your mind wanders, then let it wander. Don't get hung up on remembering how it "should" be.

FILM STRIPPING

(To be used as you are writing, not while playing poker <g>)

Imagination is a muscle, which you must use daily to keep it oiled. Try to structure your writing for the same hour each day, until you get into the pattern and rhythm of your story.

As you can see, visualization techniques are something I favor. If you don't have someone who can read this out loud to you and then you help them, you might try taping the instructions first before you close your eyes.

Close eyes. Concentrate on a place you've seen, visited, saw in a film–something you want to use in your story.

Pretend your mind is a sound camera taking a scene. Are you getting all the sensations the camera can get—the weather, noise level, colors of food, flowers, clothes, etc? What about the people and their complexions, body language, conversations? What scents would you smell—grass, perfumes, fresh paint?

If you're doing a historical, pretend you are there—in the past. After taking several deep breaths, look down at your feet and describe the shoes you are (would be) wearing. Are you male or female?

What life is about you?

Who's there with you?

What food are you eating and with what (if any) utensils?

See the clothes you're wearing, and hear the name you're being called.

Smell the flowers, the sea, or the city around you.

Think of an important event in the lifetime of the person you are in your mind. Perhaps it is the birth of a child (what was it like), your first lover, a ride on a wild horse with the wind streaming through your long hair?

How old are you? Move forward in that life.

What happens when you die?

How do you die?

Who is around you then?

Have all your secrets been told or is anything still hidden?

Now go back to your first scene and focus on the people. Overhear them talking.

Why it's two of your characters!

What are they saying?

Open your eyes and write for ten minutes without speaking on what you just saw. Let the words flow.

Then, close your eyes again and go to a scene at each major point of your story.

See the heroine's apartment, meet her roommate, see her at work, meeting the hero, see the sparks fly, see the scene where they commit to each other. Imagine it all.

Choose three or four vivid or important details from these scenes to depict the moment and make it memorable. Impressions must be strong and vital to you. If they aren't, don't choose them. (i. e., his hand trembling as he gives her the engagement ring; how she firmly grasps his hand, see the tears in her eyes.)

EXERCISE:

QUESTIONS TO ASK WHILE PLOTTING A ROMANCE

While these apply to romance novels, especially, they can be used for any novel. (These questions appeared in my article in ***HOW TO WRITE A ROMANCE***, Falk, and Crown.) You will see that these point up how the character affects the plot. If you are not writing a romance, just glance over them briefly because some of the material will apply to other genres.

HERO:

Is he loveable?

What flaws does he have?

Is he a perfect, handsome ten or not?

What has made him the way he is?

How vulnerable is he?

Why is he vulnerable?

What secrets does he have?

Can he cry?

What's his age?

Can you fall in love with him?

Does his name stand out?

HEROINE:

What are her strengths and weaknesses? Is she career–oriented, and if so, what career?

How does she meet the hero? How do the other characters know him?

How would you rate her looks? Since readers must identify with her, don't make her perfect.

How sexually aware is she?

How experienced? What's her age? Do you want to be the heroine?

Do you cry when she cries?

Is her age plausible for her career?

Does her name stand out?

Do you know her as well as your best friend, or better?

SITUATION:

Is the situation plausible?

Is it something you can expect to happen as an everyday occurrence?

Is the situation original?

Is the situation contrived?

Does the situation present enough natural obstacles on its own so you won't have to fabricate some?

LOCALE:

Considering both their careers, is this locale likely?

For the lovers?

For the story?

Have you accurately described the area and done research? (Nothing upsets a reader more than knowing the writer hasn't done proper research—like having the desert winds blow east from the Santa Monica Mountains—as I once read!)

Can you transport your readers to that locale by your description—without force feeding them?

Is locale an element essential to the plot? It should be.

LOVE SCENES:

Not all books require these, and if you are writing mystery or romantic suspense, they often occur, they are there, off page.

Are you convinced that the lovers are in love when they tumble into bed?

Is the love scene too sensible? He should be perfection in bed.

How long is this love scene? (In the romances, you want lots of foreplay and afterplay.)

What are they doing to avoid a commitment? (A must in romances.)

Is he the only one for her?

How does she show she loves him?

What were the turning points in her feelings?

How does he know she loves him?

What was the turning point in his feelings?

Are you writing with all your senses—sight, smell, touch, hearing, and taste?

SEPARATION:

What drives the lovers apart?

How long do they stay apart?

Is what's driving the lovers apart realistic? Or is it a big assumption and misunderstanding on the hero/ine's part, which can be easily resolved?

Will the reader believe that the hero/ine really believes this misunderstanding has forced them apart?

If you are doing a mystery, what prevents the hero/ine from reaching his/her goal?

OTHER WOMAN, OTHER MAN (or other obstacles)

Have you created a convincing other woman? (In romances, the cold bitch is out.)

The other woman can be a family member, ex–girlfriend, ex–wife, but these roles should be downplayed.

Have you created a convincing other man? He can be a confidant of the hero, friend, her old beau, or ex–husband. Neither of these people should be the ultimate reason for the lover's separation.

OBSTACLES: SECOND ROUND

Have you decided on what other obstacles can possibly drive the lovers apart? Check again with your original situation.

Then drive them apart again—for a plausible reason.

MORE LOVE SCENES:

Can the obstacles be momentarily dropped for his or her passion?

Does this lead to another love scene?

Can they yet admit their love for each other—or are they still scared?

This might be a good time to consider it, but even if they love each other, they shouldn't be sure of commitment yet.

MORE OBSTACLES:

Can they make a life together? This is usually a heroine's doubt.

Can she fit her life into his? His into hers?

RESOLUTION:

Are you certain there are no dangling ends? All obstacles should be resolved by now. All other subplot ends are tied up. Are you convinced that the lovers really like each other and can make a happy life together?

MAKING YOUR STORY FRESH

1. Avoid opening the story in a moving vehicle. Instead of having the protagonist on her way to an encounter, have her already in the midst of the action as the story starts. Whenever possible, begin with action and/or dialogue.
2. Don't overload circuits—keep background information in Chapter 1 to a minimum and dribble the material in for the first quarter of the book. Then you can gradually add more. Start slowly and prime your engine.

3. If you are writing a romance, remember it is a wonderful fantasy. Don't use depressing subjects. If you're doing a more realistic book, then make it realistic.
4. Avoid using stereotypical people like "the other woman" or Scottish housekeeper, black nanny—in romances, children who are too "cute," villains who are too evil. No one is ever totally evil.
5. Don't have coitus interruptus—or telephone, doorbell ringing. If you're going to have a sex scene, then have one.
6. Describe your characters in sections. Don't have them gaze into a mirror and see the whole of their lives appear before them.
7. Don't separate your hero and heroine too long.
8. Don't let others solve the problem for them.

One of the things I teach all my writing students—fiction and screenplay—is to have passion for their subject. If an author doesn't have that passion—which always shows—how can the reader?

BEGIN NOT AT THE BEGINNING

I am a hooker, but most people don't want to be grabbed. So instead I'd like to seduce you—into reading or watching my stories. I turn you, the reader, on by making the beginning so alive and exciting that you want to continue.

A tight beginning is crucial if you are writing something that can be put down or if the channels can be turned. If the recipient is not hooked immediately, you have lost them. Plain and simple. This is why, on the new Dracula series, they have an eight minute teaser—so you won't change the channel.

Because scripts, especially, must be read before they can be seen on screen. Your writing must be visual and sensual. This applies to books, as well.

BORING BEGINNING

Hooking the viewer/reader into your beginning is really not all that difficult, but most new writers seem to have problems with beginnings. They start out with boring background material and long drawn–out explanations of how the character came to be where she is.

One of the worst ways to start is with the heroine just waking up in bed and starting her day.

I use the feminine pronoun since "Woman in Jeopardy" is one of the most popular types of stories these days.

The trouble is, if we don't already care about the character, then we don't care why she is where she is. Often the incidents in the prologue are interesting, but have nothing to do with the story. The writer "just thought they fit in nicely."

While it's true that you want to know your characters as much as possible before you start writing, not all the knowledge considering those first few pages are the most crucial for the story.

Most editors and story consultants tell me that if the first three pages don't engross them, the script/novel goes back into the envelope. You could, of course, revise, but it's better to get it right the first time.

Your first three pages must be visual. We'll go into words that are visual later.

It should START WITH AN IMPORTANT ACTION.

Tell us why this moment is different for the character than any other moment she's ever before experienced.

THINK STRESSES

Disagreement, change, pressure, and fear to force the issues. What are the stresses that the character is dealing with? And then think of how it can get worse.

In ***THE NET***, Sandra Bullock's character was a loner. She was dealing with the stress of her mom in a nursing home and she was trying to work through a difficult computer virus she had discovered. When she thinks she gets the answer, the problem gets worse, because her contact at the company dies unexpectedly . . . and now someone is after her for the disk.

MAKE PROMISES YOU INTEND TO KEEP.

If this is a romantic comedy, start with a hint of romance. If it is mystery, start with the dead body or some other problem that can quickly get worse.

Again, using Sandra Bullock's film***, WHILE YOU WERE SLEEPING***, as an example, you learn immediately that she works as a teller for the CTA (Chicago Transit Authority.) Very soon after, you know that she is desperately in love with one of the passengers who comes to her station every day, but who has never even noticed her. You learn the bleakness of her life. And then . . . she witnesses his accident, rescues him and tells his family that she is engaged to him. Uh–oh!

The beginning must do several things–

1. Transport the reader into your character's world. Establish the daily life of the character.
2. Introduce the character situation and actions of the character in their new world.
3. Create empathy with the hero and become that character as we root for the character
4. Set the mood and tone of the story–be it thriller, comedy, or sci–fi.
5. Elicit emotion.

INTRODUCE OR FORESHADOW YOUR MAJOR CHARACTERS

I just read one short story where the author started it as a letter to the character's mother. Boring and dull. Make sure that your major characters are doing something or something is being done to them. Don't just have them walk into the room and say hi.

WHILE YOU WERE SLEEPING did not start with Sandra's early childhood or with the hero's family life. It introduced the two main characters at the tip of a situation and then foreshadowed the events that were about to take place.

PROTAGONIST/ANTAGONIST

Help the reader to choose someone to root for and identify with, and recognize whom to fear, suspect, or dislike. You might want to go back to the character chapter and refresh your memory here. While it should be clear who is the bad guy, you don't want the villain to be totally black nor the protagonist totally white. No one is. Color in shades of gray and browns, not just white and black. They might be killers, but they'll take time to rescue a dog in the street.

WHAT'S AT STAKE?

Establish what your major character has to gain or lose. In Eastwood's movie, ***ABSOLUTE POWER,*** he played a burglar who, while robbing a rich home, witnesses a murder, but not just any murderer—The President of the United States. He has a lot to lose if he comes forth and a lot to gain if he keeps quiet, but can he live with himself? In this case, it was only his conscious at stake, but truth of a murder. (That is one example of black and white.)

WHAT ARE YOUR CHARACTERS GOALS?

In this case, Eastwood started out with one goal but ended up with a totally different one, exposing the murder.

What obstacles have to be cleared? What milestones have to be reached? In ***ABSOLUTE POWER,*** Eastwood had to get the information out and he had to make sure he was believed.

ESTABLISH THE SETTING

Give us a visual picture as quickly as possible. I don't just mean EXT. and INT. shots. Give us a feel of the rich man's home that Eastwood is breaking into, give us a feel of the cold Chicago wind on the L–track as Sandra Bullock takes tickets. A good writer must be able to make the reader see what he is seeing, so that it can translate into good scenes for the director and producer. (This applies to novels, as well, since the reader must be able to immerse himself in the story.)

THE BEGINNING MUST FORESHADOW THE CONCLUSION.

It hints at where the opposing forces will collide. A robber who does not uphold the law has truthful information implicating the President, who is supposed to uphold the law.

SET THE TONE—the overall personality of the story. Don't try to set records for figures of speech used, resist temptation to use puns or throwaway humor. In the words of a well known Hollywood reader, KISS them—***KEEP IT SIMPLE, STUPID***. Remember the average reader has, maybe, a 6th grade education. Script readers, which is who will read your material first, get bored easily and are looking for a reason to reject. Junior readers at publishing houses might have an advantage, but they too are overworked, underpaid, and looking for a way to reject your book.

NOTHING SHOULD BE PERMITTED IN THESE FEW PAGES THAT DOESN'T CARRY IT'S OWN WEIGHT.

If you find your own interest waning, then the readers most certainly will. Take a survey of missing elements and rewrite.

GOOD BEGINNING

A good beginning grabs. It starts with action, dialogue, and a problem. True, there is some narrative. There has to be. But the narrative is carefully placed and blended so that it captures the reader's attention. Be careful of having too much narrative and description up front. We need to get introduced to and know your characters. For most stories, a problem must be established by page 7, or certainly no later than the end of the first chapter. Be careful of having too many flashbacks, false beginnings (where your character dies at the end of Chapter or Act 1), start with dreams, voice overs (this is especially important for scripts), have too much detail (especially true for science fiction or fantasy stories where you are trying to set the scene), prologues, or a laundry list of introducing too many characters (especially concentrating too much on their physical features.)

Everyone here in Hollywood is a potential writer and almost everyone I know: the waitress at my coffee shop, the gas station attendant, my lawyer, my housekeeper, the police captain, and numerous others have stories and maybe even written scripts that are waiting to be sent to Spielberg. Some of them are junk, some are decent, some are good, yours has to be better.

The good start is much like a journalistic lead, using the five W's—who, what, where, when, and why. For example, in ***TAME THE WILD HEART,*** my Irish historical: "who" is Roxanne Alden, "what" is she's a spy, "where" is Dublin, Ireland, "when" is James II's battle with William III, 1690, and "why" is because she hates James.

Once you have hooked your readers into identifying and caring about the character's problems, you can fill in background material and then introduce the other facts explaining more fully how she came to this place and why. But the beginning must set the scene and set the mood.

Use all your senses when starting a story, because it is the senses that help the reader identify with the situation. Think about what you would hear, see, feel, taste, smell, and intuit from a place.

"The hot desert wind gusted over the barren landscape, blowing painfully hard particles against her already parched skin" sounds better than "The wind blew across the desert."

PROLOGUES

Well, what about prologues, you're probably asking.

I would stay away from them. It's rare that an author can successfully use them. Most of the times when I've bought a story with a prologue, I skim the prologue because I'm bored and I've picked up the story only because I know that author will give me a good read. However, if the writer is new to me—I don't trust them yet. The prologue might very well turn me off.

WHERE TO START

The next time you're ready to write, go to chapter 3. Yes, that's right. Skip chapters 1 and 2, and see if you can summarize them in one or two sentences, or perhaps a paragraph. Chances are chapter 3 is where the action starts, where the problem is. Chances are this will be a far better opening for you.

I know it hurts to discard those first few precious scenes, but don't worry, you'll get to use the information later—maybe in a flashback. Or maybe that information really wasn't ready to be used.

Start with action, use the journalistic lead, and you'll have a stronger beginning and a better story. No matter what you are writing.

There are two kinds of story beginnings. The direct version which starts with character, setting, or problem. (A character) Joy had hair the color of squash, and fourteen freckles across her nose, plus others she really didn't want to be seen. (Setting, which sets a mood) The great dark trees of the big woods stood all around the house. As far as one could see, as far as one could travel in a day, there were only trees. No houses, no people, just the woods—and the trees. (A problem) No one ever had a sister like Ramona before; or "The murder of my sister is what brought me to Penporth Island?"

Good description is necessary in a narrative scene.

The indirect way of starting, which can be more interesting, but is often more difficult, is starting with dialogue or action. It's harder because you have to get the action going while hooking up into and establishing the character as well.

EXERCISE:

LOOK AT SOME STORIES —books and scripts. There are several places on line where you can read scripts for free.

FIND AN OPENING THAT HOOKS YOU AND ONE THAT DOESN'T. COMPARE THEM.

Scripts can be bought (or downloaded for free) from a variety of places in LA. See the address list at the back of the book. Or go to the library and check out a book of plays. (Not exactly the same format, but you will get the idea.) Some scripts are even in bound form in libraries, especially if you have a college library near. (If you live in LA, the Writer's Guild Library on Third and Fairfax has scripts available to be read in the room.)

WRITE YOUR OWN OPENING IN THREE VIEWPOINTS.

Decide who is the best to be the vocal character of your story.

WRITE YOUR OPENING USING CHARACTER, SETTING, OR PROBLEM.

Use your senses and describe the scenes, but be concise. Remember, you are allowed maybe 110 pages on a whole script. (Not 110 pages for just the beginning.)

In script writing, less is more. They prefer a leaner description, but enough so they can see the setting. You don't have to describe the Jacobean chairs or the wide maple desk, but you can say an ornate attorney office, and let the reader and set designer imagine it.

THEN WRITE YOUR OPENING STARTING WITH DIALOGUE.

See which flows best for you. There is no rule, as each story has it's own voice and a lot of that depends on the character you want telling the story.

Some other openings that work–setting the genre, tone, and identity of the hero.

1. Big action–an action hero–cop, spy, etc. and big action sequence like ***RAIDERS OF THE LOST ARC*** or ***GLADIATOR.*** You can use this only if the hero's every day life involves action, because emotion grows out of conflict.
2. The same action opening, but the hero isn't there. It's a big occurrence with lots of action–as much as five pages. Then you cut to the hero in his ordinary life and show the comparison. The reader will see that the character's life has no action at all like a waitress pouring coffee for her customer. We with our superior knowledge know that she is in for some real surprises—and danger.

3. Prologue—the opening of the wound. This can be distant or closeup. Think of Tom Hanks and Daryl Hannah in ***SPLASH,*** where as a child he encounters the mermaid for the first time**.** In my current script, I show the mother's murder and thereby set the tone. Anticipation is created.
4. Flashback—a prologue where the first scene starts in the distant past or the flash starts in present and then flashes back—***TITANIC.***
5. The everyday hero is introduced in his ordinary life before the conflict comes. The first person we see and hear about is the hero.

NOTES

SEEING THE WORLD THROUGH ROSE'S GLASSES

VIEWPOINT

Probably one of the hardest things to master—and one where new writers fall down the quickest—is viewpoint. The problem comes both in choosing the proper viewpoint and in sticking to that choice.

As you've no doubt read, there are three—actually four—viewpoints used in novels: The first person, third (singular), omniscient, and second. As I said, however, prologues are discouraged by most agents. So are flashbacks. Use them judiciously.

The second or "you" viewpoint was popular in an earlier century, especially when writers often gave "asides" and lectured the reader. You'll seldom see that in a book today and only the very unusual and esoteric novel can carry off something like this. (Even if you have the talent, very few books warrant this type of treatment.)

The first person was also very popular last century and still has its moments now. It's best used for very emotional books such as gothics and mysteries where the character/reader identification is the most crucial.

Most new authors find this the easiest to work with because saying" I dreamed of Manderlay last night," creates more immediate empathy than "Rebecca dreamed of Manderlay the other night."

In fact, many new writers find it's easier for them to write their book in first person—since they can get into the characters' heads better—and then they go back and change to third.

However, use of the first person is limiting. You can see, hear, or experience only what your "I" character is doing. It's rather difficult to sustain in a long book.

Susan Howatch succeeds with this style in ***CASTLEMARA,*** only by doing several different first person viewpoints in different chapters, as does Norah Lofts in many of her historical novels. But it takes a certain type of book and a certain type of author to be able to carry this off. Most editors do not like first person novels; nor, as a matter of fact, do most readers.

Third singular is the best for short books. While you are supposedly limited to the sights and sounds experienced by this character, you can describe and have narrative, which your character isn't experiencing. With this approach, it's much easier to fill in background material, as well as subplots since you can go into another character's view and with good transitions return to your main character without the reader being jarred.

Last to consider is omniscient style. This is the most overused and abused type of writing. What it means is that the author can jump from one character to the next, and get into several different characters' heads, but too many new authors attempt this and fail.

REJECTION

Writers fail because they don't have proper transition from one viewpoint to another.

They fail because they switch views in a single sentence or paragraph—making it impossible to know who is thinking or saying what.

They fail because they don't let us sufficiently into one character's head before jumping to another; but mostly, they fail because they don't understand what they're doing.

Editors I've talked to say that one of the most common reasons for manuscript rejection is viewpoint switching in the first few pages, so that one has to go back and line by line trace each section to try and determine who is talking. Even then it's often impossible to tell.

IDENTIFICATION

Since the reader/editor must identify with the heroine/hero and must become totally caught up in the fictional world you are creating, it's necessary that you stay with one character until that identification is established. If you're writing a romance, you want to know from her viewpoint what it feels like to be falling in love and not know if your love is returned. Your reader—as s/he reads—must feel that s/he is the character.

Keeping your viewpoints straight also keeps up the exquisite tension necessary for page turning. If I identify with the heroine, then all the terrible things happening to the heroine are happening to the reader (me).

When I curl up with a book to escape, I become whomever the story is about. I therefore resent characters that are too naive to be believable. I feel, in such cases, that the writer is writing down to me. One gothic I read, the heroine was so stupid. She went down a dark path with only a single flashlight. The author neglected to tell us that the electricity in the tunnel had been cut. We find that out only later. Something like this is important to tell the reader.

Switching back and forth from female to male viewpoint in a romance doesn't give me enough identification with either—unless one viewpoint (the person whose story it really is)—clearly dominates.

How you use your point of view clearly defines who the character is and whose story it is. Those trying to write suspense will find that tension is diluted when viewpoints switch too often.

EXERCISE:

TAKE A BOOK WHOSE VIEWPOINT WORKS FOR YOU, PERHAPS ***CASTLEMARA***, OR JUDY BLUME'S ***SMART WOMEN***.

BREAK THEM DOWN AND ANALYZE—

WHY DOES THIS WORK FOR YOU? WHY DO YOU THINK THE AUTHOR CHOSE THIS VIEWPOINT?

WHAT WOULD THE STORY BE LIKE IF IT HAD BEEN TOLD FROM ANOTHER CHARACTER'S VIEW?

WHY DOESN'T THE SAME TYPE OF VIEW POINT WORK FOR YOU IN ANOTHER BOOK THAT'S SIMILAR?

WHAT HAS THE AUTHOR DONE HERE TO MAKE YOU (THE READER) IDENTIFY WITH THE CHARACTER?

Remember the character who changes the most, the one who affects the action, is usually her view point character.

MULTI–VIEWS

Omniscient viewpoints are like watercolors on crisp paper. You want the colors to remain distinct and not to bleed together. You want to know who is talking and why. Take a glass of colored water (story) and put more water (more viewpoints) into the glass. The more water (viewpoints) you add, the more diluted your story becomes so that not even the deepest color (emotion) can touch your reader. And if you don't touch your reader, they won't touch your books.

When writers (myself included) experience writer's block, it's usually because we're having problems deciding what point of view to use and from whose vantage point the majority of the story should be told.

Look at ***GONE WITH THE WIND.*** It was told from Scarlett's view. Had it been told from Rhett's, Ashley's, or Melanie's, it would have been a totally different story. By changing viewpoint, you change the story. It's Scarlett's story, which holds the whole book together because she is an active character, and one who is seen and acts in almost every scene. This is a key issue for a viewpoint character.

Again, returning to ***SHARK TALE,*** the viewpoint character should have been Lenny, the shark.

If we're doing a story about a teenage girl and have her mother inviting the teen's boyfriend over for dinner, and have the mother persuade the girl that she's pretty—then the story is the mother's and not the girl's.

Therefore when choosing your main character, you want one who is active and is acting on her life, doing what must be done to achieve her goal, and not one who is waiting for the world to come to her. Passive heroines like Amelia of ***VANITY FAIR*** are out—no matter what you are writing.

When you are starting with third person, you need to get right to the point and start the problem; things need to start happening.

VIEWPOINT MEANS BEING INSIDE THE CHARACTER'S HEAD. KNOWING THAT CHARACTER'S THOUGHTS AND FEELINGS.

In order to grab the reader's attention, we must make them FEEL LIKE the main character and CARE ABOUT THAT CHARACTER'S PROBLEM, WHICH YOUR STORY IS SOLVING.

It's necessary, even when using multi–viewpoint, to stick with things that only your characters can know and experience in their world. They're not going to know or care what's happening across the ocean—unless it directly affects them somehow. Both the third person singular and the first person viewpoints are much like a horse with blinders. However, it's easier to switch into narrative or another character if you're working with third person.

Time is needed to create a feeling of real identification with the one character. If you get into another's viewpoint by accident, it will not only be confusing, but it may be fatal for your story.

If you must change character viewpoint before the end of a chapter break, then use white space to indicate the transition to a new personality. The effect, otherwise, is very jarring. Another trick I use are stars *** to help with transitions of viewpoint, time, or location.

Remember, too, you can never kill off your viewpoint person or the story dies too. I recall one of the very first stories I ever wrote (I think I was about ten years old.) was the "Diary of Rita Sun" about a young girl who is stranded on a planet and fears the natives are cannibals. I had written it from first person and I realized as I neared the end of my story that if I had her killed or eaten, there was no way this story would ever find its way back to earth, or that it could be logically told.

Lecturing the reader is not something you want to do—though I have seen it come in from students and clients alike! (They seem to think that if they are writing a historical they can be as leisurely as the writers of that period, but just the opposite is true.)

Again, knowing the character and who s/he is, knowing why s/he reacts the way s/he does, will help you with deciding viewpoint since everyone determines events differently. If you remember playing "telephone" when you grew up, you know what I mean. As the message went further down the line, it changed according to who was hearing and who was telling.

EXERCISE:

FOR EACH SCENE ASK YOURSELF:

WHAT IS THIS SCENE DOING?

WHAT IS THE PURPOSE OF IT?

WHO IS THE SCENE HAPPENING TO?

WHAT ACTION IS OCCURRING?

WHAT IS THE CONFLICT?

CAN YOU DO THIS SCENE ANY OTHER WAY TO KEEP FROM CHANGING V. P. ?

HOW WOULD IT BE TOLD IF FROM ANOTHER VIEWPOINT?

Because no scene should be wasted, you need to ask for each scene:

How is character revealed here? Dialogue? Visual?

What is revealed about the character's values, attitudes, and needs here?

Does this scene reveal any character change or growth in terms of self–perception, emotional growth, or the ability to act?

What is revealed about the conflicts—both internal and external?

How is the story moved forward?

Does this scene create any anticipation or suspense? Is anything new revealed here or does it repeat things you already know?

Could this information be revealed in any other fashion that would be more exciting?

How are secondary characters handled here?

Does this scene seem to derive from what has come before? Is there cause and effect?

Is what's happening here the consequence of something or is it static and arbitrary?

What is the tone and nature of the scene?

Is it active, passive, quiet, noisy, large, intimate, funny, sad, tense or light?

Finally, is it a necessary scene? If you have other characters telling the heroine's story, then it isn't her story. As I said in the chapter on characterization, despite what Thackery thought, it wasn't Amelia who was the heroine, but Becky Sharp.

EXERCISE:

WRITE THE SAME SCENE (any scene from the story you are now working on) USING ALL THREE VIEWPOINTS.

Do this again for your beginning.

How does it feel different?

WRITE THE SCENE FROM THE HERO'S V. P. AND FROM HEROINE'S. (You'll notice, I hope, despite being the same events, how different they are seen.)

READ A BOOK IN FIRST PERSON, THIRD, AND OMNISCIENT:

How do they differ?

How did you feel about each story?

Did each flow for you?

Did they feel right for that story?

How would it have changed if another character had been chosen? How much of the third book was devoted to each of the different viewpoint characters and how did the author make the transitions from character to character?

What differences did this make to the story?

Could any of the viewpoints have been left out?

WRITE YOUR FIRST DRAFT IN FIRST PERSON TO HELP YOU IDENTIFY BETTER WITH THE CHARACTER. THEN SWITCH IT TO THIRD BEFORE YOU SEND IT IN and note the difference.

YOUR OWN VOICE

Editors and readers are always asking for writers with their own voice, their own unique style. They say they can tell on the first page if the writer is natural, open, engaging.

So how do we develop an appealing voice?

1. Relax and let the writing flow. Many writers, especially those who are professionals or retired academics, have to throw off the constraints of writing "correctly." Their tone must be made more casual, and more accessible to the average reader.
2. Concentrate on paring down those long winded sentences or abstract pretentious words. Replace it with shorter sentences. Use more sensual words and appeal to the reader's emotions. The shorter the sentences and shorter paragraphs increase the pace of the reading and increase tension.

3. Try choosing one person to write to. Pretend you are writing a letter to a friend—a newsy letter full of descriptions.
4. Read authors whose voices you enjoy and learn from them. See how they immerse you in the story world and their character's lives.
5. As I said before, try writing in first person and then change to third. First person is limiting, but in third you can add more description and experience for the character.
6. Add the thoughts, reactions, and emotions of your character. Evoke as many senses as you can. You're your character through thoughts and actions and not just words. (This is for novels and not for scripts, though there are ways to show this in script form.)
7. Read your story out loud and listen to the flow. Take out convoluted sentences and clunky words. Sometimes it helps here to hire a freelance editor to go over your work.
8. Give each character their own voice based on their history and education. Add their pet expressions and personality. Try stream of consciousness journaling for your character if you are stuck.
9. Finding your own voice can take time. It might take several novels or drafts before you find one that is comfortable to you. It's not something that can be taught, but will come if you are honest with yourself and let the words flow. You might have different voices for different genres or types of writing you are doing.

NOTES

TALK IS CHEAP: DIALOGUE

Dialogue is one of our basic ways of communication, of getting our thoughts across. The same goes for your characters. But unlike talk in the real world, our realistic story world dialogue must serve more than one purpose. Dialogue should be thought of as action.

80% of dialogue just sits there. It doesn't advance the plot or tell us anything about the character. Do you know people who are all talk and no action? They never get anywhere, do they? You don't want that for your story.

Hitchcock said, "Rely on action to tell your story, resort to dialogue only when it's impossible to do otherwise."

Remember that dialogue does not always translate well, especially when you are doing a script that is being sent overseas. (Over 60% of the movie market is international.)

Every word you write in your story should do dual duty; you need to be aware of individualistic speech patterns for each of your characters.

Good dialogue not only gets the message across, but aids characterization, develops the story, shows your character's state of mind and thought, provides new information for the reader, and explains something—without sounding teachy—or picks up the pace of the story.

Think about the character, her goals, and what skills are needed for this character to obtain the goals she wants in this story.

How will she attain the changes?

Think of your characters in terms of animals, flowers, musical instruments, and natural scenery. What would they be? A lion, a mouse, a hyena or one of the many other animals? Would they be a violin, a flute, or a bass drum? Would they be gentle as a spring breeze or a gusty wind?

Think of your character's history. Where did they grow up? Do they speak euboynics (urban slang)? Southern? British? Were they raised in a proper household? Did they have an education and if so how much? These things all affect the way your character speaks.

Other ways to help with characterizing the dialogue are choosing two negatives and a positive for a villain, or two positives and a negative for a hero, or all neutral traits for one of the other people. Remember that no one is all good or all bad. And each of us, even the most saintly, have parts of us we would not be proud of or at the very least we would keep to our selves. And even the worst of us, killers and the like, play with and enjoy the company of pets and small children. Though I won't deny that there probably are people out there who are totally evil, you rarely come across them. Anyone who is too dark or too light is unbelievable, and believability in our story and in our dialogue is what we are striving for.

Choose different traits for your two characters talking, and emphasize them. Perhaps one has chutzpah (spirit and assertiveness) and the other is passive–aggressive. Pick three character traits for each of your people from the list in the appendix, and keep them in mind when writing for these characters.

FLOW

When people talk, four things happen: they think, they look, they move and they speak.

These four items should flow smoothly into one another, be indicated, or implied. "I heard what he said, thought about it a moment, looked up at him and then, gesturing, I responded."

The cat throws up on the rug. In a split second look to see that this is so. I think about what to do, and then I move, speak, or scream at him, distracting him.

You shouldn't do everything so ploddingly, but this is the order things are usually done in.

If the reactions are in a different order—then the character appears to be (or perhaps is) having difficulties.

Imagine if you will: She screams, and then turned to say, "Oh, it's you, honey?" You wonder about her stability or you think she has just been scared.

Verbs of "saying" (responded, questioned, queried, asked) should be limited. Please leave the "growlings" and "barkings" for animals. In fact, you should be able to tell which of your characters is talking by the speech and sound of their voice alone.

When writing, I often isolate the dialogue of one character and see if it sounds like her. Would she really say that? Why did she say that?

Sometimes a "he said" or "she said" is needed for clarification, but not often. If the dialogue is flowing, the verbs will be verbs of action, as in: "Martin, bring me a coke!" She stabbed out her cigarette. "And add some rum too."

We know by the use of a name whom the speaker is talking to, and we have a visual picture of what she's doing.

Dialogue is not just two people talking. You need to show their surroundings as well as make the plot turn. Another good method of dialoguing is having one character ask a question. The other ignores the question, but answers what would be the next logical question.

As a general rule, dialogue questions should never be answered yes or no. Not only is that boring, but it brings no information to the scene.

Action is often the best way to describe who is talking and what is happening without having to resort to the "saids." And while they're talking, let's hear the crickets and smell the cut grass. Smell is, in fact, one of the most sensual of all our senses. Use it to bring this dialogue to life.

Make a list now of what you have smelled during the day (sea air, manure), what you have tasted (bitter coffee grounds), felt (sweat, heat, cool breeze), touched (rough paper, smooth rocks), and heard (husband shouting at his wife, TV blaring, loudspeakers at the airport), and don't leave out our sixth sense. Intuition is one of our most important and least respected senses.

Dialogue is a form of action.

Though we often don't realize it, action is divided into two parts. The decision to act is first. Then comes the action itself.

Action: how they come to that moment, and how they show that action brings out the emotion of the character. Is sometimes lacking in stories and scripts.

The decision to act is what clarifies the character. Both the philosophy and emotional aspects of the character must be included. It need not be shouted boldly from the rooftop, but it should be hinted at.

Visual aspects are important in novels and scripts. The description of a character as a leggy, bimbo blonde affects the rhythms of her speech so that her dialogue tells us more about her than miles of narrative might.

Show what is happening there. "You're late!" She twisted the napkin into a tiny ball. (Anger)

The house she'd been building with the restaurant's matchsticks collapsed beside her water glass. (Frustration.)

She stuck her tongue out at him. (Lightheartedness)

Her tongue slowly traced the contours of her lips. (Seduction)

Her fingers loudly drummed on the Formica tabletop. (Impatience) Showing the action also creates a pause necessary to change tones and change moods.

"You're late." Mary pushed the hair from her eyes. "I really love those roses you sent."

This gives Mary a chance to recover from her anger and change to warmth, which we know she's feeling for the hero.

Tags like these also make the character more visible to us. We know that when she's angry, she pushes the hair out of her eyes or plays with the ring on her finger. Keep that as a tag for her and her alone.

PICTURING YOUR PEOPLE TALK

Scenes must be visual and colorful. There are at least a two dozen names for each color...each a slight shade different, each expressing a different feeling. Describe your room right now using the basic colors–red, yellow, green, blue, black, white, gray. Then look at the pages on color and chose various shades of those colors from the list. See how that makes a difference in the feel of the sentence and in what they are saying.

Remember that reading is a visual thing as well as a phonetic one.

In every scene, even where there are two people talking something needs to be happening. Just having two people talk—or talking heads—as it's called, can't be done without boring the reader. Even if you have her throwing a chair while she yells at him, make sure the scene is not static.

Dialogue, alone, without surrounding narrative is like two actors on a stage with no props. We need to know what's around them. On the other hand, you don't want to bog down the scene with too much narrative and too much description of clothes, food, weather, etc. It should be there only if it moves the story.

Speech needs to be sweet. Simple. Hollywood uses an expression KISS—keep it simple stupid. Remember your average reader, at best, has a 6th grade reading level. Junior readers and readers of scripts hired by the studio have a short attention span. If you bore them with long words and long descriptions your work will be back in the envelope or deleted quicker than you can say "manila".

Unless your character is one who habitually uses big words, the thesaurus stays shut. (That doesn't mean you can't use bigger words in your narrative, but, since most people don't use big words, you need to keep your dialogue realistic.)You also want to watch redundancy. Repetition of words and phrases, even in dialogue, is boring unless you have a reason such as a specific tag line for a character.

Shakespeare was a great writer, but often, to get a point across, he would have his actors say the same thing over in several different ways. Hamlet is a good example. Today's soaps remind us for two weeks after the event about the brother who murdered his ex–wife in a rage of jealousy and is now being released from prison.

You don't need to do that.

Nor do you need to use local slang, though some verbal mannerisms will show through. If your character speaks in fits and starts or with a lot of explanations, then that will tell us something about the person—but too much of this and it will bore us.

LIST TWENTY DIFFERENT WAYS OF SAYING "YES" WITHOUT REPEATING.

It can be done. Each time you respond you will see how each character can be expressed differently from "Oui" to "Yeah, Ma'am."

A man does not talk like a woman and visa versa. If you read the Mars versus Venus series, you quickly see that men like to explain things and like to solve problems; women often talk mainly to air their feelings.

FOREIGN AND SLANG

Rephrasing grammar is okay, but not if you're having a lot of misspellings. "Oi think 'e ain't gonna go, Govn'or," is difficult for a reader to wade through, especially if this is an escapist book—"a good read."

One student wrote a book totally in black dialect. The story could have been interesting and it seemed to be one worth telling, but it was difficult to get past the first page because of the peculiar spellings. I was forced to stop and sound out words every few steps. The pausing, rather than the flow, made me put the book down and not give it the chance it should have had.

A few things consistently used, like dropping the "h" for cockney dialects, are all right but they must be limited. Better instead to rephrase the grammar and write: "How you say 'kiss?' " ***N'est ce pas***?

If you are using foreign phrases keep those to a limit. It's rude when there are lines upon lines in Spanish or French that are not translated. You must explain what you are saying or don't have it in the story. Perhaps you can have one character be unclear of the meaning and ask what is being said. The other character can summarize it or answer it in a way that makes it clear what was meant.

For example, if I say in Hebrew "***Ah ne rozeh neskya***." The other character might respond with: "What did you say?" or, if he supposedly understands, he could say, "You want a kiss?" or you could have him kissing her. As I hope you've guessed, that phrase in Hebrew means "I want a kiss. "

Also you need to be careful of using slang words, costume, or music that will date your story too much—unless of course you're writing a historical. Then be absolutely sure you have your time right. I was doing a medieval book and realized I could not refer to a Christmas tree, because they were not used in England until Prince Albert's time.

SETTING AND MOOD

Dialogue and narrative combined are used to set mood; for a relaxed atmosphere use long, flowing sentences. To show tension, fear, or excitement use short, choppy ones.

All dialogue should have tension and create suspense. There are several ways of doing this. If the hero is in danger, is in an unfamiliar environment, and feels the danger, that's suspense. If we, the viewer, know about the danger coming up and the hero doesn't, that puts us in a superior position and makes things scarier for us the reader.

Here are some ways to create suspense. When a crucial tool or weapon fails at the final moment, a natural disaster occurs to the hero, a ticking clock. When we know the other person has an ulterior motive, a situation impedes the hero with the ticking clock; the hero is in a trap, or the hero is confronted by a force he doesn't understand. The hero's dignity is at stake and he must decide if he can keep his dignity or not. Any situation where one of the characters is afraid, where there is a battle or situation leading to battle, where two people want the same thing, or where the hero is caught doing something he shouldn't will create suspense. Other ways are of two opposite type people joining together for one goal, and where we know that the enemy has spied on our hero and knows his plans. There are many other ways of producing tension and suspense. These are just a few suggestions.

TESTING YOUR WORDS

Speaking out loud is an excellent way not only to hear speech patterns of the characters, but also to check if the words sound right to your own ears. If not, change them until the voice is that of your character.

As a screenwriter, I often have a table read—where actors get together and read the lines of my script—when it is finished.

EXERCISE:

LISTEN TO A CONVERSATION ON THE PHONE, THE SUPERMARKET, THE BUS, THE STREET, ETC. TRY TO COPY IT VERBATIM AND SEE WHAT WASTED WORDS THERE ARE.

LISTEN TO A PLAY OR READ ONE. ANALYZE THE WORDS. Do they move the story forward? Are there any wasted words? What is the subtext of the story? How are these words different from what you might hear on the bus, in a cafe, on the street, etc?

TURN ON THE TELEVISION, BUT DON'T WATCH—JUST LISTEN. HEAR THE WORDS USED AND HOW THEY ARE USED. FEEL THE TONE, THE PAUSES AND THE HIDDEN MEANING.

Then write what you think the character is like, merely from what you've heard. Only then look at the picture and see how close you've come.

WHAT YOU REALLY MEAN: Subtext or not.

The subtext is the intent of the words and is often used in scripts. The subtext is what the characters truly mean when they're saying something else. The soap operas used this commonly. A character can sound like he's giving a compliment and really be insulting you. You might have the character saying "I hate you," but his tone, attitude, and everything that's gone before will be saying "I love you so much that I can't live without you. Please stay."

More so than a book, subtext is crucial in a script. The subtext should not be told by inner monologue, but should come out with action, dialogue, and our knowledge of the character.

EXERCISE:

MAKE UP A CONVERSATION WITH PEOPLE MEETING ON THE STREET IN REAL LIFE AND THEN SEE WHAT WOULD NEED TO BE CUT FOR A STORY. We want believability, not necessarily reality.

COMBING THE SCENE

When you are writing dialogue, the scene is slowed because you are taking a fine magnifying glass to the situation, rather than skimming across the top as you might do if this was narrative. But dialogue, in it's own way, is action and needs to be treated as such. Dialogue adds to the intimacy of a scene—intimacy that is difficult to achieve with narrative alone.

OPENINGS

Dialogue combined with action is great for openings. "I knew it was murder!" He stared at the body in front of him.

EXERCISE:

WRITE TWO PAGES OF DIALOGUE INTERACTION BETWEEN TWO CHARACTERS WITH NO TAGS, NO ADVERBS, ETC. ONLY THE DIALOGUE. EACH CHARACTER'S SPEECH SHOULD BE SO DISTINCTIVE THAT THE READER IS NEVER CONFUSED AS TO WHO IS SPEAKING.

THEN WRITE THE SAME DIALOGUE USING ACTION AND TAG LINES.

Wherever you can, cross out he growled, she laughed, or items such as that. It's rather hard to speak and laugh at the same time. Either write, "I'll get that?" She laughed. Or write, She laughed. "I'll get that." Never use, "I'll get that," she laughed.

Ellipses are used only for tight emotional scenes where, if spoken, the actor's voice would tighten and maybe even break.

Don't . . . over use.

BE SURE THAT YOU BREAK UP NARRATIVE WITH DIALOGUE AND VISA VERSA.

Look to see: does each passage of dialogue move the story forward, or convey information? Is the speaker easily identified without tags? Is their contrast in their speech? Finally, does it SOUND right? In scripts, your dialogue should not be more than five lines before you break for an action or narrative.

Questions-

Is my dialogue active?

Is it as lean as it can be?

Is it realistic?

Is it individual to each character?

Does my dialogue reveal exposition invisibly?

Is my dialogue emotionally impactful?

Does my dialogue have subtext?

Is my dialogue error free of spelling or grammar mistakes?

Does my dialogue sound good out loud?

Have I read scripts and learned from the masters?

***

RESEARCHING THE HISTORICAL, SCIENCE FICTION OR FANTASY

Historical novels are good, readable stories, which teach you something while they are entertaining. A lot of authors I know stay away from history because of the massive amounts of research needed to do a historical. While your facts have to be right, there is a limit to the research you need. It all depends on the type of book you are doing.

If your book is a biography, then you must, of course, read everything on that person's life and the era in which s/he lived. If it's a historical mainstream piece, you must again know life styles and historical events as well as political personalities and traits of the people of that time. If you are writing a costumed romance or drama (like ***THE SCARLET PIMPERNEL***) where history only mildly comes into play, while you need to know dates, times and places, your main emphasis is on the characters—what they would wear, how they would talk to each other (be careful of using too much formal dialogue or slang), and currency used at that time. The knowledge you gain should be like a slip, protecting and covering your story, but not peeping out from the hem of your story. It's a hidden skeleton, which supports you, but never shows. Your plot in the historical romance needs to focus on the love relationship and use history only as a backdrop.

Historical books enthrall readers with a past time and place and with knowledge they don't have. But even in history, or the future, people are and were very much the same. They might have had different dress and manners than ours, their moral code might have other rules than ours, but they had or will have the same passions, lusts, and hates as we do. Once you identify with the characters, you can ask yourself "Given these circumstances and given the rules of life at that time, how would I react?"

HEROINES

You must remember that women in the past did not have the freedom that we do today. I don't know what women of the future will have—that's up to you the science fiction author. An accurate, believable recreation of the time and place means living, breathing characters. Motives stand out here, as elsewhere. This applies to futuristic people as well. We don't care what they look like, even if they have five hands and three heads, but their emotions and manners, and their motives, will make them real for us. (Remember the humanistic traits we talked about in character building.) And if, as in the past, liaisons between those not linked through marriage are "unaccepted" in society, you must show their passions to be so great as to overcome any social disapproval they might encounter.

LOCALES

Don't forget, even if you are writing about your city—but 100 years ago or 1,000 years in the future—it is still a foreign place and must be described as such. It must be made visual for your reader. Your story can be a chronological list of events, it can be an exciting work of fiction, or it can be a blend of both.

Research is also necessary when you're doing contemporary novels. Those who read mysteries and police procedurals, those who read Westerns and young adult novels, are going to know when you've erred. If you're giving your character a career, make sure you know enough about it and if possible have someone in that field read the novel over before you submit it.

MY START IN HISTORICALS

My own interest in historical fiction began in junior high when my Early America history teacher talked to us about the wagon trains going west. She would have us close our eyes and imagine that we were one of the women crossing the plains or the desert with the caravan of wagons.

We had to think of the life we left behind and what we had to look forward to. We had to imagine the Rocky Mountains in the distance, hear the noise of the babies crying, the oxen bellowing, the sweat dripping down our homemade cotton dresses, and our hair stringy as we trudged along in fear of Indian attacks at any moment.

We would sit about the fire, bone weary, and listen to the sounds of the night. They were women and men, just like us.

PLOT IDEAS

History, or the future, for those who like it, is a wealth of material for plots. You must chose a time period in which you feel comfortable, since you will be living with it for several months. Even if you are not doing a biography, many of the real characters of the time can be used as secondary characters in your story. Best plots come from time periods with a lot of conflict. While the American Civil War and Revolutionary War are periods much used and overdone, editors still read them—as long as they haven't just read three other books in the same time period!

ACCURACY AND SUSPENDING DISBELIEF

I, myself, insist on accuracy and don't like lying to the reader, but many other writers have no compunction about this—as long as it tells the story. Therefore, when doing research and reading other fiction written about that time, verify facts you might glean from those other novels.

In order for us to suspend disbelief—since sex was not taken lightly and marriage for love was almost unheard of until recently—the story of these two characters in history must be so powerful that it defies the historical rules. The heroine would, of course, be totally virginal since most women—especially the nobility—knew nothing at all of sex.

This brings me to the status of your characters. In a historical, to make proper use of the time, the characters must be of the nobility (even minor nobles are all right), but they must be those who are affected by this battle or that change with the king. Most peasants, as long as they had their land, their few bushels of grain, and could pray at their church, didn't care who was king and so were not affected by the political intrigues at court.

KNOW YOUR FICTIONAL WORLD

Knowing about your fictional world also means knowing what they would have eaten, and what they would have regarded as common. You can't have an "electrical feeling" to describe the meeting of the hero and heroine since electricity wasn't yet discovered. Nor can you have oranges, sheep, horses, bananas, limes, or chickens—nor say a man then was cocky or sheepish in the Mexico of Aztec times—since these items didn't come to Mexico until the Spanish invasion.

Again, knowing your world means knowing what your people would have seen as they entered the kitchen or palace. You don't have your housewife describing the table as she walks in or the items she's using, unless there is something unusual about them, but you can make use of them in conversation. Rather than saying, "I walked into the kitchen and saw the wood hewn table with the silver toast tray, etc." You might say, "Mother took down our silver toast tray and placed it on the uneven table, which father had fixed only last year."

There are several series which go into The Daily Life of England in—(Georgian, Regency, Victorian) times and Daily Life in Spain during the Inquisition, etc. The library is your best friend here, but so are used book stores.

EXERCISE:

CLOSE YOUR EYES AND VISUALIZE A SCENE; WHAT SMELLS, SOUNDS, FEELINGS ARE THERE?

WRITE A SCENE—OUTSIDE OR INSIDE—FROM THIS TIME PERIOD AND VISUALIZE IT—GIVE US A HINT OF THE TIME AND OF THE CHARACTER WITHOUT BEING TOO WORDY.

TAKING NOTES

YOU ARE CREATING YOUR WORLD, ESPECIALLY IF THIS IS SCIENCE FICTION OR FANTASY, AND YOU MUST BE CONSISTENT WITH THE RULES YOU LAY DOWN FOR YOUR SOCIETY. MAKE A LIST OF THEM—WHAT WAS THE ECONOMICS LIKE THEN? WHAT MONIES DID THEY USE? WHAT PLANT OR ANIMAL LIFE DID THEY HAVE? ARE THERE ONLY TWO SEXES STILL? (Think of ***AVATAR*** where they have sexual experiences through their tails.) If you're having a mad passionate sex scene, you must know the clothes he has to tear off to get to her. Accurate costume is important.

When starting to research a time period, I find going to the children's section is the best, since books for kids are written in the simplest terms. If you go to the adult section first, the books usually assume that you already have a knowledge of the period and the situation. Kids books can give you your basic plan, and from there you can fill in with more details from the adult books.

Maps of the area for that time period are also helpful. Sometimes you can't get maps of that exact year and must be satisfied with something close. While it's not necessary to visit the location, I find it fun to do—after I've done my research and my first draft. I wander the area as a tourist, absorbing the facts and feelings about me. You'll find questions often come up while you're writing and if you've visited the location before writing you'll say—, "Gee I didn't see that." And probably have to make another trip and long distance call.

Remember to keep ALL your receipts for the flight, food, gas, museum entrance, photographs, etc. It's all tax deductible as a writer. (Talk to your accountant, but last I knew you had seven years to deduct before it was not considered a hobby.)

Read old diaries, old newspapers, and all the documentation you can find. You must recall, too, that writings are influenced by the time period. If you're reading a section about Anne Boleyn when she was in favor, the material will say what a wonderful loving queen she is. If it's just after her beheading, when the King was trying to marry Jane, the material will say she's a bitch and a whore. If you're reading about the American West, you'll find the Indian are always the bad guy and the white soldier the good guy.

We know, of course, that not all the officers were perfect, but history portrays them this way. You must take historical material you read with a grain of salt—which by the way was a mark of nobility (to sit above the salt). If two supposed eyewitnesses disagree, use the most plausible.

While language should be authentic, as they might phrase things, and while swear words such as "God's blood!" and "God's death!" are used, you still want your sentence structure to flow and not have the reader stopped trying to understand a passage. Your readers are modern, even if your story is not.

The amount of research you might do can be enormous, and only 1/3 will appear on the paper, perhaps another 1/3 will remain in your head, and the final third will disappear, but it's necessary if you are to live that period in order to write about it. You have to know enough so that if you were magically transported back into the court of that time, you would know not only the political things, but what laces and satins were being worn, what fashions, who was sleeping with whom, and the layout of the city. Reading about other events, which occurred in other parts of the world at that time period, is helpful for establishing your sense of the period.

HIRING OTHERS TO RESEARCH

If you are limited by time and place, you might consider hiring a professional researcher. These people can either give you the facts you want—which is all right if you need to check only certain data—or give you book lists to choose from.

I prefer to do my own research, since by reading the material at hand I might come across a single sentence that will perfectly describe the home I want to portray or a character. It might, in fact, be hidden in a very dull, boring diary, which I've waded through the whole morning. But that one nugget, when I find it, is usually worth my time. Had I hired a researcher, he would have given me the facts I needed, but I would have tasted none of the period's flavor first hand.

Most reference librarians have a free service and will be glad to help you with a fact or two. If you are still having trouble locating material, then the researcher can obtain a list of books for you along with their pertinent data. Most libraries belong to an inter–library loan system and can obtain the books for you from elsewhere. Since I like to mark my books, I usually make Xeroxes of the pages I want to jot notes on.

The essence of the place and the person is what we are seeking and because of it, your setting is almost as important as your characters. ***Architectural Digest,*** the magazine, often features old homes and castles. Look at that if you can't actually travel.

ALTERING HISTORY

While you can alter characters—fictional—you shouldn't alter facts. A firm grasp of history is needed because your reader will know if you have your heroine being presented to James I at a party in 1603 when he died in 1601. And for medieval falconers, the wrong bird on the wrong hand can do you in with readers.

Because these historical books cover a bigger scope, multiple–view points are permissible. But it's important to chart out your time line so that you know where each of your characters is at a given moment in time. And don't think you have a captive audience just because you caught them with your hook. You must continually have suspense—even in the historicals. Each chapter should end with a cliffhanger.

DESCRIPTIVE

For costume, I find a book called ***WESTERN WORLD COSTUME*** by Carolyn Bradley, 1954, Prentice Hall, to be very helpful. It is now out of print, but can be found in libraries. There are many costume books and several should be available to you.

Dover Books also makes a series of cut out dolls for various time periods and dollhouses, which you can cut and set up on your own. Great for visualizing your characters.

The Douglas Guides, for dollhouse makers, which describe different period homes, is also helpful for certain eras.

For titles and addresses, I find the (British) Whittaker's Almanac to be the best. It can be obtained from the libraries here or you can purchase it from London bookstores.

USING YOUR INNER KNOWLEDGE

If, during your writing, you can't find a detail, then gloss over it and check it later. Usually your common sense will prove you right.

Since you must keep history in mind at all times while writing, make sure your readers know where they are by starting with historical facts like: "The King's birthday had come and gone, and with the new year of 1794, came the crushing news of the British defeat in India."

Don't be afraid to ask questions. Experts at the reference desk in the library, the university, or the work area will always be happy to help you and answer your questions.

Not all historicals have to be set in the distant past; and in fact, one must know their world just as well if they are doing science fiction, fantasy, or the occult. The reader will believe you only if you make it believable.

Remember again—manners and morals might have been different but the motives were the same. Know them.

Emotions should never be forgotten while writing history. These were living people and should come across as such.

EXERCISE:

SET A TIME LINE FOR YOUR BOOK—BE IT PAST, PRESENT, OR FUTURE. Go back to the time chart in the character chapter and in the appendix. (Look at various Time Lines Books available from Touchstone Press.)

WHAT ARE THE RULES GOVERNING UPPER CLASS AND LOWER CLASS IN YOUR TIME?

WHAT ABOUT RULES GOVERNING RELATIONSHIPS, MARRIAGES, AND RELIGION? HOW DID WOMEN FARE?

WHAT WERE SOME OF THE MAJOR BATTLES?

WHO WAS KING, QUEEN, RESIDENT, OR LEADER? WHAT WAS THAT PERSON LIKE? BENEVOLENT, TYRANT?

WHAT CLOTHES WERE WORN FOR DRESS OCCASIONS AND FOR WORK?

WHAT TYPE OF WORK WAS DONE? HOW MANY LOWER CLASSES WERE THERE? HOW DID THEY HAVE FUN? WHAT DID THE UPPER CLASSES DO FOR FUN?

The imagination can invent anything, and if you are setting this in the year 3500, then you must know your world so you can show us.

FLASHBACKS, FORESHADOWING, AND TRANSITIONS

Finding the right place to start your book is almost as important as the book itself. Too often new authors start too early. They believe that EVERYTHING must be told about the character and the situation, when, in fact, the less you can get away with telling at first the better. New writers need to learn how to start with action and put the information into short flashbacks, or expositive dialogue, which won't look too obvious and won't bore the reader.

FLASHING

You don't want Jim, who has obviously known and been dating Mary for several years, to say suddenly "What do you mean—you have a brother?" Unless, of course, we, the reader, know that material has been kept from him. Nor do we want him to say, "Tell me how your brother got into jail." But he can comment,"Tom did have a motive for killing Susan. "Your heroine would respond, "He's innocent. He's been framed. He shouldn't be in that awful jail—and I'm going to find out who's put the blame on him." The situation is brought out here and you don't feel as if you've been framed.

In those few words we know all we need for the moment.

Flashbacks should be short, dramatic, and done when the character is at rest. Action should not be stopped. Choosing the proper moment is tricky and often it's best if you do a little at a time, making a suggestion here and an inference there.

In general, flashbacks tend to be annoying and we avoid them as much as possible, since they take us away from the here and now and can be confusing. Flashes in a short story are the most troublesome and if there is a way to dramatize the information with action and dialogue, you're better off doing that.

The most important fact in the book is to hook the reader first with the problem—and then you can give a history of the characters, but only bit by bit since the action of the characters should speak for them. What happened to bring him to this point in the story can often be told in dialogue and action with another character, but again, you want to keep the relationship of the characters in view. If a man has lived with a woman all her life, he's going to know that she doesn't like dogs and for him to suddenly exclaim as if he didn't know—merely because you want to get the point across—is not going to work.

A good example of where a flashback is properly used is in the western book where the gunfighter is walking down the street, finger itching to reach for his trigger. Now that the reader's attention is captured, we can mention BRIEFLY that Todd was here to defend his darling sister's honor. We have the shootout, and as he lays dying with her cuddling him we can have her flash back on the scene which brought him here.

Because the human mind reacts strongly to threatening situations (and maybe your life does flash before you as you think you're drowning), you don't want to stop the action by putting in a long explanation. We would not have told the gunfighter's story as he's walking across the street. Only as he's already down and at rest, and we have hooked the reader, can we talk about his problem.

FITTING YOUR RESEARCH IN

New authors, because they have done so much research and want to put it in, often become preachy and tell us things about the character, which do not move the story forward. Ask yourself—what does the flashback have to do with this problem? Can the story succeed without it? A long, drawn out, detail–by–detail description of the past takes the reader away from the present, from the urgency of now. Frustration builds up. If you really think it's necessary to have this material in the book—then start your story earlier—at another problem setting. To use a similar situation, if you take three hours to convince your boss that you want off at 2:00 p. m. , 2:00 p. m. will have passed!

Properly done, flashbacks can build urgency and create more sympathy for the character, but you're best trying to keep it to a few sentences and worst when you try to force that information. For example: she saw the pink sweater at the bus station. It reminded her of the pink sweater in the window she and Tom used to walk by, of all the fun they had, and of the book store they had met in., etc. This very diluted round about way of getting into the flashback doesn't work.

FLASHBACKS SHOULD FLASH

Each story will dictate its own rhythms. But a good rule is to continue forward from your opening until the reader's curiosity about the past outweighs curiosity about the future.

Moving back and forth from present to past is done by appropriate verb tenses, and indications like "now" and "back then."

--Begin in the simple past tense "John watched the storm."

--Go to Past Perfect: "He remembered how Polly had hated storms."

--Feel the past: "He could still feel the softness of her hair on his shoulder."

--Return by appropriate words to simple past: "Now, twenty years later, he wondered how she was."

***

TRANSITIONS

Another problem, which plagues flashbacks, is poor transition. Most authors forget that transition is the most easily done merely by leaving a blank space of several lines, sometimes with asterisks, in between the paragraphs (as I've done above). Blank space can indicate change of scene, change of character viewpoint, passing of time, whatever.

USING TIME

Time is a good suspense tool to keep in mind. If time is something the character struggles with, then time should be established at the beginning of the story—year, month, day or hour—depending on what's crucial for them to know. For each new scene, you should be aware of what has already elapsed in time.

Time passing can be illustrated, too, by objects such as a bird bath in the garden—being covered with snow, welcoming the first bird of the year, having birds come to drink from it, and covered with leaves.

Of course, the lead in must flow smoothly and effortlessly. Another method often used is to repeat the words.

"Tomorrow will be different," she thought.

"But tomorrow was even worse."

Repeating the same words from paragraph to paragraph should be handled judiciously. Doing this too many times makes it look as if you are being redundant.

EXERCISE:

WRITE A FLASHBACK, INTEGRATING IT INTO YOUR STORY. THINK OF THE SCENE YOU'RE WRITING AS IF YOU ARE ONE WITH THE ACTORS. ACHIEVE INTIMACY WITH THE STORY. SENSE IT! For flashes to work, you must have a connection with the present story and the flash back must feel as if it is present and immediate.

STUDY TWO EXAMPLES OF FLASHBACKS FROM BOOKS—NOTE THE TRANSITIONS. HOW WAS IT DONE? DOES IT WORK FOR YOU? This means learning to read as a writer and not a visitor. Enjoy the story but keep your eyes open for techniques.

FORESHADOWING

Foreshadowing, like flashbacks, makes use of time. Foreshadowing gives clues, which can be as simple as one word, or as long as a whole scene. They are an indication to the reader of what might happen; they are tension builders and warnings of things to come. As page–turners, they are necessary for every book.

These are—in the plotting structure—what are often called the pinch points, and what key in the reader to the dramatic event in the middle or the crisis in the resolution.

Foreshadowing must be done for characters you want to introduce as well, especially if they won't be appearing until later in the story. Otherwise, the multitude of new characters and ideas becomes confusing. Set the reader up—but gently.

In the movie, ***YOUNG SHERLOCK HOLMES,*** they say a good detective observes. The same goes for a writer. We are trying to detect what makes a good book and why one book sells well and another doesn't. It's a mystery to almost anyone in the industry and yet clues are there, if we look.

EXERCISE:

FIND TWO EXAMPLES OF FORESHADOWING IN A NOVEL—AND WRITE THEM DOWN.

***

NOTES

THOSE TORRID SCENES: SEX AND VIOLENCE

These two items sell books, but are they necessary? That is, are they necessary for your story? Do they push the plot forward—or have you, the author, just put it in because you think it will help sales? If sex and/or violence don't give us further insight into the characters and it doesn't flow naturally with the story—then it shouldn't be there.

KNOW THE GUIDELINES

It's important to know your market, know the current guidelines, and know who your reader will be. If you are writing for the romance market, or for the women's market, violence (as in rape) is out. At one time, there were books with violence and rape in them. But it was soon proven that women do not fall in love with their rapists, and that rape, being a male–oriented lashing out against women, should not be used in romance novels.

While you might still find some novels with rape, it is only because the editor thought the story on the whole was a good one and was forced to overlook it, or perhaps, for that one novel, it fit in. Though usually the rapist is brutally murdered and has his just desert. Any type of violence is frowned upon in the romance books, ask yourself if it fits in with your story and then see if you can't accomplish what you want to say in some other way. If not, then put it in, but gently.

NO RAPE

Rape is violence and sex without love is pornography, or at the very least lust and not love. I once had someone while I was doing a travel assignment, call my room with an indecent proposal. He knew that I wrote romances and assumed that I, therefore, was ready for "some fun because there was sex in the romances." I explained to him that it was essentially to show the couple in love first and since I did not love him, he could take a hike.

CONVINCE US IT'S LOVE

To put sex in the books, we must be convinced the couple loves each other before they climb into bed. This is especially true in historicals where the morals and codes were so much stricter. For example, in ***SHRIEKING SHADOWS***, I have the couple (who are married) have sex because it flowed naturally with the story—after all, he wanted an heir and thought this woman was his legal wife.

MORALITY

Morality is important even in the contemporary romances. If she has had sex before, only the hero really turns her on. He, too, might have played around before—but now that he's seen her, there is no one else for him. This applies even if they're apart for some time. In the historicals, she's almost always a virgin (usually sixteen to twenty years of age).

SENSUALITY

Love scenes have to be both physical and emotional experiences. Since they are larger than life, we have no impotence and no boring sex. Relationships here are the ideal, and of course, the infatuation heightens the experience. The love does last.

By definition, sensuality is the purely animal or physical part of human nature, the lusts of the flesh, the quality or state of being sensual, devotedness to the gratification of the bodily appetites, and free indulgence in carnal or sensual pleasures.

Sensuousness is defined as relating to the senses, addressing the senses, suggesting pictures of images of sense, characterized by sense impressions or imagery addressing the senses (description or for pure satisfaction), producing an agreeable effect on the senses, something conducive to physical comfort or content (mild breezes), highly susceptible to influence through the senses.

Synonyms might be sensuous, sensual, luxurious, voluptuous, sybaritic, or epicurean—which all have to do with providing gratification of the senses.

It's a good idea to find some other words for penis besides "manhood" and "tool."

Because romance books are fantasy, good books to read are ***FORBIDDEN FLOWERS*** and ***MY SECRET GARDEN*** by Nancy Friday.

In romances, the rules are to use euphemisms for genitals, and only the top of the body is described, not the lower part. If you read a porn book, you'll see the difference between that and a well-done romance. In the romances—if you use subjects such as incest or homosexuality—treat it very, very lightly.

MALE AND SEX SCENES

Most men, it seems, have difficulty in writing sex scenes for women's books, since men appear to think of sex as a mechanical act and women think of it as an emotional act. You'll notice in reading the romances that there are several pages of foreplay, kissing, and touching before the act, which is briefly mentioned. The average sex scene lasts about three pages with quite a few emotional metaphors and the body is shown to be alive through the senses.

SEXUAL TENSION

But even if sex is not performed in the book, sexual tension is a must. That's making total use of the senses and creating the chemistry from across the room. Slight comments, gestures, touching, and looks can all be used for sexual tension. Be careful, however, of catch phrases like "the moment she saw him she felt weak-kneed and her heart pounded." This is already cliché. Remember there was no electrical charge in historical books.

WHAT TURNS YOU ON?

If you're writing sensual things, ask yourself what turns you on? Do you like walks on the beach at sunset, fires, moonlit nights on the sea, and the soft glow of a lamp? What turns you on in bed? Soft warm lips, piercing thrust of the tongue, kisses at the base of the neck, smoothness of his shoulders. Don't be heavy–handed. These scenes must be fantasy and light.

The setting is also an integral part of the love scene and should come alive for us as much as the act. If you are doing a historical, it's crucial you know the clothes they must discard before making love.

EXERCISE:

FIND TWO SEX SCENES FROM BOOKS AND COMPARE THEM TO A PORN NOVEL.

WRITE A SEX SCENE USING ALL THE SENSES, BUT NO CLINICAL TERMINOLOGY.

WRITE A SENSUAL SCENE—with all the tension—BUT USING NO SEX.

MOODS

To get into the mood for writing the sensual scenes, some authors recommend soft music—Schubert, Braham's, Mozart, or other romantic songs. Two of my favorites are Neil Diamond's, "I'm Glad You're Here With Me Tonight" and "God Only Knows How I Love You." Scented candles, perfumed linen, fresh flowers, a bubble bath, or lace and satin negligees help you set your mood, too.

Sex scenes can be funny, tender, or hostile depending on your characters and their moods.

EXERCISE:

TRY WRITING THE SEX SCENE YOU JUST WROTE IN THE OTHER TWO WAYS. MAKE USE OF THE SETTING, MAKE USE OF THEIR CLOTHES.

Remember love must be enduring, it must be pleasurable, and mostly it must fit in and flow with your story.

Senses, however, can be expressed in other ways besides with sex. A comparison of senses will heighten the tension—if for example, it's a beautiful spring day and your character feels suicidal. The chirping birds and balmy air will be in more contrast than if he felt in love, and happy with the whole world.

Think of certain smells, tastes, sounds. In writing ***LIGHTING AND FIRE***, my biblical romance about Judge Deborah, I had to think of the stink of the cities with the camel dung, and the bells of the animals, the braying of the donkeys, the sounds of the hawkers, not to mention the heat and dust. I had to see it, taste it, smell it, feel or touch it, and hear it. One single word or phrase can center on a moment and bring it out of the ordinary more so than pages of description.

***

METAPHORICALLY SPEAKING

Visual or sensual writing means making the reader see, feel, and experience what your characters are seeing, feeling, and experiencing. Often you are coming from an experience that you, yourself, might have known, or that one of your friends might be familiar with. But how do you get it across to the reader? How do you share your thoughts and words so that they can feel that same experience?

Metaphors and similes are one way of writing in which you go from the familiar of what they might know to the unfamiliar of what your character is sensing. Metaphors help cement old feelings to new information, elaborate abstract ideas, and help in problem solving.

William Gordon, author of ***SYNECTICS,*** has devised a system of helping to "break out" our thinking. Traditionally, it's been said that writing is a mysterious process. It cannot be taught, but according to Gordon it can. As most of us writers are considered to be "irrational beings" already, we are ahead of the logicians with his approach. Mr. Gordon says that the irrational state is the best for exploring and expanding ideas. In other words, the crazier our thinking is, and the more we "go for it," the better our stories will be.

As they say, "the devil is in the details." Rather than saying "he took some pie" try—the fork sliced through the crumbling crust and pierced the ripe cherry. He added a spoonful of whipped cream.

Metaphoric activity is initiated by asking you evocative questions. These open–ended questions draw your subconscious into the present. It can be done in–group form, often known as "shooting the bull," or it can be done individually.

We are naturally conservative and lazy, often choosing the easy answer. The purpose of these exercises is to stretch our brains and push us just that little bit further to make our writing special.

DETACH–COMPARE–NEW CONCEPTS—FINAL RESPONSE

There are four steps that we go through in choosing our metaphors. First, we must detach ourselves from the present idea or problem. As we choose the easiest answer, we engage in speculation about other possible ways of looking at the item we want to find a metaphor for. This is usually a direct analogy, which compares two objects or concepts. For instance, compare a wheel of a car to other objects, which rotate. First, you might come up a with can opener. The comparison doesn't have to be identical in all respects. The function is to merely open up a space for new ideas to come in. We then move from the general to the particular, like going from a wheel, which spins, and thinking of the blades of a can opener, which also spin, to a helicopter.

In the third part, we return to the anatomy of the creative process. We draw out one of those new concepts, stretching it like taffy, going from that helicopter spinning, to the orbit of Mars, or the spinning of a seedpod.

The "final response" in the process is one that appears totally autonomous of the original idea, but has subtle relationships. In this instance, you might have come up with the curve of a hoop snake. It's round like a wheel and yet totally unlike it. Other answers could also have been chosen.

DETACHING

As you detach yourself from the problem and make a general comparison, you put aside your concentration on the object and let whatever will occur come to your mind. Speculation starts as you play with the idea, and come up with an autonomous idea, which leads to the inspiration or invention to solve your problem.

We've all seen parodies of method acting when one has to "be a wave" or "be an orange." In writing, however, we have to be what we are not. Even if the character is a part of us, they are not us, more so if we are trying to describe an inanimate object.

Being something else requires an extensive loss of self and goes through several processes. There is the first person description of facts. If you are "being an engine," your first step might be to say, "I feel greasy" or "I feel hot." But these are facts we already know and there is no new view of the auto engine here.

Then we must identify with the emotion. And often we'll get common emotions, but no new insights. Perhaps you'll say, "I feel powerful."

As we empathize and identify further with the item, we begin to feel emotionally and kinesthetically like the subject. This is, of course, easier if we're working with a living object, but it can be done with an inanimate one, too. "I feel like my parts are racing around. I'm always in a hurry," might be one answer. Or, "I feel exploited. I can't determine when to start and stop. Someone does it for me," might be another.

EXERCISE:

- COMPARE YOURSELF TO A PHYSICAL OBJECT. HOW WOULD YOU LOOK IF YOU WERE A BULLDOZER? A FLOWER? A CATERPILLAR? HOW WOULD IT FEEL TO BE A SCHOOL? A WATERFALL? A CLOUD? HOW WOULD YOU THINK?
- TRY SEVERAL METAPHORS, BUT LIMIT YOURSELF TO PHYSICAL DESCRIPTIONS.
- IF I WERE A ________________, I WOULD LOOK LIKE A ________________.
- BE THAT AUTO ENGINE. WHAT DO YOU FEEL LIKE? DESCRIBE HOW YOU FEEL WHEN YOU'RE TURNED ON, WHEN YOUR BATTERY IS DEAD, WHEN YOU COME TO A STOP LIGHT.
- HOW WOULD IT FEEL TO BE LOVED? (Not in love but the emotion love.)
- HOW WOULD IT FEEL TO BE HATED? TO BE AMBIVALENT?
- IF I WERE LOVED, I WOULD FEEL __________.

Now combine physical aspects and empathasize with the emotions.

- HOW WOULD I FEEL IF I WERE A LONELY CHILD?
- HOW WOULD I FEEL IF I WERE STOOD UP ON MY VERY FIRST DATE?
- HOW WOULD I FEEL IF I HAD AN "A" ON MY EXAM?

You might find it necessary to work through the first person description of facts, the emotion, and then the empathy. But it does work. If you look at the 1970s craze of "Pet Rocks," you know that emotions and feelings can be assigned to non–living objects.

Another type of comparison is called the "compressed conflict," in which you take two items that are totally different and find something which binds them together. You must go through the first process here to observe and speculate about the item. Then find two words in your description of the other metaphors, which seem to fight each other—as shy and aggressive. How is a computer both shy and aggressive?

Essential to the compressed conflict is the idea of combining paradoxical points of view about the same object or idea. The more ways you can see the object you're working with, the better you are.

EXERCISE:

- TAKE A TOPIC
- SUGGEST A DIRECT ANALOGY AND DESCRIBE WHY THAT IS LIKE THE TOPIC OR ITEM.
- BECOME THE OBJECT. WHAT DO YOU FEEL?
- TAKE TWO OF THE DIRECT ANALOGIES AND FIND CONTRASTING WORDS, WHICH CAN APPLY TO YOUR ITEM.
- COMBINE THIS AND FIND ANOTHER DIRECT ANALOGY BASED ON THESE TWO WORDS BUT RELATED TO YOUR OBJECT.
- RE–EXAMINE YOUR ORIGINAL IDEA.

You should have developed a new understanding for the original object. These processes are designed to help make familiar the strange (if you're describing a time period or experience which you think few of your readers will be able to relate to). It works especially well with historicals and science fiction. It also works visa versa by helping you to see familiar objects in a new light.

Let's say you want to describe a kid who's a pest, always in trouble. First, we compare him with inanimate objects. Words like a drill and a hurricane might come up. Then we become the drill or the hurricane. How do these feel? One might be powerful and twisted; another might be out of control and tired.

Take two of the words, which seem opposite, like "tired" and "twisted." Use that to form your new analogy. How are the hurricane and the drill alike? How do these apply to the boy? Well, if you were to "become him" you might say you were tired of twisting in and out, and felt out of control, but couldn't stop unless someone else stopped you. The boy and the drill both make a lot of noise, and disrupt "things as they are."

EXERCISE:

Try now to compare an auto engine to something else.

AN AUTOMOBILE ENGINE IS LIKE A ______________________ BECAUSE:

(Detachment) 1.

(default)2.

(spec) 3.

(autonomous) 4.

(invention)5.

You could say a storm is like an engine because it makes noise.

THE PROCESS

1. Play with your idea. What is a (poem)?
2. Select key words. (It doesn't have to rhyme, lets your feelings out, and uses different kinds of words.)
3. Choose something outrageous to compare it to. (How is a poem like an automobile? Both are self–propelled. Once you start it, it seems to go on its own. When you're writing you sometimes have trouble getting the motor started.)
4. Pick an animal that's like the object. (How is a poem like a giraffe? It has a lot of parts to it. It stands above everything else and looks at things in a different way.)
5. Select one of the words here such as "above," for discussing the poem. (How does it feel to be "above"? You feel different. You can see things ordinary people can't. You start feeling superior if you don't watch out.)
6. Make a list of words that have been mentioned dealing with the item yet seem to be opposite in some way. (Perhaps two animals chosen might have been a giraffe and a snail. These animals are different, but each can represent a poem. The snail being that poetry examines things in minute form.)
7. Think of the giraffe and the snail together as you're writing about the poem. Think of them holding hands! Compare and feel as if you were there.

***

MAINSTREAM AND GENRE WRITING

Even though I consider myself a professional, I never stop taking classes, and never stop learning. Because each writer has his/her own way of plotting, characterization, etc. I seek out and listen to other writers. I like the way I work and yet there are times when I do have that horrid writer's block. Then I find that by processing my work another way, I can get past that block and adapt.

One of the teachers I've learned from is the late Ruth Mitchell of UCLA. Here are some of the things Ruth taught us.

1. The most important and most specific item is written last, since it always catches the most attention. This applies to sentence structure, paragraphs, and chapter endings. The item stressed is at the end. An example might be: "The mansion sat on the hill, built of clapboard that had been weathered for over 100 years, wood decayed in places—from the broken porch stairs to the window sills that had collapsed."
2. Because language is rhythmic, it should also flow easily from objective sentence to subjective as in:"The apartment had a faint odor. She crinkled her nose." This is action/reaction. She looks at something and has a reaction to it. Alternations occur all the time in writing, since you go from objective to subjective or stimulus to response. Compound sentences have subjective viewpoint as the response. This is especially important in plotting, since whatever the villain does, the hero must counteract.
3. Even if you are taking a cliché of setting, you can make it different by using action/ reaction and by use of experiences and the senses. Think about what image of the scene you want your reader to see—a close up, a medium, or a wide shot. What does what you are saying tell us about the character right now? What does it tell us about the world around him? Use emotions in your sentences. A man struggles with the hose rather than he placed the

hose down. Think, what in the moment do I need the reader to pull from my story? Read your work out loud and see if you are missing anything. If you don't feel the emotion then the reader won't either.

4. Make similes work. They should agree with each other. For example: "A hot gust blew her hair like champagne colored ribbons." That's nice but "A hot gust blew her hair, like desert wind ruffling the sand" is even better. Relate unfamiliar objects to familiar objects. "His dream, the driving ambition of his life, was to make Destiny as well known as any other big name act in the world." Change those last few words to: "as well known and respected as the Beatles, as sliced bread, as peanut butter and jelly, as the Berlin Philharmonic."
5. Eliminate relative clause markers wherever you can. In other words, stay away from that and which. Reading: "Coming out onto the shaded quarterdeck, which rose in a half moon around the main deck, she stopped." And then read: "Coming out onto the shaded quarterdeck, a half moon around the main, she stopped." Or: "An ugly phrase that had surfaced in her mind stared at her, permitting no evasion of its implications: biological warfare." And: "An ugly phrase surfaced in her mind: biological warfare."
6. Use fragments to foreground information. Like: "The last note, a brilliant high C effortlessly produced, stunned the audience. Complete silence." Or: "Estelle smoothed the silk over her hips. Finished at last."
7. Use dashes to lighten and brighten. It keeps the reader awake. For example: "True to his word, the mate had loaned her several books, but they had always been brought by someone else." Or: "True to his word, the mate loaned her several books—always brought by someone else."
8. Use parallelisms whenever possible. Read: "His white teeth flashed in a wicked smile as he discerned her discomfort. His grin grew more pronounced as he in turn studied her." And: "His white teeth flashed and his grin widened as he studied her." Or: "People were bound to be about where lights were, she reasoned." And: "Where there were lights, there were people, she reasoned."

9. Read magazines like Vanity Fair and Newsweek. Collect their verbs and use more imaginative verbs in your writing. "The tiny blue compact car arduously made its way up the hill." Or: "The tiny blue compact car chugged up the hill." Made is a word that is useless in its blandness.
10. Always write active words and not passive. He runs (or ran) is better than he is running. Avoid words like is, are, and ings or ly's where you can.
11. If weather is important to your story, then make use of it. It's your language that sets the tone.
12. Give the reader credit for his imagination. Infer and imply things, don't force feed. In "her red curls bounced out of her bonnet as she clung to the wooden rail of the main deck." We are implying a different time period and that she is on a ship.

Visual symbols are available in every scene. Hitchcock—a master of them—used several in Psycho. When we first see the hotel, there are flowers everywhere, but by the time Marion arrives all the flowers are dead.

Beginning writers sometimes get so wrapped up in their plots that they forget to look at the story through the character's eyes. (One reason why the timeline helps so much.)

Ruth felt that most writers faced such typical problems as clunky sentences which go on and on, wrong words, inaccurate expressions, or infelicitous juxtapositions, too much explanation or trying to tell too much, beginning too soon in the story (she calls this the introduction syndrome), not writing consistently from one point of view, pointless scenes which don't move the story forward, and insufficient RELEVANT details.

Telling too much is as bad as telling too little. But often the writer, knowing the story and character as well as she does, thinks the reader understands and leaves holes in the story.

EXERCISE:

REWRITE THE FOLLOWING SENTENCES AND INDICATE WHAT THE PROBLEM IS:

1. Her phone rang softly (she had had the phone company put a damper on the bell, so that it wouldn't scare her out of her wits when it interrupted her thoughts) and Mike answered it for her.
2. Because she was five feet ten inches tall, stretching felt wonderful.
3. The crew was enviously busy.
4. She accepted their compliments but kept watching anxiously for the one person who did not come up to commend her.
5. She wondered if the television audience ever realized that behind every on–camera reporter who looked like they were just blithely telling them about the pictures they saw on their screen, there was a harried and frantic writer.
6. Bonnie wondered what Hollis would do were he here and concluded that, despite her newness as the latest member of his sales staff, he would want her to extend every courtesy to a prospective purchaser.

Don't be locked into your words. Be willing to revise and rewrite, but not so much that it stalls you. Art Holcomb tells the story of one writer whose first chapter was so brilliant, but the rest of the book was blank. The reason, fearing failure he kept on rewriting the first chapter until it was perfect and couldn't get passed. He couldn't go on.

Don't go talking out your plot to everyone or your brain will think of it as a completed story, and your creative spark will suffer.

Continue writing your story until the end and then go back and revise. Don't worry, you will get plenty of editorial or production notes from the people writing the checks.

Do not rely on spell checker or grammar checker, they are often wrong and miss things. Have other people proof read your work, because no matter how many times you read it over, you will miss something. It's human nature to read into it what we think is there. I hire a freelance editor to look over my material before I submit to my agent. It's not unusual for a studio reader to toss a script if they see two or more typos or grammar errors on the first few pages. It's a small price to pay for looking professional.

MAKE A LIST OF YOUR CHARACTER'S ACTIONS IN GETTING HIS GOAL OR ATTEMPTING TO REACH THAT GOAL.

THEN NEXT TO IT, LIST WHAT REACTIONS THE VILLAIN HAS TO THE CHARACTER'S ACTION. (This can be done with the timeline seen in the index.)

HOW THEN DOES THE CHARACTER REACT TO THE VILLAIN'S ACTION, AND VISA VERSA?

(The time line shown in the appendix is good for this.)

It's like tying a shoelace and bouncing from one side to the other.

A villain does not have to be human. A villain can be time, weather, land, or a spirit.

Remember, you must have a life and death happening, a reason for the characters to go on, for the reader to keep reading.

What's important at stake? The suspense, as in Jaws, where we know that there is danger coming, will keep us reading. A ticking clock, knowing that the protagonist must get something accomplished by a certain time and certain date, will keep tension going.

We'll talk about this more in the mystery writing section, but suspense is developed by meticulously developing the risk and danger, time and action, character and conflict. But most new writers, while they start to develop the suspense, forget to climax it.

The readers will get tired of just reading and holding their tension up if there is no pay off. That climax must be fully dramatized; it must be seen, experienced, felt, and sensed. There should be a genuine doubt about the outcome.

You must have a strong protagonist, someone whom we can identify, and someone we can love. There must also be doubts that he will succeed in his goal.

And if you run your stories past these, you should keep the reader reading.

When asked what genre their book is in, many students blithely say mainstream—even when it's obvious their story is a romance, historical, western, adventure, sci fi, or mystery. Why is this? Most writers, when asked who the reader they are marketing their book towards, will say their book is for everyone. That's the wrong answer. No book is going to attract everyone. Readers are in niches. Women like certain books; men like another; young teens like yet another. The writer has to decide who he is writing for.

Writers, especially those from academia, like to consider their work literary masterpieces and push aside the fact that they are really working in one genre or the other.

Perhaps it's because many of the genres seem more "common" or more for the masses. The fact is, genres got their start with the penny pulp stories or mass market paperbacks that poorer people would read for entertainment, because they couldn't afford the then classics of Shakespeare, etc. Many young struggling writers at that time, Dickens and Poe among them, wrote for the penny pulp or mass market trade because it was all they could sell, and it helped them learn and polish their craft.

All the genres, at one time or another, suffered under the negative tinge of "Oh, you read those books." For a while, it was sci-fi and westerns, then it was mystery, and now it's romance.

When I taught at USC, I worked both with the masters of writing group and with the adult education center. The later ate up what I said about writing commercially, whereas the master students felt offended when I suggested how to make their work more successful. They wanted to do what I called "belly button writing" (writing from "the soul") and didn't care about getting their work published.

It's for this reason many of the students aspiring to be "literary" writers do not want to admit, or cannot see, that they are writing for the commercial market. They are writing to sell; they are writing for the masses. Many are insulted when you try to explain to them what commercial writing is, compared to what they are writing.

Writing the genre is not writing–by–number, despite what tales you've heard about formulas. The fact is most genre books are exceptionally well done and take as much time and craft to develop a good story, especially considering the guidelines that must be used in writing them. Yes, there are those that are just tossed off, and they show.

What exactly is a mainstream novel, and how does it differ from genre writing? You won't believe this, but even mainstream has a type formula of its own. The trouble is that, mainstream is a catch–all phrase for any type of book that combines more than one genre or doesn't easily fit into one genre glove. Its guidelines are not as precise as the ones for romance, mystery, et. al.

Even so, there are a few givens in a good mainstream. These books are much bigger not only in word length, but in story. Some of the words which come to mind are international scope, global passions, high melodrama, and overwhelming obsessions—revenge, hate, lust, love for country, or high ambition. Mainstream novels, like genre, take you to the height of glory and depths of despair.

In order to really succeed, the stakes have to be made more personal. In ***TAKEN,*** not only is the story about human trafficking, but the cop's daughter has been kidnapped. In ***DEEP IMPACT,*** Tea Leone's family is about to die.

Some books confuse a student because they appear to be genre, like Janet Dailey or Tom Clancy. Why have these books and authors made the successful crossover when others in their field have not? The reason is the subject matters they've chosen and the depth and heights of emotion which their characters feel as the story evolves.

Most mainstream books encompass more than one location, almost all deal with more than one character's story and these intermingling plots have emotion dripping from them.

Their love scenes, if they have them, may not be as steamy as the romance novels, but they also are not as "delicate." Common, and sometimes crude, anatomical terms are used in an effort to show the "real" world.

Characters in the mainstream must overcome more than normal problems. In fact, superhuman endurance is required and justice MUST prevail in some fashion. For all their glitz and glamour (and these books have quite a lot of that), for all their marvelous life styles, which most of us only dream about, these people suffer deeply.

The night time soap opera , *Dallas,* is a great example.

Every drop of emotion is wrung out of these stories, and no they don't need a happy ending, but they must have a satisfactory ending.

Mainstream metaphors—with a central one used throughout—are so sensual that the reader can feel and see everything as the character's life blood is slowly drained away.

And even once they have perfected their craft and are ready—if they wish—to go on to mainstream, many genre writers stay where they are because they enjoy the challenge of writing unique stories using tried and true guidelines and because they know, mainstream or genre, they can deliver a satisfactory read.

IDENTIFY YOUR MARKET—Who is the target audience for your book or script? Don't say everyone because not everyone will want it. Is it geared toward the male teen, female, family, or older? And how will you let them know that your project exists? One friend, whose hero is Latina, I suggested they approach some of the Spanish stations to place his ads. The publisher or producer is going to want to know this and as a business person—which every writer must be—this is something you should know.

ASSIGNMENT: Study a genre book similar to what you are writing, You'll notice that most mainstream books do not deal as heavily with the sex scenes, but if you feel it flows with your book—and only if you've been reading that genre will you know—put it in. (Though if you look at two recent books, ***THE GABRIEL'S INFERNO*** series and ***50 SHADES OF GRAY,*** they consider themselves mainstream—mainly because they are bigger and longer than the genre guidelines, but they still use many of the same techniques.)

Study a mainstream with elements of that genre—i. e., a Harlequin romance and Barbara Taylor Bradford's ***WOMAN OF SUBSTANCE.*** Compare the writing styles, length of sentences, metaphors, tone, distance, senses, and emotions.

UNRAVELING THE MYSTERY OF MYSTERIES

With the changing of the markets of gothic, suspense, mystery, and romance suspense, it's important to understand the difference between the genres and how to construct them.

Despite what most of you think, there really isn't any secret to writing a mystery or suspense. You've already probably done it, if you've written anything at all. All stories are mysteries because we're constantly asking the question — do the hero and heroine get together? Does the hero obtain his goal and defeat the villain?

We plan the obstacles they will face, foreshadow the problems they'll encounter, and give clues as to the final outcome. In short, any story, romance or otherwise, is suspense.

I've used the words "mystery" and "suspense" interchangeably here, but in fact they are two very different types of stories.

In a mystery, the crime has been committed and we must go along with the detective to find out who did it and why. The villain is unknown until the end of the story. Although it opens with a crime, additional crimes might follow to further twist the story.

For mystery, the best person to study is Edgar Allan Poe, since he did almost every kind, including the locked room and study how it is done. He explored the who done it, as well. This is the most common today in combination with an open murder which occurs up front, and the revenge mystery, among others.

There are several forms of mystery: the detective, the horror, the adventure/mystery, romantic/mystery, and the literary or character mystery (sometimes called the "cozy"), and the police procedural.

The detective story is an intellectual one. The major thrust being the unraveling of the puzzle. It's an aggressive book. The detective takes the problems, attacks them, and gives chase to the solution. There must be fair play for the reader. Whoever your detective is, he or she must relate to the readership—be it teen, hard boiled man, a couple, or a senior citizen.

The literary "cozy," or amateur mystery, is another form which Agatha Christie specialized in, often has a lot of "talking heads"—dialogue—since quite a bit of thinking must be done. Writers like Agatha Christie and Martha Grimes, an American writing in the cozy style, emphasize character development. These books are slightly slower placed and in a self–contained closed society, like a small village. Motativation is all–important here. These books are clean with no foul language or senseless brutality and no graphic sex. Justice is always meted out in the end. Teens can do their own forms of cozy—like a small high school or vacation community. But teens generally like more action than a cozy allows. My own Fanny Zindel series, ***RED SEA, DEAD SEA*** and ***BAGELS FOR TEA***, a senior amateur, belongs in this category. My book, ***A GATHERING STORM,*** from Silhouette is a perfect example of a teen cozy detective.

Romantic/mysteries often have a male/female team with witty dialogue and romantic tension along with the mystery. The old TV shows, *Remington Steele* or *Moonlighting,* are good examples of this. Harlequin has a special line of intrigue books that use this technique often.

The horror story, of course, has lots of emotion in it and you might want to consider combining the elements of the adventure with horror. The horror mystery is not as intellectual and clue oriented as the detective mystery. This is the heart thumping, stomach–tightening story where the hero/ine is the intended victim, where they're more likely to come eye to eye with the killer in a room at midnight.

Hard boiled thrillers are tense, tough, and cynical. Good and evil are not clear cut here. In some of these, the legal system is as corrupt as the criminal activity it is supposed to be protecting from. The heroes here are anti–heroes and often seen in the detective novels of the 1930s to 1950s. Dashiell Hammett and Raymond Chandler are good examples as are currently Sara Paretsky, Sue Grafton, and Libby Hellman's Georgia Davis PI thrillers.

Other thrillers can be medical, legal , political, historical, espionage, erotic, or crime. They feature high excitement, tension, anxiety, and often unexpected developments. They tell tales of terrorism, corruption, and conspiracy with plenty of heart pounding suspense as they overcome nasty obstacles and threatening situations. Examples of these are the ***BOURNE IDENTITY,*** anything by Dan Brown, Tess Gerritsen, Stieg Larsson, and Libby Hellman's ***HAVANA***.

Historical crime such as mysteries written by Lindsey Davis, Jeri Westerson, Barbara Peters, Rhys Bowen, and Tasha Alexander are great if you're fans of ancient Rome, Egypt, WWII, the late 1960s, or anywhere in the past. These require less technology and more leg and brain work to solve the crimes. Like historical novels, a lot of research is needed.

Police procedurals attempt to show the inner workings of the police force as they investigate crimes. Sometimes readers know the perpetrator from the start, but often the police detective (and thus the reader) does not. Writers who do this genre must know the forensics and procedures they are writing about, which vary from state to state and country to country. They also need a good understanding of the court system. Some of the best examples of this are Ian Rankin, Peter Robinson, Michael Connelly, Louise Penny, and Paul Bishop, who, himself, is a detective in real life.

Noir fiction, also called roman noir, is closer to the hardboiled thriller, but the main protagonist can sometimes be the victim Gillian Flynn's books are a good example of this. I don't especially like these because the endings are too lose.

Often in the espionage mystery, characters are more deeply analyzed. It is the human under stress. These are psychological novels as opposed to the problem novel for the mind adventure.

Don't get me wrong, no matter what type of mystery you're doing, you still need to know your character and set him up. The sounder the mystery, the more psychological the story.

The suspense, on the other hand, usually has a more amateur detective who is lured into the problem against his or her will. Someone is after them for what they know or the threat they pose. It's a lot like the horror story with lots of creaking stairs, and whispering branches thrown in. The villain can be identified at the beginning—either to the reader and/or lead character—but not why? In suspense, the major violent crime comes at the end. The object here is to foil the villain.

Gothics are often classed in the suspense section. The basic difference between gothics and romantic suspense is that the gothic is usually historical and often in first person, whereas the romantic suspense is almost always contemporary and sexier. That's not to say gothics can't be contemporary, or in third person. They can and often are. Using my own book, ***SHRIEKING SHADOWS,*** as an example, I can say that gothics can be sexy. ***A GATHERING STORM*** is my teen version of a modern gothic. Classed as such, it had difficulty finding a home until the editors decided gothics were coming back.

Often the gothic is, however, more suspenseful and mood oriented than the romantic/suspense, which has more action in it.

The romantic suspense is probably the hardest to do, since you must essentially write two stories at once—a romance and suspense. The majority of the romance editors I spoke with who wanted this type of story say the main fault is either too much romance or too much suspense. A good romantic suspense should be 50–50—half romance and half suspense.

Before taking pen to paper, or fingers to computer keys, it's best to decide who your reader is going to be. If you are writing a hard–core guts and action story for men, you'll write in one style. If you're doing a young adult mystery, then the adventure/mystery—with lots of action and lots of emotion—is the best.

In doing this type of book, you might even want to have two simultaneous plot lines going with indications of where they intertwine, since each story requires its own foreshadowing, obstacles, and clues as to the ending.

The bond you establish between your protagonist and reader is what will carry you through any good story—but this is especially true with a suspense/mystery.

If you are writing a romantic suspense, the protagonist should be a woman, not unlike yourself—perhaps with some cunning, but not a lot of training. If you are writing for teens or children, the protagonist should be a teen or a child, not much older than your reader. The reader must be able to relate to what the hero/ine is feeling, thinking, and going through for him to enjoy the story. In the New Adult genre, the heroines are in their late teens or early twenties, no older than twenty-two years of age. This is so the young adult audience can relate to them. Stories like Hunger Games and the Twilight series fit here.

A major difference between a teen mystery and an adult one is the use of violence and the type of crime. Death can be used, as I did with ***UNHOLY ALLIANCE***, or you can use other problems with equal effectiveness. In fact, the next book in the series, ***A WEDDING TO DIE FOR,*** uses drug overdoses. My editor at Fawcett wanted less violence in the book and more action.

It's like tying a shoelace and bouncing from one side to the other.

A villain does not have to be human. A villain can be time, weather, land, or a spirit.

Remember you must have a life and death happening, and a reason for the characters to go on, for the reader to keep reading. What's important at stake? The suspense, as in ***JAWS,*** where we know that there is danger coming, will keep us reading. A ticking clock, knowing that the protagonist must get something accomplished by a certain time and certain date, will keep tension going.

Suspense is developed by meticulously developing the risk and danger, time and action, character and conflict. But most new writers, while they start to develop the suspense, forget to climax it.

The readers will get tired of just reading and holding their tension, if there is no pay off. That climax must be fully dramatized: it must be seen, experienced, felt, and sensed. There should be a genuine doubt about the outcome.

You must have a strong protagonist, someone whom we can identify, and someone we can love.

And if you run your stories past these, you should keep the reader reading.

The mystery/suspense is complex in that our heroine's aim must be larger than life. She must want to do something, prevent something, or help someone. This drive should bring out extraordinary achievements in her. She is committed to a goal, which to her, is more important than life itself—if need be.

Presupposing the crime, the heroine must have a desperate reason for wanting to solve the problem. She must go into it enthusiastically—often without thinking and often foolhardy. The reader must believe her motive for going into the situation. If you think her reasoning sounds too dumb, a good trick to use is, "I knew it was probably foolish to go to the cliff at night by myself, but it was an obsession with me. I had to go." That helps the reader to know our heroine isn't a dolt, just determined.

The hero/ine must be seeking justice as my heroine in ***DECEPTIVE DESIRES,*** now a screenplay, ***LOGAN'S LAND***.

The best plotting is wasted if we don't care about that character. The more we care, the better the suspense. Even if the reader does figure out who did it on page 15, he'll stay with you until the end, because he cares about that character you've created.

What the clue says and where it is put must be related to your character. A clue cannot come out of nowhere and neither can the actions of your characters. Everything must be kept consistent. For example, Tzipporah, being a rabbi's daughter, would not willingly break the Sabbath, but she felt finding the murderer was a good reason.

The primary clue, which is the one that gives you ultimate proof, is often a little known fact, which only the killer would know. These might be like doors, almost always open in the direction of the hinges, or that riders always mount horses from the left side, or that a woman puts on the head of the sweater first and then the arms, whereas a man puts on the arms first, or that the law of motion dictates that when a moving vehicle stops, everything is thrown forward.

The detective finding this would know for sure who the culprit is, and therefore, this clue would not appear until the final few scenes. Other clues, leading to red herrings (suspects) and to the killer, as well, are liberally placed throughout the story. But each story needs one primary clue.

A good clue must also be well buried. The reader's attention should be diverted at the clue's introduction so that he isn't aware of the importance until later, if at all. In ***UNHOLY ALLIANCE***, I used a gum wrapper as the key clue. Another wrapper appears just as Tzipporah discovers her cat's been catnapped.

Clues should not be withheld, but it's all right to place false clues, which will mislead the hero and make him think that one of the red herrings is responsible.

Starting with your principal clue puts you a step ahead. Then you must decide how to bury your clues. If it's too obvious, the reader will feel cheated. If it's too deep, he'll feel angry. The writer must play fair with the reader and keep the clue within the knowledge of the average reader. And if it's possible, they won't know something, educated them before the clue is dropped.

Secondary clues are what the reader first sees since the primary clue will be revealed only at the end. These secondary clues can help establishing not only legitimate proof of guilt, but can be used to lead to the other suspects. The clue can be a trigger, as well. It can lead the hero into further trouble. Sometimes the best thing is to bury a clue in the middle of the most exciting part. This distracts the reader so he won't notice the clue is there.

Some physical clues might be: footprints in the snow, dog doesn't bark if he knows the owner, behavior patterns of people.

Animals are great to use as sub—characters. If you have a cat who hates men, and the heroine comes home to find the apartment ransacked, but the cat contently sitting, then the villain has to be a woman.

Clues need to be logical and do need to be planted. I read a Dell Supreme where the story was well executed until the very end—when we were surprised with the guilt of the villain since there had been no hints or clues as to her identity. That is a cop out!

Since you must tie up loose ends at the end, any clue you've used must be explained. Therefore, you want to keep your extra clues down.

Another problem comes when the hero is given a secret knowledge that the reader isn't—like the suspect has a .44 Magnum and the bullet in the body was a .38 Special. The reader should be given all the details the hero has, and then some. The reader must see and feel all the clues the detective has or they'll cry foul play.

Even the setting and dialogue come into your plotting in a realistic fashion. They must be something your reader can understand. That's not to say foreign locations like the Greek isles or the streets of Edinburgh aren't fabulous and spooky; they might be. But if your protagonist is a ten–year–old child, you'd better have a plausible reason for him being there. You'd better have things there he can relate to**.**

Settings, themselves, are very important. Often they come alive and behave like characters. The house in Phyllis Whitney's ***RAINSONG*** is an excellent example. You want a place, which can be moody, and threatening, yet which can seem innocent and perfectly natural all the same. Cornish islands, Cape Cod resorts, and small isolated towns are fine. The trick comes in being able to make a big city department store seem just as threatening as an isolated island.

You naturally need plenty of places to hide, with lots of long shadows. Factual accuracy is important, but you also need elements to build up the romance as well. In short, you need sensuality.

If your protagonist is a youngster, you'll have to worry about parental supervision. The parents will need to be immobilized so they don't get in the way of the kid solving the problem. They can be latchkey kids, kids with folks on a vacation, on a babysitting job, or even a paper route. They must have a believable life for the reader to believe them. Ten-year-olds might not care about drugs, about the war in Lebanon, or nuclear bombs—unless they are personally involved. They'd be more concerned if their teacher died mysteriously of poisoned peanut butter sandwiches, or if someone disappeared at a carnival.

Teens might be into marathons, American geography or traveling. With high school, they'd have more freedom than the ten-year-old, but they'd still be restricted. In ***UNHOLY ALLIANCE***, I had to have reason to keep the adults out. Since the sheriff didn't believe her, Tzipporah and her friends had to solve the case by themselves.

The same goes if your heroine is to be romantically involved. Her situation must be believable—especially if you're putting her out in the midst of an island with no one but herself to look after her. Why is she there? What brought her there? In ***A GATHERING STORM***, she is sent to Cape Cod because her mother is getting married.

No matter who your protagonist is, the perils and conflicts in the book lie in the threats being real, in danger, which your reader can understand.

EXERCISE:

MAKE A LIST OF PERILS—BOTH NATURAL AND ARTIFICIAL—WHICH YOUR HERO/INE CAN BE SUBJECTED TO WITHIN THE COURSE OF YOUR STORY. THINK OF PERSONALITY, LOCATION, AND TIME.

Examples might be: falling rocks, a cave–in, hurricane, runaway horse, being pushed off a cliff, being locked in a freezer, being confronted with rats (or other nastiness she doesn't like). Remember, they must all be logical for the time, place, and personality. Ask yourself what you're most afraid of. Don't worry about making a fool of the hero/ine since her determination is what got her into this mess and her determination is what will get her out—we hope.

The mystery/suspense is a plot, which has to be entangled, much as a spider's web. What the writer knows is not yet evident to the reader. It's impossible for us just to sit down with blank paper and write a mystery. No, I won't say impossible, but you'll certainly waste a lot of time and effort, not to mention paper. You'll find it easy to get your characters into trouble—not so easy to get them out.

For this reason, it's important to know where you are going before you start out. Yes, we are talking about outlining again. I've heard this phrase many times, but it's true—you aren't going to drive to New York without a road map, without knowing what highways to take, what detours will lead you where, and where you'll stop for the night. Should you attempt this, you'd get lost awfully quickly.

The outlining of your story will help you decide where to plant your clues. As we said, they must be placed throughout the story, and usually in inconspicuous places so the astute reader can see them, but not necessarily realize they are clues. Each clue will later somehow point to the killer. I found backward construction really helps here. Not only can you know where to plan and foreshadow, it also helps when you're stuck on a part and don't know where you're going. You can simply take up with a different section of the book and merge the two later.

Ask yourself, what is the basic question of your story? As long as you have a "why," the reader will continue turning the pages. You, as the writer, need to have an answer—not only to know where you're going, but also to know where you'll stop for the night. What clues will you plant for the detour? You need to know not only what and who is threatening the heroine, but why? (Please don't use drug smuggling. It's been done to death!)

After you've fixed your clues, you need to list all the people who might possibly be the cause of the problem or crime. Who are they? How did they come on to the scene? More importantly, what are their possible motives, opportunities, and methods for the crime, and for trying to harm your innocent heroine? These folks are called red herrings—and you need to have several of them.

You need to have the reader believing that one of these not so innocent bystanders did the deed. Then you need to determine when and how the hero/ine finds out this person isn't the one. Often the trick used is finding the primary suspect dead half way through the book, putting the reader back to square one. In ***UNHOLY ALLIANCE***, the first suspect is arrested. Tzipporah and her friends think they're safe, but not for long.

Of course, you don't want to have too many false suspects because then you've got too many people in your book. Two or three is the average.

When I'm doing a mystery, I keep a note above my typewriter. WHAT ARE THE HEAVIES (RED HERRINGS) DOING NOW? This is because all–writing, but mystery writing especially, is an action/reaction story. For every action the hero takes, the villain takes one to counteract that.

EXERCISE:

MAKE A LIST OF THE POSSIBLE SUSPECTS FOR YOUR BOOK, THEIR MOTIVES, THEIR RELATIONSHIP TO THE HEROINE, AND WHAT CLUES SHE WILL FIND TO MAKE HER THINK THEY ARE THE VILLAIN.

CREATING DANGER

This is especially important if you are doing a gothic or romantic suspense, since the heroine almost always believes the hero to be guilty—while loving him nevertheless. The man she loves must be a prime suspect and must have an established motive. Even in the teen gothic***, A GATHERING STORM***, I had the heroine suspect her boyfriend and in ***UNHOLY ALLIANCE***, Tzipporah suspects Paul for several chapters.

Although I've put sex in my gothic, sensuality does not mean sex. It means using the senses—all of them (hearing, taste, smell, feel, sight.) Creating a suspenseful mood means using all your senses.

VIEWPOINT

Viewpoint is essential for the right mood. Most gothics and mysteries are done in first person because of the immediacy it creates. That doesn't mean you can't write a good suspense piece in third person. You can. It just means you have to work harder to stay in her perspective. Again, it's important to know what house you are writing for and what that editor requires.

Viewpoint can even be someone other than your protagonist. This can be helpful since he can include things you might not know about. It is cheating a bit, but it's one way to get information about without it sounding too much like exposition. A good example of this is ***SHERLOCK HOLMES.*** Here the story is a lot of dialogue and conversation about the crime. If you do decide to work in first person, it's important to remember the heroine can't know anything, which she, herself, does not experience first hand or isn't told. Several children's detectives use secondary characters to relay the events, since the smart kid solving the crime wouldn't be relating events in a way that the ordinary reader would see them.

EXERCISE:

WRITE A SUSPENSEFUL MOOD: A girl being followed home on a dark street, a storm coming up, or a chase scene.

Terror can grow from dialogue, as well as anything else. Sometimes the threat can be underscored with just a few words. The atmosphere of a terror scene is important; the senses must be evoked totally so that we can react emotionally to the silent house, the dark path. The main character must change and be affected by what's happening.

In using terror, delay is a tool often used and the moment is stretched out with terrifying pauses, while the reader feels the fear of the unknown along with your heroine. Each second in this sequence is magnified from the moment she steps out of the house, hears the creaking of her foot on the gravel path, feels the presence of someone watching her, listens to the silence around her, sees the darkness, etc., and each step forward needs to heighten this terror until we are sure she is doomed.

The quickest way to destroy the bond between reader and character is to have inconsistent behavior. You must remember that humans are basically conservative beings. They will do only as much as they have to in order to achieve their goal. Therefore, they plan the simplest way and go farther only when thwarted.

VILLAINS

Because the villain doesn't want her to reach the goal, the villain will do all in his power to defeat her. When she realizes her first step isn't working, then she must reconsider and take another and yet another. Each of these steps must have obstacles. Once again, she must dedicate herself until so much has happened that even if she wanted to turn back, it would be too late.

For every action the character takes, there must be a reaction from the villain.

Since the villain is the power center of the story, he must appear—at least in name—early and often. He has to know something about the heroine so the perils he puts her in are perils, which really affect her. (The villain of ***SHRIEKING SHADOWS OF PENPORTH ISLAND*** knew Tamara couldn't swim, and therefore, tried to drown her. He didn't realize he was dealing with Vicky and not Tamara.) You must know what your heroine is most afraid of and what she cannot do.

At each step in the book, ask yourself, how the villain is going to obstruct this. Don't forget, villains are human too, with goals of their own. They should be painted as clearly and with as much depth as the hero/ine. If you want cardboard people, take out the shirt cardboard and draw them! Don't write them.

SAGGING STORY LINE

There are usually three rising crises before the final climax comes, and at the blackest moment, we can't imagine how the heroine will succeed. It's true we like her, but we must be sadistic. We must make her suffer. We must think of ways in which problems beset her. Ask yourself, what the worst possible thing to happen now is. How can your reader suffer more with her?

Because sagging middles are the death of us all, you need to know beginning, middle, and end before you start. Then, it's also a good thing to fill in your turning points, which foreshadow and lead up to each of the crises.

Deciding how long your book will be will also help with the plotting. If you know how many chapters you'll be dealing with, and how long each chapter will be, then you can have one strong scene towards solving the mystery and one strong scene towards the romance in each of your chapters. Of course, you'll have several minor scenes as well.

Villains, of course, are all hopelessly conceited. They never believe they will get caught. They know they'll get away with their crime and are often quite bold about it—especially towards the end of the book.

CHARACTER MOTIVE

All of the protagonist's motives fall into two categories, self–preservation (of money, family, status, fear of blackmail, physical threats, a personal desire for revenge), or on a larger scale, preservation of life or ideal beyond her own interests. (She can be committed to a helpless friend, to her country, or her standards.) Basically, she knows if she doesn't go on something terrible will happen to someone she cares about deeply.

OUTLINING

Before starting to outline, you need to have a checklist. You need to know what crime was committed and what problem is there. (If you do have a murder, it should occur no later than chapter three.) Some writers even prologue this first murder event as I did in ***UNBORN WITNESS***.

It's crucial that you set up the rules for your world and foreshadow everything. For instance, if you are writing a paranormal where ghosts are the norm, then you have to established early on that ghosts are allowed in this story and the rules by which they function. Can they walk into walls? Can they read minds? Know it before hand so that your story will be consistent.

Then you need to know what other problems will complicate the story—and/or the relationship. Again, what else can go wrong? What are the motives involved for the murder, attempted murder, or crime? Everyone who is suspect must have had an M. O. M. : method, opportunity, and motive. Other accomplices for the villain need to be considered as well. They may or may not be suspects themselves.

Finally, you need to remember that justice must be done in the end. The villain must be found, the hero/ine must be saved and the couple must admit their love (if you're doing a romantic suspense). She must not realize until the end that the hero is innocent of all she suspected him of. Even so, she loves him desperately.

Be careful of coincidences. Surprise your readers. Surprise yourself by letting your characters take over. I find by writing fast, I make the action fast. Simplicity and clarity are two important parts of good action writing. "The blade flashed," and we see a knife being thrown. Excitement follows, but it's not wrapped up in similes, and metaphors. Show the reader what, but don't lead him by the hand. Let him feel it just as you should be feeling it. Use your senses for the best tension.

A mystery has a seven–step framework (usually with murder as the basis).

1. The inciting incident (of the body being found).
2. The solution. (Usually the wrong one.)
3. Complications. Make things difficult for hero/ine. Don't be afraid to have them suffer and put them in jeopardy.
4. A period of confusion.
5. Hero/ine gets clue or hint and begins to put it together.
6. The real solution—with explanation, wrap–up, and tie–up of loose ends together.
7. Who, how, and why it was done.

Of course, you don't have to be locked into this, but today's reader demands characterization plus plot. He wants to feel informed about something he didn't know before reading your story.

There is also the three–act drama, which can be used for any kind of writing.

1. Something happens—the inciting incident.
2. The back–story of what led up to it.
3. The conclusion.

In this, the hero and heroine should be introduced in the first chapter as well as the villain. The first act should end upbeat so that we think the characters will get what they want.

Read books on abnormal psychology, police procedural, visit the crime labs, visit the federal courts.

Remember, all stories are suspense, and you can do it, if you want. Research is important but our books are only as good as the characters and the clues.

Ten final rules given by Don Sobel, author of Encyclopedia Brown series, are:

1. Bury the clue—not too deeply.
2. Play fair.
3. Keep in the storehouse of reader's knowledge or help her out.
4. Do not begin writing before having an outline.
5. Be sure you have a primary clue, which depends on facts.
6. Sprinkle false clues and make them a proper part of the story.
7. The simpler clue the better.
8. Have several convincing red herrings.

9. Be careful of too much violence in a kid's mystery.
10. Be passionate about your story.

There are several ways that you can create suspense.

The first, as we have already stated, is the ticking clock device. If we have to defuse a bomb, the ticking down of the clock will lock us into the action taking place. The problem is this has been so overdone it's become a cliché; on television shows it's as subtle as being bludgeoned with a hammer.

Remember, we talked about cliché traffic accidents? Meet cliché ticking clock. But suppose we use another device? Like water pouring into the hold of a ship, and our heroes are battling to keep it afloat? A train running wild toward a crowded station and our heroes trying to stop it? Remember the movie, ***SILVER STREAK***? A ticking clock device doesn't have to be an actual ticking clock. Anything that signals the action slowly building toward a climax will work, even the ticking clock, if done with finesse and subtlety.

Stretching time is the opposite of the ticking clock. Again, it requires subtlety. If we bring our hero into a dangerous climatic scene, we can stretch the suspense by describing the place, painting it very heavy or dark and foreboding.

Remember to use all the senses: see, hear, smell, touch, and taste. I mentioned before how Dean Koontz stretched out a scene in ***TICK TOCK*** by simply describing a beast as it advanced on the hero, the eyes, the sounds, the way it moved, how it smelled, so while one part of the reader's mind is absorbed in the details, the other is screaming for the hero to run.

Again, do it with finesse. SHOW, not TELL. No eyes rolling with, or filled with horror. No clichés. And end it before it becomes obvious.

We talked about the ticking clock and stretching time devices before. How else can we tighten the screw?

Write about a placid scene where everything is normal, but twist one thing out of place:

Sally carried her laundry basket down the second floor hallway, aglow in sunlight, streaming in through the west windows, setting off three clown pictures hanging on the wall. She stopped to study them, pleased at the purchases she had picked up Saturday for two dollars at a yard sale. Not junk. All her years spent in studying art screamed of their quality. Something reminiscent of Renoir, Monet, or Manet. She had unearthed a treasure, for sure, whose worth she could not guess until she could get them appraised. What were they doing in a yard sale? Why would anyone want to get rid of them? For two dollars? She shook her head and glanced at her watch. She would have to hurry if she wanted to reach the club in time for a pre–lunch cocktail. She turned left into her bedroom, filled with the morning sun.

Okay, so you see it? Actually there are a number of red flags here, but only one thing really out of place, vastly out of place. If she's hurrying for a luncheon date, what's that glow streaming in the west windows? I also added the morning sun in the bedroom just to make sure you didn't think it was a screw up, but it's really over doing it. There's a difference between a subtle hint and overwriting. The first is trusting your readers' intelligence to not let it get by them, the second is a poke in the ribs and saying—"D'ja get it?"

All else being the same, we could rejoice with Sally at her great purchase, but with the sun business, the questions of the art work bargains becomes an ominous foreboding. The next time we come back, what's that red smudge on one picture frame? And the following time, are they on the opposite wall? See? You could work it just as well with everything being perfectly normal, but say the lights on in the daytime. Then a picture askew. A window cracked. Each step tightening the screw.

Another way is to leave something out of a normal setting, something that would ordinarily be there and is not. No stove in the kitchen. No commode in the bathroom is just an example. And the thing doesn't have to be tangible:

Sally walked through Harry's library and stopped midway, glancing around at the pale green walls, the curtains lining windows that she had helped pick out, and the hanging art work he had collected so lovingly over the years. She would have to box them up. But what had stopped her in mid–stride? She glanced around again, breath held, then exhaled at the vacant whisper of the place, an emptiness that had expanded and filled the air like a foul odor seeping up from a sewer pit.

How long had Harry been in the grave? Less then twenty-four hours. Yet the spirit of the house had fled. Which, of course was ridiculous. The feel of a house can not be turned on and off. Can it? No, what had changed was only her perception.

Let's break this down. What had changed was Sally's perception. Or was it? We get tension from her holding breath. Something's not quite right. Then there is the off slant feeling by the use of a vacant whisper, and foul odor expanding to fill the air. Notice, none of these things are actually present in the room, it's the use of narrative description that gives us the uneasy feeling. Then the questions arise. If the spirit fled, what had taken its place? And we imply that it surely had, by over emphasizing that it hadn't. Remember, we can negatively set things up by overstating the positive.

Okay, we talked about the ticking clock and stretching time devices, and how we could write a scene adding one thing out of place, or leaving something out that would normally be there.

Finally, we can use an unknown place, and the things found there to ratchet up the tension to a breaking point.

Sally descended the candle–lit stairs into the cellar of the manor house. A long subterranean passage stretched under its full length. Torches, ensconced in holders at twenty-foot intervals, sent shadows licking across dark stone walls as they flickered in a breeze that ebbed and flowed and tasted of salt. Somewhere the passage connected with the sea.

She hesitated on the wooden platform, glancing back up at the stairs, then down the long row of torches. The shadows would make slow going on the rough stone floor, but they aided her as well. If someone came the other way, she could hide in them, or race back to the stairs.

She started out, one foot after another, careful of falling. She passed the third torch before she paused, listening, aware that something had changed. What? She glanced back toward the staircase to see it had been swallowed in the darkness. Not only had the candles burned out, but also the first torch. Burned out or blown out. She crossed over to the torch, thinking to use it to illuminate the way back. It hung too high on the wall for her to reach. The next one looked lower and she hurried toward it. Then stopped. Something had changed again. She turned and the last two torches winked out. She rushed forward for the torch, but again it was out of reach. And on to the next as the one behind puffed out, leaving only a black void where there had once been stairs. And if the others went out, she would be trapped with no way out. She hurried forward and the torch she popped out passed, and then broke into a run as the next one went out, racing along the passage to keep from getting caught in the blackness that followed along, chasing her down.

Well, you get the picture. So, we're off in a dark setting. You could scream cliché at me, Sally being in a place she shouldn't really be, but she has a rational escape route set up so it's not really a cliché. Then as she moves along, we start tightening the screw by cutting off her escape. At first it's one light, way back, then the popping off torches move closer to her, and finally blinking off in front of her so she has to race to catch up, filling her with the terror of being trapped in the dark, driving Sally toward some unseen horror—or something.

In this example we used light as our driving force. But couldn't we use something else? How about the snakes in ***RAIDERS OF THE LOST ARK***? Or the rats in ***THE LAST CRUSADE***? Take notes when you're viewing movies. When Hollywood avoids the clichés to build tension, they do it right.

But couldn't we even use something else? Something that is completely innocuous?

How about red roses? What a lark when they first arrived. She smelled rich scent and held the stem where the thorns had been clipped off. Secret admirer? Someone from the office? Or someone from the dancing class she was taking? That would be more like it. Dancing, dining, flowers. They seemed to go together. When the second dozen came, it was even more intriguing, but when it reached twenty dozen in one day, coming at half hour intervals, from florists all over the city, some of the sun had gone out of it. This was no longer just an admirer, secrete or otherwise. Now the roses were like hammer blows beating down the gates to her castle, until finally she yanked open the door to scream at the deliveryman, only then did she realize her mistake.

You see. Of course all this is TELLING rather than SHOWING, but I'm trying to give you the idea of how to build suspense in a paragraph rather than actually writing the scenes. Anything done with finesse can be used to build suspense. You don't believe me? I will not argue with you. Just know that I have your address. And tonight, when you turn your light off, make sure all the windows are shut. And locked. How about the door? Did you remember to put the night latch on? And set the alarm? Then you have nothing to worry about.

Unless?

Unless I am already inside.

In a closet perhaps. Under a bed. And maybe I'm a spirit–thing crammed into the top of an uncapped ballpoint pen. Waiting for you. Waiting for—

No!

Do you see what we mean by suspense . . .

VIOLENCE

The amount of violence you might put in a murder mystery depends on the type of book you are writing. If you are doing an amateur sleuth, such as Mrs. Polifax or my own, Fanny Zindel (***RED SEA, DEAD SEA*** and ***BAGELS FOR TEA,***) the murder scenes are not graphic and are handled as gently as possible.

If you are doing a police procedural or hardboiled detective novel, then graphic is okay . . . to a point. Tom Clancy does some great scenes in his books as does Patricia Cornwall.

You want your scenes to be as realistic as possible. Read about forensics, ask questions, and do your research. Most police and others are happy to answer your queries. I have also taken courses in profiling and investigation from Knowledge Solutions, an online program. (www. corpusdelicti. com)

There are several basic books on forensics, which should be in every writer's library, including ***THE BOOK OF POISONS.***

EXERCISE:

Write your murder scene in various stages of graphic description. See how it affects you.

Read at least two murder scenes and compare them.

SOME MYSTERY SUBGENRES:

As near as one knows they are:

I. Mystery.

A. Cozy/Traditional.

1. Older Citizen.

2. Accidental Hero/ine.

3. Occupational Hazard.

(These people are in a profession that leads them into situations where crime happens, but are not police nor private detectives. Usually it is a profession like forest ranger, veterinary, insurance agent, etc.)

4. Woo–woo elements, but not a mystery/fantasy cross.

(Anthropomorphic animals.)

5. Juvenile and Young Adult.

B. Private Detective.

1. Hard Boiled.

2. Comic.

C. Police Procedural.

D. Cross–Genre.

1. Mystery/Science Fiction.

2. Mystery/Fantasy.

3. Mystery/Horror.

4. Mystery/Romance.

5. Mystery/historical.

E. Suspense/Thriller.

1. War.

2. Conspiracy–Criminal or Political.

3. Spies.

4. Biological Disaster (caused by humans).

THRILLER NOTES

1. The protagonist can't solve the problem through any normal means (calling 911 etc.).
2. The problems faced affect the community, even society at large (scope).
3. The solution involves some violence or illegality (by protagonist).
4. Subcategories are the political thriller, the disaster thriller.
5. The hero's motives must be highly defined to justify extreme, risky actions.
6. The protagonist must be out to preserve or restore a threatened society or group.

7. The key event is a counterthrust at the antagonist.
8. Hero progresses from ignorance to knowledge.
9. The climax creates a substantial change in knowledge and perspective on the issue addressed.

To me, the terms "thriller" and "suspense" are interchangeable, And most mystery subgenres can qualify if they meet the basic criteria, which is: someone or many are in constant danger, the reader cares, and the object is to stop the perpetrator of the violence.

It can work in a police procedural as indeed it did in ***SILENCE OF THE LAMBS***. It can work in the PI novel, if the PI or one of the other characters is in constant danger, and it can even work in the cozy—I think ***TEN LITTLE INDIANS*** is an example of a thriller in the cozy.

The watch word of the mystery is "solve"; that of the thriller or suspense is "prevent."

For that reason, I think most serial killer books are suspense and mystery because the object is to stop the killer from killing more.

Not all thrillers are mysteries, and neither are all mysteries thrillers, but a mystery can be both.

I think the term thriller is generally interchangeable, but I can think of cases where that might not be true.

***

HALLOWEEN HAUNTING AND OTHER SCARES

Beyond suspense there is horror. Horror is a genre of its own and has its own rules. Much of the information learned in mystery writing still applies. In mysteries, you are worried and concerned for the protagonist. In horror, you are ready to jump out of your skin. But horror is also being disgusted. I can be horrified at seeing an autopsy and the body parts all over the room, but it doesn't mean I am scared. I am scared when I think that my body parts may be the next to be spread out over the room.

There are several things to think about in writing a horror.

One of the main features of horror is fear of the unknown. The more we know about something, the less we fear it. The less explanation and the more hints of horrid things, the better it is for the story. The information about the monster, therefore, should unravel one step at a time. The story needs to be kept in the dark because we fear what we do not understand. Even if your story takes place in broad daylight, it is in a strange place, a place where you (the protagonist) do not feel comfortable. Life and reality unravels one slow step at a time.

The key is an impending doom of dread. So we only see fleeting glimpses of the monster, his shadow, or other evidence of his existence, such as shredded papers, glow in the dark eyes, a child's ball rolling down the stairs when no one is there, acrid smells—like the smell of putrid bodies, or strange noises in the hall. It is the fear of violence that keeps us on the edge of our seats as the monster plays with his food.

Another is the loss of free will. You have no choice but to fight the monster. Our character loses control as she tries to fight the monster.

One of the key losses of free will is love. In my script, ***DEVIL'S DAUGHTER***, Kim the protagonist falls in love with the little girl, Alex, whom she is taking care of, even though everyone tells her that Alex is evil. Despite what she knows and what she sees, she risks all to save the child . . .

Sex also makes us lose control so that stories of incubus and succubus are also good myths.

Fear of being lost and fear of death are, of course, two other big fears. So are other almost universal fears such as insects, spiders, snakes, and fire.

Keeping the reader/viewer off kilter is the key. If the star is murdered early on, then all is up for grabs. After all, we believe that the hero will over take the monster.

The protagonist is always alone against the world. Everyone whom he/she thought could help them was either killed or became one of them (***ROSEMARY'S BABY***.) Emotional attachments become a liability. Even people you trust turn against you. That old man next door could be the leader of the cult.

Unexpected violence and gore is upsetting and leads to more dread. We are doing things that seem perfectly normal—taking a shower, shopping at the grocery store—when all of a sudden someone comes after us; everyone in the grocery store is a zombie and we are the lunch meat. Take the ordinary and make it dangerous. Bad things happen suddenly and without apparent reason.

Many people think of horror as violence without a story. Bodies being cut up and guts splayed everywhere. That isn't necessarily the case and a good horror story, even though it might have its share of that, does it within the realm of the story. It is not gratuitous violence for violence sake. However, there are those who say there should be some sort of horror every ten to fifteen minutes in the movie, or every other chapter in the book—at least.

Shock is good. Shock but schlock shock is better . . . There is always some sort of comedic relief to let the tension go like a cat or a poodle. In one movie, there was the scratching at the door . . . could it be . . . no . . . we can't answer but we do . . . oh my Lord . . . it's just the poodle...and we let down our guard, while chiding ourselves for being so foolish, then the monster breaks in through the window.

Locations are another key spot in horror stories. They are usually limited with the action taking place in smaller areas. I mean if we can escape the snowbound hotel in Colorado or the isolated motel on Route 12, we would. You need a plausible reason why the protagonist cannot escape—no gas, isolated in the woods, a space ship, snowstorm, etc. There is no choice but for them to face the monster. In the movie, ***OPEN WATER***, the couple went on a snorkeling cruise . . . only to be left behind. The ordinary became extraordinary. They could see things above the water, but watch out...what just nudged against your foot. You can't see below the water, can you?

Religious beliefs often come into play here and are usually challenged. When we go against the belief system, we face the unknown. Jonathan Ryan's book, ***THREE GATES OF THE DEAD***, is an excellent example of this.

EXERCISE:

List some universal basic fears. Why are people afraid of them?

List some of your own fears. Why are you afraid of them?

What does your protagonist fear and why? How can they be used in your story?

List some places where you might be vulnerable. List places where you feel uncomfortable or scared.

List ordinary places and see what extraordinary things can happen there.

Let's talk about the villain for a moment. He needs a back story. He must be plausible and needs to have some human (or total lack of human) qualities. (After all, no one ever can really kill him, they just stop for a bit, but he comes back in the next sequel. Evil can never be killed.) Actions establish character, but don't take them for granted. He must have an MO—he always kills by sticking them on poles, with a machete, or by hanging.

We have to understand where he is coming from. Jason Voorhees had a pleasant childhood and could have grown up fine, but seeing his sister having sex with her date on the sofa when she was supposed to be taking care of him was a sense of betrayal, and from then on he went after young teens, especially young teens about to do it. Freddy Kruger was killed by town folks for molesting young kids, wronged by society. Therefore, he came back to have his revenge and really molest the kids using their minds. The mother alien was not going to let Sigourney Weaver take her children, no matter what. Now, what's the dark shadow in the corner?

KILLER ENDINGS

Have all your story threads been tied up? Subplots? Have you foreshadowed everything? If not, go back and do so.

The reader feels disappointed if the question asked in the beginning are not answered. Will she find the man who killed her husband? Will she chose the right man? Is your ending too predictable? How could you twist it?

Has your theme been sufficiently proven or explored? The theme is the way the character makes his choices. In Star Wars, Darth Vader chooses violence and evil, while Luke chooses the force.

Knowing the ending will often help you with the beginning, because you will know where and how to plan clues that logically (but not too easily) lead to your end. Some writers write their end first and then plot backwards from it, so that the cause and effect becomes more natural.

If you do not know your ending, you do not know your character? In one story, a mobster who had values, stuck to his value to the end, even though he was killed for it.

The crisis–where the choice is in front of you, the climax—when you make the choice, and the resolution–the after emotion are MUSTS in any story.

Paradigms for endings are several:

1. Central dilemma—where the character wrestles the whole story with the question and it builds to his decision. ***GODFATHER*** is a good example. Little dilemmas led up to his big one, when he finally had to decide to join his family in crime or lose them.
2. Projection—when the character fears the worst. He feared being alone and now he is . . . but he can chose not to be there.

3. The character arc being established and fulfilled. He has been hurt, wounded, and needs the courage to live again. What goals can't he achieve and why? What are the external problems he must overcome before his internal journey is complete? The external problem must be dealt with before the internal.
4. The character is set up and his growth is sacrificed. He must face his fears in ***LA CONFIDENTIAL.*** The theme is prominent here.

Which ever your ending is, if you have plotted it before, you will have a better direction on how your character will behave.

FINISHING TOUCHES: THE TITLE

Titles are almost as important as the story, but not quite. I do know people who have gotten carried away and created whole stories to suit one title.

On the other hand, a title can—if good—convince your editor that this book is worth reading. Those who put UNTITLED or give the editor a choice of several titles appear as wishy–washy writers who don't know their own minds. Editors like to think you know what the story is about and therefore can choose a title that is snappy and short.

Bear in mind that most titles are changed before publication—I've heard it's because editors are frustrated writers, but it could also be that titles, like the synopsis, are one of the things writers have the worst time with.

ONE TO FOUR WORDS

The title should be from one to four words—three is probably the best. It should somehow indicate the setting, mood, time, or genre of the book. For instance, romances usually have the words lust, fury, storm, passion, frenzy, satin, wild, fire, or desire in them. Western novels might have tombstone, grave, guns, horses, desolate, or wilderness in them. Science fiction might have planet, earth, alien, magic, fantasy, queen, knight, or the like.

Often there will be a working title for the author's use alone and the real title will suggest itself only as you are writing the book.

HOOKING

The fact remains you do need a title which will hook the editor when you send your material in—if only so they can properly code their cards.

Titles are not copyrighted and so you can use titles from other sources, but you want to make sure that these titles haven't been recently used and that your story won't be confused with them. I was upset recently when Zebra used a title similar to my ***TAME THE WILD HEART*** on Sylvie Sommerfield's book (***TAME MY WILD HEART***). But there was nothing I could do about it.

And the recent film I just finished, which I had called ***THE UNBORN,*** had to be changed because too many films out there had that name. So it became ***UNSEEN WITNESS***.

In Hollywood, a producer might even like your title so much that he'll option the book or screenplay merely to use your title and change the story completely. Since he could have just used the title, the producer will often do this to avoid legal hassles and accusations later on. Most of the time, the title, which the author chooses, is not the best for the story and needs to be changed. A good title will inspire you and push you into continuing your book, if you are stuck at any point.

EXERCISE:

WRITE THREE TITLES FOR YOUR STORY USING ONE, TWO, AND THREE WORD COMBINATIONS. MAKE IT SOMETHING THAT RELATES TO YOUR PLOT, GENRE, OR CHARACTERS.

Example: one student was writing about a homosexual priest and we came up with the title *WITHOUT BLESSING*.

LOOK AT TITLES THAT CATCH YOUR EYE. WHY DO THEY ATTRACT YOU? DO THEY TELL YOU ANYTHING ABOUT THE STORY?

***

POLISHING THE ROUGH STONE: REWRITING

Writing is rewriting! That is a plain and simple fact. There are very few things that come out perfect the first time. Despite what some popular writers tell you, a good book is not written in four days, ten days, or even a month. A first draft might be written in that time period, but not a polished draft. Mea culpa. I admit to being one of those writers who bragged about writing a book in a few days, but that was in my infancy when I thought everything I wrote was golden.

I usually advise my students to write a "vomit draft" where everything tumbles out. It's much easier to go back and rewrite material that is already written and it helps you to get the initial pressure off your brain.

Yes, it took only ten days to write my Cagney and Lacey book, but then I had to do four rewrites!

Nothing is perfect and especially in screenwriting, everyone—from the producer, director, and even the actors—seemed to want to give you notes. Revising is something that every professional writer must do.

Let your manuscript go for a day or two and then pick it up again. Read it out loud, listen for the rhythm and sound. Where can you make it more sensual? Where can you use more metaphors? Have you explained things clearly enough?

It helps to have a friend, preferably a writer, to read your work to, since when one is close to the story, it's difficult to judge if the writing is flowing or not. Another writer or even a reader is a good bouncing off place. They will be able to tell you if something works for them or not. Judge who you are giving your work to with care—a family member or good friend might say it's wonderful because a) they believe in you and you could write anything and they would say the same b) they don't want to hurt your feelings, or conversely, they could be jealous of you and tell you it's bad—when actually it's not. The green monster of jealousy is a terrible thing to be with.

Writing groups are great for encouragement and comments as to what works and what doesn't, but be aware that these are only opinions. At the start, I was so overwhelmed with comments that for each note I was making changes and doing massive rewrites. The story became totally different than what I had originally planned. I found out that if three or more readers have a problem with your story, then consider changing it. Otherwise, you are the author and creator and it is your story. You need to do what is right for your "baby."

Also you need to consider the credentials of who is evaluating your work. Are they published or produced writers? Or are they, like you, novices in the field. (This doesn't mean they can't have some good notes, but listen to your heart.)

When you are rewriting—and now that I know, my material is often rewritten four and five times, not to mention being looked over by a professional editor before it's sent out—check for inconsistencies in hair color, check to see that you are using active not passive verbs, that "was, were, would," and other to be verbs are changed when possible. Saying, "She ran," is stronger than "She was running."

You also want to make sure that you don't intermingle "ed's" and "ing's" to often in the same sentence. "Grabbing at the food, she wolfed it down," could be rewritten to, "She grabbed at the food and wolfed it down."

"That's, and's, and which's" are other problems you must face in your rewrite. See if the sentence sounds better without them. Usually you'll find that's the case! (But sometimes not.)

Your beginning might be great, your end dynamite, but if you have a sagging middle, the whole story will fall apart. Can you kill any of the middle chapters? Can you make things worse for your characters? Ask yourself what would happen if —?

It's nice to have self–confidence, but we can't be in love with what we write—either with the chapters or with the outline. Remember the outline is supposed to be just that—an outline, used as inspiration. Have you tried to keep too much control on your work or have you let the characters roam free and become what they wanted to be?

If you aren't laughing at your own work, in terror, or horny at the appropriate moments, then the writing isn't strong enough. Your story is special but you have to show the reader that it is more special than others he's read, and fresher in approach.

There is a danger in too much rewriting and holding the manuscript for too long. At one point, we must let our children grow up and our manuscripts go. It will probably never be totally perfect. Even after I've received my galleys, I see things I want to change—and I can't. But I am the only one who knows. However, you don't want to mail off your material without a final reading. I can't tell you how many times I thought my computer–spell check would catch mistakes— and it didn't.

Grammar and spelling are a big thing to watch out for. Sometimes, because we know our story so well, we read what we want to see and not what is there. This can be fatal for the book or script. I know many readers who, if the first few pages have a lot of typos or grammar errors, they will put it down.

Commas are one thing that confuse many people and you might want to check out the article, ***13 RULES FOR COMMAS SO YOU DON'T LOOK LIKE AN IDIOT***, It can be found with an internet search.

REJECTION LETTERS

If that horrid rejection does come your way, and you have a list of other publishers to send the manuscript to, then you won't feel at a loss. There are several types of rejection—the form letter (which could merely mean they were too busy to make comment), the form with handwritten note (which means they were interested enough to comment and be sure you send other work to them), and the letter of rejection (in which you should consider rewriting, because they are obviously interested in you and you're that close to acceptance.)

When someone—an editor or producer—gives you a note. Sometimes you think they don't understand your story. They might say, we need more romance here or ask if the culprit is a girl? I had one producer ask what would happen if we put a monkey in the story? A monkey? I was flabbergasted.

They are not always saying what they mean. You have to analyze the note and look at the scene. What is unclear about that? It turned out the "monkey" producer had really misunderstood the scene and with a few words of description, I was able to correct it. In another case, when the note did not make sense, I went back and reread the story and realized that I had not planted enough clues and not foreshadowed what was to come about.

Know ahead of time you're going to get some negative notes. Common notes include—characters not being likeable, or not being active in the goal. You might hear, "the story just lies there." Often that means that you were using too many passive words and not enough action in the dialogue. Make sure the person giving you the feedback can really express what they mean. Also, make sure the intentions of all the characters are clear.

Don't overwrite, but make sure that all your clues and situations are set up. Sometimes, that's only a matter of a few words.

Understanding notes are an art of itself. Don't go home feeling miserable and rejected. Don't get super defensive and argue with the executive, editor, or producer. It will only lose you points. And don't necessarily take what they have said literally. Know, too, that they feel it is their duty to give notes, even if they don't seem to make sense, so they feel that they are doing something worthwhile in their job. A producer who doesn't give notes, is not a good producer.

The secret is to eliminate the objection. Ask them what else they didn't like? And what else upset them? Be friendly, open, and constructive.

I often tape my sessions with the producers so that I can review them later. Sometimes, when they are first coming on, it feels as if you (and your baby) are being attacked, and you fail to hear what they are really saying.

Writers that do not take notes well do not work in the business very long.

It's important, also, to know who you are sending your manuscript or script to. Do they specialize in science fiction? Are you are sending them a historical that could be an automatic rejection, even if they like your writing?

Research that editor or producer. Try to meet them, if you can, at conferences or meetings. In Los Angeles, there are always meetings being held by the Writer's Guild, Women In Film, Hollywood Networking Breakfast, Breaking Into Hollywood, and other groups where you can physically shake hands with these people. If you know something about them, it impresses them.

Treat them as they want to be treated. At one conference, an editor was mobbed with people pitching her stories. I went up and simply asked if she wanted something to drink. When I brought her back a soda, she was so grateful, she asked if I had anything she might be interested in. That was my first young adult book sale. It was something I had not expected, but you have to remember that when you make it a win–win situation, everyone comes out happy.

Now, put your book down for a few days (even a few months if you can afford the time) and go back to it. You will see it with different eyes.

Being a writer means never giving up. I wrote seven books, before my 8th book became my first published book. Later, I was able to go back and revise four of those seven into published books and manuscripts that I started years ago, which didn't sell then, are coming around and being asked for now.

Just the other day, I learned that a TV show idea I had written up five years ago had finally found its way into the hands of someone who was excited about producing it. Persistence... and faith... pays off.

Both publishing and Hollywood run in cycles. What's hot now might not be hot next year. Then again in five years, it might make a come back. I had started working on a vampire historical last year but because the industry has been overrun with vampires, I put that aside. I will wait until next year when it will be given a fresher chance.

Keep everything you write. All of your drafts. You never know when you can make use of it. A script that I wrote eight drafts on has come full circle. I decided I like the first draft the best and am revising that right now.

Keep going and good luck!

QUESTIONS TO ASK YOURSELF

Are all my characters necessary for this story?

Are all the loose ends tied up?

Have I told where I could have shown? Have I made full use of the senses?

Can I say this with more interest?

Can I chop some of the dialogue?

Can I kill off any of the characters?

Can I come in later in the scene? Can I get out earlier?

Does everything match—hair color, eyes, and spelling of names?

Is everything told from the proper viewpoint character?

Do my transitions from viewpoints, or in time, flow smoothly?

Is there anything I can cut out?

Are the verbs active?

Is dialogue brisk? Have I any foreign words unexplained? If this is a foreign setting, am I being too much of a tour guide?

Do I have too much dialogue? Is the dialogue and action well integrated?

Have I taken for granted the reader knows everything I know? Is anything unclear?

Have I been redundant anywhere? Have I said the same thing twice? Do I have several of the same words appearing in a short time, or a similar gesture? (I have a horrid time of sucking in lips, and pressing lips together as overused gestures.)

Did I hook the reader in the first five pages? If not, try to start with a later scene. Established readers can tell in one page if the writer knows what he is doing.

Did I establish the mood on the first page?

Does my beginning hint at my ending?

Does my beginning hint at the problem?

Did I give an indication of the major conflict, where the book or story is going and establish time frame—by the end of the first chapter or first few pages of the script?

Does my work have: a strong opening situation? Conflict? Universal problem?

Crisis points in which all appears to be lost and the viewpoint character struggles to win? Climax in which the viewpoint character wins and ending where all lose ends are tied up?

What is the theme of my book? Have I crossed any countries too quickly (for that time period)? Are my historical facts accurate. Have I had a full nine months to my pregnancies? Does all make logical sense in relationship to time?

How many flashbacks have been used? Have I made careful use of them?

Have I kept the character in character?

Is my plot believable? Are my facts accurate?

Have I overworked phrases or gestures?

Have I destroyed the mood by unnecessary description in the middle of the action?

Is my story too "internal"?

Can I make my story more visual?

Do I have mundane "what" where my character seems to do something just for the sake of doing something and not for the sake of the story? We don't need every moment of the character walking to the door or sitting down. Start the scene where they are already seated in the meeting.

Does the protagonist solve her own problem? Or do I have acts of God coming to the rescue?

Am I preaching my theme?

Have I followed whatever guidelines might be necessary?

Did I write a salable synopsis?

Do I have an active, action packed blurb?

Is my logline short and snappy?

Have I stayed with the proper viewpoint? The more viewpoints the harder it is to sell the story?

Have I stayed in the genre?

Have I varied sentence length?

Have I tried to be cutesy or smart?

Is my dialogue stilted? Be sure to break up long passages.

Is my climax too abrupt?

Have I been too wordy? The shorter the work, the tighter it must be.

Do I know the market? Have I a list of publishers I want to send the book to? Have I a list of publishers or producers that I want to send the story around to? Do I know my target audience?

Can I say anything in fewer words?

Have I shown rather than told?

Is there any place I can break up dialogue with descriptive phrases?

Any places I have too much narrative and can use some dialogue?

Does each chapter add to the story and move it forward?

Does each chapter end on a cliffhanger?

Does the book end when the story does?

Can I eliminate any "he–said" or "she–said"?

Do my people say words or do they cough, smile, laugh, and shrug them?

Have I checked proper definitions?

Have I mixed anxious and eager, like and as, their or they're?

Do their eyes dance around the room—or do they gaze?

Do I have too many pet words such as "very, perhaps, little, began to, it was, I guess, I think, I started, only"?

Does my character overuse any gestures or phrases? (I mention this a lot because it's one problem that many writers have.)

Have I used all my senses in each scene? Can I see it flashing on the screen before me?

Have I kept my metaphors in the same line? Or have I mixed them?

Is my character likeable? When you get notes that he is not, sometimes it's only a matter of a few words—like having him pet the cat—that can change things.

Have I made a final reading before mailing it off?

PROCRASTINATION

I know many writers—or would be writers—who talk about writing, but never get to it. Sometimes, they talk so much, they talk the story out of them. Sometimes, they finish one draft of a book or script and then let it sit because they are afraid of taking it out. They are afraid of failure, but failure is just another challenge.

In the beginning, there were words, and the words said anything. Write just to fill up the white space in order to start the words flowing.

Copy what you wrote the day before. Add a line. Copy and crumple the words until new words are moving so fast, you no longer have time to tear up the pages and throw them away.

After you've written chapter one, tackle chapter two. Take it one step at a time. Save the fine–tuning for last. Hopefully, you have an outline to guide you. If you don't have an outline, do it after you finished the first draft. (It's okay to have notes to go on while you are working.) Keep writing and don't revise until you have finished your first draft.

Give yourself 15–minute deadlines during the day.

Bribe yourself with rewards: eat, exercise, be merry with friends, shop.

Create a time schedule and stick to it.

Be realistic.

Establish a routine and make it a habit. Try to work in the same place every day. One student wrote one page every night from 8:00 p.m. to midnight. At the end of a few months, he had his book.

Begin in the middle and write the parts that are clearly in your mind and tie in with the rest later.

Expect rejection, but don't let it bog you down. You can swim.

Do your busy work in less creative time periods. Know what times are best for your writing. (Mine is morning.)

Get your dirty laundry out of the way. Make lists of other chores, which "worry you away" from your writing.

Work on something else when the major project isn't working.

Talk to anyone who will listen to you.

Buy a notebook, and on the clean empty pages, write a title and one line of what your story is about.

Agree to working five minutes a day on your writing. You'll probably do more, but even if it's only the five minutes, you'll accomplish something.

Don't wait for the right time because you'll never find it.

Set small goals for yourself. Baby steps get across the stream as much as giant ones.

Know that you are changing not only your life, but the life of your readers.

Listen to anyone who will talk—you never know what gems of dialogue you might come across.

Read something or watch movies. Listen to movies without watching the action. See if you know who is speaking without looking.

Spend money—preferably on a computer. And put the bill where you're forced to look at it daily.

(Remember to keep all your receipts as it can all be tax deductible.)

Add—be committed to your goal of being a writer. Do five small things daily toward your goal—write a few pages, do a little research, call a bookstore, let others know you are working on a book. One writer set the date for the book launch party and invited all his friends. He kept the date in front of him so that he knew that he would have the book finished by that time.

***

QUERIES AND SYNOPSIS: YOUR SELLING TOOLS

For many writers, the most difficult part of writing a novel or screenplay is the synopsis, the narrative summation of your work. It's also a necessary art to master. Part of the problem lies in knowing just what a synopsis involves. What makes it different from an outline, a summary, a treatment, a query, or a partial?

EVERY BOOK NEEDS AN OUTLINE

As stated before, I am a firm believer in this, though there are still many writers that balk at outlining. However, every book submitted—even if you are sending the whole manuscript—you must have a synopsis with it. Every screenplay must have a logline. (More about this in the screenplays section.) This holds true for all submissions, but it is especially the case when you want to sell your book on a "partial."

A partial is the first two or three chapters of your book. Most editors will ask for this after seeing your query, but if you are a new author you will often be required to finish the whole manuscript before seeing a real contract.

The "partial" is a tool best used by established writers. I often sell manuscripts on a detailed synopsis and two or three chapters. Mind you, these aren't just any chapters. These are the first two or three. The editor wants to know that those first few chapters will be dynamite. On a rare occasion, a not–yet–published author can also sell her book on the partial system, but mostly the editor will only indicate the desire to see more.

Some publishing companies such as Dell and Silhouette, however, have a new system for weeding out stories. They ask unpublished writers first to write a query letter. If that passes muster, the writer will be asked for a detailed synopsis and the first few chapters. Finally, they will be asked for the whole novel.

The query letter is a sliver of the bones used to build your synopsis. It should indicate time, place and type of novel—especially if the company publishes more than one kind of novel. The query should indicate the major characters, their problems, and their relationship to the other major characters and how the problems are resolved. This should be no more than three paragraphs.

The query should also indicate what qualifications you might have or special research you might have that has prepared you to write this book. The whole letter should be no more than two pages—but preferably one.

You want to find out the name of the editor and spell it right. If you can find out the name of an assistant editor, you're even further ahead, since they don't get half the mail. And if it's addressed personally to them, you'll get better attention.

A query example might be:

Dear Editor:

Enclosed find my partial of ***TAME THE WILD HEART***, a romance novel of about 85,000 words, which takes place in James II's court of Ireland.

Roxanna Alden, nineteen years of age, niece of the great Irish general, Patrick Sarsfield, hates James for what he had done to her mother and vows her revenge in the only way she knows how—spying. She knows it would hurt her uncle, who supports James, if he found out. But she cannot let a man like James rule her beloved Ireland.

To her horror, she finds her assignment is to spy on Sebastian Steele, thirty years of age, her uncle's aide de camp.

Despite her own misgivings she is attracted to Sebastian. With the political intrigues of the day swirling about them, Roxanna must decide if she will betray the memory of her mother, or betray her heart.

In researching this book, I spent time in Ireland and at the British Museum in London.

My previous books are ***THIS BITTER ECSTASY*** and ***A DREAM FOREVER.***

Sincerely,

They don't want to start reading what they think is a contemporary novel and find the book you're sending is a historical. I think of the query paragraphs rather like the log line of the TV Guide: concise sentences that sum up the story. In fact, it's good sometimes to have a single line at the top of the story, which will immediately clue in the reader to the focus of the story.

In ***TORRID JANUARY,*** my line was: Will the D. A. prosecute the man she loves or will she first prove his innocence?

EXERCISE:

WRITE THE PREMISE FOR YOUR BOOK IN TWO OR THREE SENTENCES—AS IF IT WERE THE LOG LINE FOR A TV MOVIE.

As I said, the query also includes who you are. This doesn't mean the editor wants to know that you have five kids and your husband's a mechanic. It means she wants to know whether you have been reading in this genre for some time. Are you familiar with the types of books they buy? The editor wants to know if you've had any writing experience, if you've worked as a copywriter, or done articles for a local newspaper. They also want to know any expertise you might have which enables you to write about the subject. If your heroine is a dancer and you were too—say so.

Never say, "this would be a perfect book for you." Or "My aunt read it and she thinks it's the best thing you could buy." Again, that smacks of unprofessionalism. The editor needs to make the decisions herself.

A letter like the one above was my admission to the Tapestry (Pocket Books) line. The editor then asked to see my partial. In her letter back to me, she asked to see my detailed synopsis.

Often the words "outline" and "synopsis" are used interchangeably, but they mean two different things. A novel has a synopsis. The non–fiction proposal has an outline. The outline is, in fact, only the barest of bones and is often used by the author in plotting out the synopsis, but should not be sent. It states the facts, but seldom gets into the emotion of the story.

An outline might be:

Chapter One: Roxanna learns of her new espionage duty. Meets Sebastian as they both go into the castle together. He sees mud on her dress. Does he know where she has been? Will he tell her uncle?

Chapter Two: Attracting the eye of the King, she must fend him off. Sebastian helps her. She should be grateful, but she's angry he had to help her. She becomes ill at the ball. Uncle Patrick asks Sebastian to see her safely home to their manor.

Chapter Three: Waking after the fourth day of illness, she realizes Sebastian has been there taking care of her all the time. Has she said anything? She also realizes today is the day she must meet her contact. Can she ride back to Dublin in her ill state? She must.

Chapter Four: Sebastian finds her trying to leave and locks her in the room. She manages to get out and rides the following night.

EXERCISE:

ON SEPARATE PAPER, MAKE AN OUTLINE OF THE CHAPTERS YOU ARE WRITING WITH ONE OR TWO SENTENCES PER SCENE, AND JOIN THEM TOGETHER WITH A HOOK.

TAKE A BOOK YOU'VE READ AND WRITE ONE OR TWO SENTENCES FOR EACH CHAPTER.

This can go on for twelve to fifteen chapters (or however long you want), or you can do an A. B. C. , Roman numeral style outline for the book. Regardless, this outline does not get sent. While writing, I have an outline in front of me—

where I list each chapter and the scenes to go in it to guide me, but I also have my synopsis. It is the synopsis or the full narrative story told in present tense, which I send to the editors.

SUBTEXT INCLUDED

The synopsis, which has the motives or subtext of the story, is often the first thing read. The editor needs to know: can this writer interest me sufficiently here to propel me into reading his/her first chapters?

Most students of writing have trouble with the synopsis, because they don't understand the necessity for immediacy, for action, and for drawing the editor into your story. Instead, they philosophize for pages about the worthwhile objectives of their novel and goals of their characters—without really touching the meat of the story: the emotions.

EXERCISE:

READ AT LEAST TEN BACK COVER BLURBS OF BOOKS AND TRY TO WRITE ONE FOR YOUR OWN BOOK OR A BOOK YOU'VE RECENTLY READ (WITHOUT CHEATING). THIS WILL HELP YOU IN YOUR SHORT QUERY.

The synopsis is your selling tool. It must hook your reader/editor just as your first chapter must hook him or her. It must show you in the best light and show the editor that you know how to construct a fast–paced story. I know of several cases where novels were bought or rejected based solely on the synopsis. This especially is the case when an author tries to sell his novel on a partial.

The hook I used in ***BLOODSTONE INHERITANCE*** was:

After the sudden accidental death of her mother, Elizabeth Ann Larabee discovers a letter indicating someone other than Zebulon Larabee had fathered her. Who? Beset by curiosity, forced to sell off what she and her mother had, Elizabeth journeys to the thriving river town of Aberdeen, Illinois, to her mother's old home. She feels here she will find a clue to her natural father.

The hook to ***SPANISH HEARTLAND*** was:

Jersey Jordan couldn't believe her luck. Professor Tomas Ramirez, one of Spain's leading historical experts, had agreed to let her come study with him for the year, to live with a Spanish noble family in Seville.

The hook in ***TAME THE WILD HEART*** was:

May, 1689, Dublin, Ireland:

Hating the English Catholic King James II and his court for what they did to her mother, Roxanna Alden has become a spy for the forces of William III. Being the niece of the Earl of Lucan, Patrick Sarsfield, a man highly regarded by James, Roxanna has no difficulty in getting information to pass on. The difficulty she does have is in keeping her feminine identity a secret from her contact, and in coping with the nosey Sebastian Steele, Lord Bristol, her uncle's trusted aide.

On a misty, damp night, Roxanna is waiting for her contact on the bridge. There had been no time to change since she had to go straight to the ball that James was giving. She detests these parties as much as she detests James, but she does get good gossip there . . .

In all beginnings, I indicate who the heroine is and something of what the major problem will be, as well as the place and setting. To hook the reader (editor), think of the most crucial point of the story. This, of course, should be where your novel starts, but not always. It should be at a point where the heroine (or hero) is "gnashing his teeth against some problem" or anxiously awaiting the outcome of some situation.

EXERCISE:

WRITE A PARAGRAPH ABOUT EACH CHARACTER—NOT JUST PHYSICAL, BUT EMOTIONAL: GIVE US GOALS, MOTIVE, AMBITIONS, AND PROBLEMS. (This belongs in your query.)

When the book is first being considered, the synopsis alone might be sent to several different people to judge the merit of the story, and if it's worth considering the whole book. Seldom does a single editor have say over purchase of a book. Usually several people must read the synopsis before a decision can be made.

Dell uses queries to make sure they like the concept of the story. Other publishers also use the synopsis for this purpose. It is the synopsis, which the editor usually relies upon in the sales meetings when she must push for the acceptance of your book. It is the synopsis, which the cover artists and book jacket writers receive.

THE OUTLINE WITH MEAT

The synopsis is the outline with meat—just enough meat to give your skeleton form, but not enough to flesh it out fully. Making your synopsis too heavy will sometimes lead to a rejection. What you tell in the synopsis gets magnified tenfold. If the editor believes you will be enlarging greatly on the point mentioned in the synopsis, she might be reluctant to buy that book. In one case, I made the mistake of having the heroine, at a crisis moment, cross herself (since she was a good Irish Catholic) I mentioned this in the synopsis.

Immediately, I had a call from the editor. "We don't want religious books." The fact was, there was no real religion in this book, but my mentioning this in the synopsis made it seem so.

Told in narrative form, usually in present tense (though some writers prefer past), the synopsis includes the premise of the story, and a bit about the characters. You want to get across not only whom your characters are, but the motives they have and the emotion they're feeling. You want to show, in these few pages, the conflict which will develop between the characters as well as the conflict, which starts the book moving. This building of tension is what will hook the editor.

Major turning points of your plot, as well as beginning, middle, and end, are mentioned. If the book is sexy, then sex should be mentioned in the synopsis.

Sometimes I find it necessary to throw in a bit of dialogue or description, especially if I'm doing a historical novel. This will illuminate the character and his desires. It will also give background for your story. Again, this background is necessary if you're doing a historical.

EDITORS DISLIKE

Editors have complained of writers ending their synopsis with: "Read the rest of this exciting novel to see what happens." I can almost guarantee you that this kind of come on for an undisclosed ending will get your story sent back to you immediately. It's the mark of a novice.

Editors (and readers for producers)are putting their jobs on the line each time they buy a book or a script. They want to know what they are getting for their money. They want to know that all the loose ends are tied up and the story is brought to a satisfactory conclusion.

GRAB INTEREST

The synopsis shouldn't reveal all your secret twists and turns, but there should be enough there to grab interest. Don't be coy and cutesy, but do pack as much excitement and drama in these few pages as you can.

Not only must the synopsis open with a hook, but it must indicate the character's viewpoint—and secondary characters that will be important to your story—should be mentioned. Enough background on your characters should be given to make them believable.

If you're doing foreshadowing or writing a suspense, you're going to want to mention the clues and indicate which are followed up and how. Action must be well spaced throughout the story. Because it is not necessary to put every scene into the synopsis, the story you give the editor may not follow the logical progression of events—but you should be clear on where each part of the story comes and which scenes contribute to them. A logical conclusion must be seen.

Some writers prefer to divide their synopsis chapter–by–chapter—similar to what I did with the outline, only much more in depth. About four or five paragraphs per chapter—one for each major scene—should be done if you want to do it that way. Writers also sometimes do the three chapters and then synopsize the last part of the book in two or three pages.

I find this last method doesn't work for most editors, since, as I said, they will often read the synopsis first or send the synopsis around without the chapters. They tend to find this method boring. I find, too, that doing a straight narrative rather than a chapter–by–chapter synopsis helps the story to flow. If, for your own purposes, you want to write first in chapter by chapter, by all means do so. You will then find it is easier to make the synopsis tighter when you do it in narrative form.

Now a lot happens in between those points, but I gave the editors only enough to hook them. Enough, it turned out, to win Dell's contest and write the best synopsis for the Ecstasy Supreme line. My synopsis won that and I then had the go–ahead for the first few chapters and a more detailed synopsis.

MECHANICS

Mechanically, there is also the question of whether to single or double space. The majority of my synopses are single–spaced, but I double space between paragraphs. Since the editors don't need to edit between the lines here, single spacing is fine.

However, if you have elite type and the margins are small, it doesn't hurt to double space. Editors have tons of reading to do. The easier we make it for them, the better it is.

My synopsis can be as short as two pages—when I just have a sketch of where I am going—to as long as twenty pages. (This is preferred by Harlequin Intrigue and many mainstream editors. They want it only long enough, however, to tell the story.) A judgment is hard to make since you have to be able both to tell the story concisely and to hook the editor. For most editors, the shorter you can make it, the better it will be.

As a guideline, I would say:

55–65,000 word book == 2–4 pages for the synopsis

75–90,000 word book == 5–6 pages for the synopsis

100–125,000 word book == 8–10 pages for the synopsis

150,000+ word book == 10–14+ pages for the synopsis

These are single spaced pages, if you are double spacing, than double your pages.

EXERCISE:

POLISH YOUR SCENE LINES WITH YOUR HOOK. WRITE AS MUCH AS YOU FEEL LIKE—UP TO TWENTY-FIVE PAGES. ADD BITS OF DIALOGUE AS IT MIGHT COME TO YOU. (Don't throw this away. Keep it for when you start writing as your own guide.)

CUT THESE TWENTY-FIVE PAGES DOWN BY 5, THEN AGAIN BY 5 UNTIL YOUR STORY IS AS TIGHT AS YOU CAN MAKE IT.

Before you write your synopsis, you'll find it's important to have your plot worked out fairly well. That doesn't mean you have to stick to what you've written in the synopsis. Often, as I start writing, the story changes because the characters take over—but if the editor has bought your story on the basis of the synopsis, you're going to want to discuss any major changes with her. There are people who can write super synopses, but fail when it comes to writing the book, just as there are people who can write great books, but fail when it comes to doing a tantalizing synopsis. As professional writers, it's our job to do both well.

The synopsis not only tells the story, but also gives the editor a chance to see your writing ability. The first few chapters will tell her how well you've been able to transfer the emotions mentioned into those vital beginning chapters, which hook the reader and draw him into your fictional world. Tight, concise writing is what counts.

EXERCISE:

- Do you open the synopsis with a hook? If not, write an engaging hook for this book using the heroine's name, indicating time and place, character's profession and/or critical problems.
- Does the beginning of the synopsis establish the viewpoint and secondary characters? Does it give enough information to make the characters believable?
- Is your plot any way contrived or does it have clichés?
- Does each scene show motivation?
- Does it lead into the next scene?
- Do you plant clues—and follow up on them? Do you tell too much?
- Is each scene necessary for the synopsis?
- Just because it will be in the book doesn't mean it's necessary to have in the synopsis. Does the synopsis show enough movement or action leading to the turn–around scene?
- Is your action well spaced?
- Is the conclusion logical?

THE NON FICTION BOOK PROPOSAL

Writing a nonfiction book proposal is different than writing a synopsis for a novel. Your qualifications for being able to write this book—maybe you're a psychologist who specializes in children's issues and your book is about raising teens—is paramount.

The editor will want an outline of your chapters and what you plan on including in the book, as well as what other experts you might be consulting. They will want sample chapters, as well. However, almost as important as your abilities is your marketing plan. They want to know who the target audience is and who you plan on having buy the book. Don't say it's for everyone because no book appeals to all. Think about who might enjoy your book. One of my historical novels that took place in French Montreal and Air Canada agreed to place it in their planes as reading material.

They want to know how you plan to help with the publicity. Will you speak and if so where? Will you do autographings? (As we will talk in publicity, the publishing houses seldom contribute to this anymore and they depend on the author to do a lot of publicity on their own.) I have done postcards for my books and taken out ads for them, as well. Yes, it costs a little money, but it helps to build up your name, your brand, and your recognizability, which you need to become an established writer. It's also tax deductible.

AGENTS: KEY TO SUCCESS

Most new writers are happy of the fact they have snared an agent. I recall how proud I was when I first had an agent interested in representing me. How great that sounded—"My agent does this, says that, etc." It was a magic phrase. To new writers, it still sounds great.

The fact of the matter is that while agents are very necessary for the success of a writer, they are not magical. An agent cannot magically sell books and scripts. They are not—for the most part—teachers. They do not market your book, as one student suggested to me the other day. If you need to learn your craft, take more classes. They are, as another writer put, a "car salesman."

(Even with all my successes and the fact that I teach writing, I too constantly listen and learn, taking classes from those who have published or produced more than I have. I almost always learn something—even if I sometimes feel that they are repeating things I already know.)

Agents, especially in Hollywood, seldom are willing to pick up a new writer. They want someone who has already demonstrated he can sell and want to develop him into a bigger career. Those in screenwriting would do well to consider obtaining a manager who can assist you far more than an agent, especially when you are just coming out. The manager can then help you find a regular agent later. Since there are some managers, like mine, who deal in both books and scripts, I got a two-fer, but most novelists do not need managers.

READING FEES—PRO AND CON

I used to help agenting some of my students and others. I no longer do this due to time constraints. However, when I did, I charged a reading fee, as some still do.

This topic has been hotly debated for many years. When it comes to picking an agent, reading fees are a question for many people. There are pros and cons of reading fees. You need to find out exactly what you are getting for that reading fee. While you, the writer, may think the agent should consider herself lucky you've chosen her and should be thankful that you "are going to make her a million dollars," she sits behind a pile of manuscripts wading through them to sort out those that are passable, those which still need work, and which will sell in the current market.

She must take her precious time to read and evaluate your manuscript as to your writing ability and its marketability. If she is trying to make a living as an agent, that time spent reading your manuscript—especially if it's not ready for market—is wasted. She should be compensated for that time. There are, in fact, very few service departments that will give a free estimate on work to be done and agenting is the same way.

Reading fees should be critiquing fees if they are more than a few nominal dollars. The reading fee I charged as an agent, since I am a teacher as well, not only covered my reading time, but also compensated me for the time and skill involved in writing a critique. I would go over a writer's manuscript in depth, tell her where it worked for me and where it didn't, and what would have to be done to make it successful.

Many agents who charge a reading fee will not tell you what's wrong, but will only send you a rejection letter. A good agent (who charges a fee) would go over your manuscript in depth and tell you where it works and what needs to be done before it can be sold. Agents are, however, not God, and can never predict exactly what will make or break a book. If a book is ready for market, some agents will credit your fee to the final sale.

Readers or creative consultants for hire are popular in Hollywood. Producers, only give you one chance and they have long memories. It happened to me that I sent something, which wasn't quite ready, to a well known producer whom I met at a network event. He did not like my material and has since refused to look at any of my other material.

Often I, or other screenwriters, will hire someone to give me notes. The late Gary Schusett of Sherwood Oaks College gave me this idea. Sometimes, I will put a different name on the script and tell them that I am considering optioning the story and what do they think? The critique you get that way can, at times, be more honest. Be prepared for some criticism and don't get defensive.

If the story is not salable, most agents will not bother with you. They, too, must occasionally send out form rejection slips. Don't forget: no matter how much you might think this is a bestseller, or how much your Aunt Ellen and her best friend loved it, or how much your reading group approved of it, the agent must approve it too. Her reputation lies with that manuscript.

If you are paying an agent a reading fee then you should get something for your payment . . . but don't expect her to sell a book that is not ready. You have to remember, however, as we talked about in rewrite, that all comments are subjective. Not everyone will like everything and not every agent is right for you.

If I, as an agent, send a manuscript to an editor I know, that editor takes my word that this is a good manuscript and worthy of consideration for her publishing house. Therefore, I cannot send out something I don't believe in.

An additional consideration is that the agents, must make phone calls and send out the manuscripts at their own expense. If they don't sell your manuscript, they take a loss. This is another reason why they cannot take on things they don't believe in.

But the agent, no matter how much she might like something, still cannot sell it if the editors aren't interested, or if you the writer aren't willing to work and make the changes suggested.

A good agent and/or manager will guide your career and make suggestions as to what you should be working on now, where the market is going, and if you should or should not sign a particular contract. There are times when, despite what the agent suggests, the writer wants to sign the contract. As a writer, you have to be conscious of business decisions, and if you are disagreeing with your agent, you have to take responsibility. (In Hollywood, the manager often takes on the role of guidance, where the agent just makes the phone calls to sell.)

In order to get an agent, you need to be conscious of several things. First, you must present yourself professionally. That means sending a SASE (self address stamped envelope) big enough for the reply, and if you're sending a manuscript, big enough for that to be returned. Otherwise, make it clear that you do not expect the manuscript returned. (I wish postage didn't cost anything, but it does.)

In the days of email, some agents will take an email query, but many will not accept attachments because of viruses. You have to know what that agent or manager wants.

You should query the agent before you send your manuscript to find out if she handles this type of work. I can't tell you how many times—when I was agenting—that I've received poetry, scripts, men's action books, how–to–books—none of which I handled. A simple letter or phone call would have prevented the problem for the writer and prevented a waste of several dollars in postage.

Even if you are sending it overseas, you are still responsible to send return postage coupons (available from the post office) or a cashier's check to cover the cost of return.

The physical appearance of you manuscript does make a difference. Proper presentation will not guarantee a sale, but it will get your manuscript a more sympathetic reading. And if you're serious about this business of writing, doesn't it make sense to give your manuscript every possible advantage?

The author's name and address—as well as the title—should be on the title page, along with the approximate number of words. On the following pages, in the upper right corner, type your last name and page number.

Never bind the pages. (Unless you are doing a script and then you will need to have it three hole punched with brads.) Editors will often take a few chapters and judge whether they want to continue from there. Don't fold your pages, and don't use fancy binders or covers. They might look nice, but they increase postage costs and if you have a whole bound manuscript, it will be difficult for them to get non–stop reading time. In New York, especially, where many of the book editors are, they will take home sections of a book to read on the train. Use an envelope or box large enough so that you can mail your manuscript flat.

Book manuscripts must be printed, double–spaced, and on one side of the page only. Leave one–and–one–quarter inch margin surrounding the entire page, and be sure to use a good grade white bond paper. Never use colored paper, or thin onion skin for your top copy. Be sure to save a complete copy for your files. (In fact, I save my work in several places and have Carbonite Cloud, in case a disaster befalls my computer.)

It goes without saying that you should check your work carefully. If a page is covered with errors, it should be retyped. Even if you've run your work through the spelling checker, you must learn that the checker is not infallible. Have someone else read over your work as well. I know that despite my reading it several times, someone always finds an embarrassing spelling or grammar error.

Of course, you must always have a fresh toner cartridge in your printer. In this day of ever–decreasing markets and ever increasing competition, a new printer, if need be, and careful work is a small investment. Editors and agents, being human, suffer from eyestrain just like anyone else.

Agents do serve as a nice buffer. The editor can get angry at them, and agents are often willing to take responsibility for not allowing you to do something that they think will harm you career.

However, being with an agent is like a marriage—you have to be willing to give and take; you have to understand and get along or get out. (I can't tell you how many agents I have been through. A lot of it was due to misconception of what I thought they should be doing for me and what they thought they needed to be doing.) They do not, as in the days of Hemingway, line edit your work.

Unless you already have a name for yourself, Hollywood agents will not be after you, and you'll not be getting the chance to write the next blockbuster movie. We can't just sit around and expect the agent to get us work, it's up to us, as writers, to prove ourselves. (That's why, especially in Hollywood, networking is so crucial.) And why it's important to attend as many writer's conferences as you can especially those held in your genre – like RWA – Romance Writer's Association; Crime Writer's Association, Horror Writers, Science Fiction and Fantasy Writers.

HOW TO GET AN AGENT

1. Know what you want to write.
2. Go to conferences and talk with other writers who do have agents. What do they like and not like about them? Would they recommend you to them?
3. Talk to editors and ask for a few recommendations. Interview these agents—or any others they might want. (Though there are organizations, anyone can call himself or herself an agent. In Hollywood, agents must pay a fee to be accredited, book agents do not.) Make sure they understand the type of work you are doing, make sure they can carry out what you need from them.)
4. Ask what they've sold recently and to whom?
5. If you are signing a contract with them—or anyone—have a lawyer check it over first. Don't get stuck in a relationship, which has turned sour. (Speaking of contracts, get EVERYTHING IN WRITING, even if you are writing with a friend or a partner!! It might feel awkward at first, but you won't regret it later. I've personally run into several situations where, because we were friends, I started writing with someone and then later got screwed because we did not have a contract.)
6. Read Writer's Market or Literary Market Place. They have lists of agents. Check which ones indicate interests the same as yours. Write them letters of introduction with an SASE.
7. Do not multi–submit or Xerox letters to agents!

8. Don't abdicate responsibility just because you now have an agent. Keep informed as to the market changes and let her know that you know. Read Publisher's Weekly, Variety, and Hollywood Reporter. Network, network, and more networking. I've made many contacts, which I had my agent follow up on, at various events. Especially in Hollywood, this is a relationship town and who you know is almost (not quite) as important as your talent. Many talented writers have their work still in their top drawer because they didn't network.
9. Have a body of work to show them. Don't overwhelm them with seven manuscripts. Only give them your best, but have the others on hand so when they ask what else you have, you are prepared. They don't want to represent just a one–time wonder. They want someone who will have a career.

***

CONTRACTS: THE FINAL STEPS

If you've followed all the steps in this workbook, you have by now finished your partial, and hopefully the editor of your favorite publishing house has accepted your manuscript. What happens now?

If you have an agent, she will do the actual negotiations for you. However, while most writers are known for being "in an ivory tower," writers are at a disadvantage when they feign ignorance of the contract and "let their agent take care of business." We are a business, and as small business people, must be savvy in our own rights. Even with the agent, we need to be a part of our career and plan where we are going.

Female writers, especially, have a reputation for "writing on the kitchen table," and for signing whatever contract is presented them without arguing to get more, and for being "wishy–washy." Writers must learn how to get the most from the publishers while keeping on good terms with them.

Okay, what can and cannot be negotiated? Almost everything can be changed—if you're patient. But you also have to decide how badly you want to be published. Sometimes, you have to accept less the first few contracts, but with each contract you push for more and more rights.

Not all agents are good negotiators, and some, like I did, work in conjunction with an entertainment contract lawyer, who knows just how far the publishing house can be pushed. While some agents do get upset if you want to see a lawyer as well as them, most agents—certainly those who are mature—will understand that even they cannot argue as efficiently as the lawyer who doesn't have to stay on any editor's good side.

The subjects you will be discussing with the editor, if you are negotiating, or with your agent–lawyer, are advances, royalties, time for royalty payments, copyrights, use of your name, revisions, delivery date of manuscript, e–books, subsidiary rights—film, foreign, and magazine rights, option clauses (how much they need, what type of book, and how soon they'll make a decision on your next book), rights reversion, promo, publicity, author's copies, cover approval, galley approval, and multiple book contracts, as well as remainders and other things.

Most contracts, especially for advances under $10,000 (and you seldom sell a first book for over that, though many times it can be as little as $500 for the first advance), will be given in two parts—one upon signing of the contract and the second upon acceptance of the approved manuscript.

The publishing industry grinds SLOWLY, much too slowly for my liking. It's often happened that my editor will call up and say, "I love this book. When can I have it?" My response would be two months time (as the DELIVERY DATE) for me to finish the book. She would say fine and then my agent would talk to her—negotiating the rest of the contract.

It's important to be realistic about when you can deliver the book because once they've scheduled it, things become sticky if you can't get it to them on time. Deadlines are deadlines! Publishers respect and re–contract writers who follow those deadlines. So don't say you can get the book done in two months, if you are working full time, have a house of kids, and the book is only barely started. For your own sanity, double that—at least.

Even then, it's not unheard of for the contract negotiation to take over a month and then another month or so before the finished contracts are sent out. Sometimes, the publishers will try to put items into the contract, which you and your agent did not agree to and so it's back to the talks. Even if you can sign the contract now, it will be at least another month before you have that first check. There have been times when I have, the whole book finished and ready to hand to them, and we still don't have the signed contracts. (You, of course, do not give them the book until you have the contract.)

After that, it will take another month or so before they approve the finished draft of the book. If revisions are needed, you will have to do them before you receive the second part of your check. Make sure you do get paid on acceptance of the full manuscript—rather than on publication of the book. If you have a large advance, you might have three payments—one on contract, one on manuscript acceptance, and one on publication.

Therefore, it is not a wise idea to quit your job the day your editor calls and says she wants the book. It's also not a good idea to quit when she calls and says "We love your book and we'll offer you $2,000/3% for it."

If you agree to those terms, you are stuck and your agent cannot change it. Do not talk money and terms with the editor. Let the agent do that. When the editor calls, you say I'm glad you like the book and I think I can get it to by such and such a date. I'll have my agent call you to work out the details. If you don't have an agent, you can certainly get one now that you have a major publisher interested.

(In fact, that is what happened with my first book. I had approached one agent and they turned it down because it was a historical romance and "category" to them. But when Pocket Books called me, I thought of the first agent I could and called them. Of course, they took the job, but I don't know how much better they made my contract.

When it came to offering Pocket Books a second book in the deal, the agent held back. This was not the type of book that he represented. So I was once again agentless.)

The advance is money paid to you against your royalty, so if you're only getting a royalty of 2%, you have to work a lot harder to pay back that $2,000 than you would if you received a royalty of 6%. So ROYALTY is another thing you want to negotiate.

Many houses, such as Zebra, start you low and work you up with each book, and you have to decide if you want to try other publishers—or if you believe it's better to take what you can now and use this as a springboard. If you've not been published before, just getting your name out and showing the other houses that you can write successfully will be good. You might want to ask them at what point they expect to start making a profit (after how many sales), and then ask that your royalty go up several points at that stage, (perhaps 100,000 copies sold), and once again it should go up at 150,000 sales. The royalty should be on the retail price of the book, not the wholesale price, and not on the publisher's discount. (I said should. You cannot always get it into a contract, especially if it's your first.)

Royalty should not go down for book club sales, and optimally, you should get 90% for you and 10% for the publisher on magazine (serial), movie, foreign rights. At least, you should get 50–50%.

While you probably won't get it, you want to try for a bonus if your book makes a best seller, or gets adapted into a movie. Do not, however, expect huge bucks when Hollywood calls. Most producers have limited monies to option books and are taking the book out on spec. They have to then hire the screenwriter and get the book and script to the various studios and investors.

Yes, it sounds great having your book optioned for a movie, but most novelists have a twisted view of what happens in Hollywood when the rights to your book are acquired. Unless you are already a bestseller, chances are you will not get a lot of money on the option, and you will probably not be allowed to try your hand at the screenplay. Realize also that once you sell your book to Hollywood, your baby is gone. It will change to something you might not even recognize. I have done many adaptations where all we kept in is the main story line. Characters and situations were cut, etc. More about this in adaptation of your works.

Copyright should be done in your name, and the publisher will take care of those details. In some cases, as in work for hire where you are paid a flat fee—as I was in the novelizations—or in cases where you are working with a packager as "The Velvet Glove series," they will want copyright in their name. Again, you need to think how badly you want this book published or how much you want the work. Now, when a producer wants to option a script, you have to look at who they are and what they have done. Can they really get your script to J J Abrams? Probably not. I have optioned my works for as low as $1 just for the legality of the contract, with a sum for buyout listed, should he actually sell the script and get investors to make the movie. In fact, my book, ***THE FORENSIC NURSE***, which was later optioned by Fox, was done for free because I wanted to get it out there and I knew that the producer who I was dealing with had the clout to get it around. I also optioned my western suspense script for $1 because the producer had one specific client she was taking it to, and since westerns were not in vogue, it was a chance I was prepared to take. You need to look at what they are offering up front, what they offer when they are making the final buyout, and who they are. Just think, the other option is having the script sit in your drawer for another year—or more.

PSEUDONYMS

The use of your own name versus a pseudonym is another issue, which plagues authors. I think it's best to use your own name as much as you can. Some houses want to feel they own you and will request that you give them a "name" which, when you leave, they can keep. However, with the market becoming so glutted today, and with so many readers buying their books by author, it's important to get your name known.

If the publisher says you must use a second name, consider using one very close to your own name, or using your own name with your middle initial. For my young adults, I wrote, at first, under the name of Megan MacDonnell—merely because I didn't want adults to pick up my Y. A. book and think it was an adult fiction or visa versa. (Now, however, I use my own name.) So, if you're writing in a different genre—or writing in a predominately male or female oriented category, you might want to slant your name to that area. If you use your own name, however, it's difficult for the publisher to try and keep it later. Though some writers—especially academia—don't want people to know they are writing romance or whatever genre their book is in. If that is the case and you are looking down on the readers who will buy your book, why are you writing it in the first place?

REVISIONS

Revisions are important. Contracts can still be terminated if they are not pleased with the changes you make—and don't think you can do the changes they want. The contract should say that they have 30–60 days, at the most, from the day you send in it. Otherwise, you could end up waiting quite some time for that added check.

OPTIONS

Options are another thing you want to watch. If you can't get the option clause removed—and most publishers won't—narrow it down so that you are giving them only your next book in the same genre you're writing for, that you can sell them on a partial of two chapters and synopsis—rather than a whole manuscript, and that they will make a decision on this partial within two months. Otherwise they might hold your new idea—and keep you from selling elsewhere—until your first book comes out and the sales figures are in (as long as several years!). You should also have the option of getting other prices for your book. And if other publishers are willing to top this, then your original publisher has a last chance to match that price.

PRE-EDITING

You should have your work pre-edited before sending it out. Since editors, as we've said, are over worked and under paid. But in the rare event they do like your book and feel it needs work, they will probably farm it out to an outside editor. The cost, unless you are careful, will come off your money, not theirs.

OTHER PARTS OF THE CONTRACT TO CONSIDER

Check their DUTY TO PUBLISH. My young adult book was bought by Fawcett in 1982—my second sale—but it didn't come out until 1985, because Fawcett was sold to Ballantine and the book fell into the cracks. When they finally decided that they did want it, there were less than six months left for them to schedule it, and I had to decide if I wanted them to still put it out. If I did, I had to sign a form allowing them another year. Duty to publish means they will have the book out within a certain period of time.

If SUBSIDY rights—foreign, film and otherwise—do not sell within a reasonable period of time, twelve to eighteen months, those rights and all others should revert back to you. A clause referring to rights REVERSION should be in your contract. This includes rights to the book itself, after it is no longer on sale. (It's always hard to find if a book is out of print, but if you ask your local bookstore to order a copy and they get back a slip saying, "Out of Print," then you can take action.) Before it goes out of print, you should have the option of buying up remainders and the original plates, if you want them.

Speaking of REMAINDERS and author's copies—usually you'll get ten to fifteen copies free. Sometimes, if you are doing a lot of publicity yourself, they might give you more copies. I usually buy 100 copies of my book because I sell it at meetings and to friends. (It's very irksome when people you barely know demand you give them a free book! But there are other reasons to give people free books—people who might want to read your style for future writing jobs, or publicity.)

Once you're established as an author, PUBLICITY will be a clause in your contract. But until then, don't expect author tours or anything else. Any publicity other than general stuff the publisher sends out will have to come from you. Very few houses these days have a publicity budget, especially for genre books. Most, like my publishers, throw the tennis balls (books) against a sticky wall. Whatever sticks (not many of them) gets the publicity. All else are lost in the general shuffle.

Even if you are dealing with a known publisher, there's always a possibility that they might go under, so be sure there is a clause in the contract which gives the rights back to you should anything happen—and that you can keep the advance. This has happened to me once and it is a hassle to get the rights back to your books.

You should also be able to keep the first half of the advance, even if they change their mind on the second part of the book. Sometimes, you have to pay back that money—but only if you sell it to another publisher.

Those of you who are lucky enough to sell a MULTIPLE–BOOK contract have to be careful that they do not do cross accounting. Each book should have a separate account—otherwise it will be years and years before you see any money.

If by chance your book does get optioned for the movies, be aware that there are several types of options. You should never give them the copyright (as Torch recently wanted from one client) for an unlimited time. Time should be stated as twelve to eighteen months for a said amount up front. Sometimes they will ask for an option without paying you, but then you need to consider how much you really want this and what chance you'd get someone else to pay.

Your story price might be as high as 5% of the budget for the film. I say should since often with the scarcity of money—and more independent productions these days—in Hollywood, you are lucky to get a small portion of that. The writer of the film, sometimes, barely gets that, and more and more options are going for free.

Should your book get this far, you will certainly need an expert entertainment lawyer (not just a contract lawyer). Too many people think that a lawyer knows all types of law, but that's like going to a doctor who specializes in feet and asking him to diagnose an eye ailment. He might know something is wrong, but not how to fix it, nor how far he can go in surgery, or what the recent advances are. It's the same in law; you need someone who is familiar with and deals daily with the producers. This means someone in New York or Los Angeles.

Be aware that the publishers will try to get the best of you because that's business. Read over everything you sign and make sure you understand it—even if you have someone else doing the work for you. If there are any clauses, which don't make sense, ask your agent. If she doesn't know, ask you editor.

They don't call it show or publishing business for nothing. We love to write, but we have to protect ourselves, as well. Remember you are the CEO of your own small company. Be savvy.

PROFESSIONAL SURVIVAL

There's no question about it. Being a writer isn't easy. In fact, it's damned hard. You tend to work alone a lot. Even if you're working with another writer, writing is a lonely profession.

You have to have the 3 D's—desire, dedication, and determination. If you aren't willing to give up part of your life for the success of your career, if writing isn't in your blood, if you can give it up—then do so, because writing is heartache after heartache until you finally succeed. Even when you succeed, there is no guarantee you'll repeat that success.

Success is a term that you have to define for yourself. How many projects have you finished? How many sold? Does that mean published or produced—once? Many times? Does it mean you are making a living at your writing? (Something that is very hard to do these days.)

Being a professional writer means more than just saying, "I'm a writer." It means more than just sitting at the computer once a month. Many people tell me they want to write. My response is: "Then write." It sounds glamorous, but it really isn't.

On the other hand, you do have to acknowledge what you are doing. I know several would be writers who, when asked what they do, will timidly say, "I'm trying to write." No. If you are putting your tush on the seat and sitting in front of the computer, you are a writer—even if you are not published or produced yet.

It's difficult to make a living as a writer alone. With thousands of people calling themselves "writers" or perhaps "producers," only the best and the most determined will survive.

Even when you do make that first big break, your first sale, it still won't be Oz.

Writers are needed. The producers, television networks, agents, and publishers are all dependent on us. Yet we are probably at the bottom of the totem pole.

I am in the unique role of being both a writer of books and scripts, but even that hasn't helped me as much as you might think. In the role of the writer, I face the same problems and frustrations as any writer. Even when I was an agent, I faced the same irritations working with the editors, publishing houses, and producers.

Professional survival in the writing business means first that, while you spend as much time as possible on your projects—both writing them and marketing them— you also must spend time on yourself and treat yourself. You must have a job (or means of support), which allows you to pay your bills, and keep the collectors from hounding you. You must also have emotional support—either in terms of a writing group or family members who believe in you.

If you, like me, have a family who give you flack for not being "normal," then the network of writing friends is a must. One writer divorced his wife because all she did was complain about him sitting and staring into space. She couldn't understand that he was thinking about his story and his characters.

Being a professional writer doesn't mean only that you are a selling writer. You can be a professional writer even if you haven't yet sold anything. It also means you respect other professionals. My own agent gets only 15% commission. Therefore, she should only be expected to do 15% of the work. Network. Network and more networking. . It's not just how talented you are, but who you know, especially in Hollywood. Go to conferences and seminars. Meet people. You never know who, through the six degrees of separation, will know the proper person to get your book or script read.

The determination to succeed means you spend a minimum amount of time each day doing something towards your writing. It can be an hour; it can be three hours. It can be a half hour in the morning before the rest of the family gets up; it can be an extra half hour at the office. Perhaps you don't go to lunch with the others. Perhaps you bring a bag lunch and write during that time.

Yes, you'll get snide comments and people trying to get you off your schedule. There will be times when you face writer's block and think nothing is going the way you want it to. But you must, if you are professional, continue that writing schedule.

Even on days when I find the writing going tough, I force myself to sit there at the computer and write something, anything. Once my fingers start to get the feel of the keys, writing often flows for me. Even if it merely means rewriting and copying what you wrote the day before.

Having the habit of writing a few pages each day (perhaps you've set a goal of three pages or one scene), you'll have a completed teleplay or novel by the end of the year. It may not be perfect yet, but nothing ever is the first time.

Being a professional means you do not wait for the muse to strike you. It may sound very lovely and romantic, but it doesn't get the writing done. The muse comes only when you hold a whip over her and demand she come.

It always seems that at the most crucial moment, when I must finish something, life comes and interrupts me—with a double deadline, screaming cats, an accident, or other untoward circumstances. The ordinary problems of living often interact negatively with our physical and creative well–being.

By definition, writers are "crazy and neurotic." I know that's what my own family thinks of me. Writer's block is part of being a writer and comes upon us sometimes when we least have need for it. For each person, the trick of getting out of the block varies—sometimes from person to person, or even block to block. What works one time may not work another, but you do have some control over it.

There are two different types of blocks. The first type is of the external environment—physical discomfort with the room too cold or too hot, interference from family or a new child in the house, not enough sleep, fatigue, and illness. All of these keep you from your best concentration.

The second type is internal—usually it's a form of fear. Writing is putting you on the line. It's having people look at you and feeling foolish if they don't like what they see. It's having them know (or think they know) your innermost secrets. (Just because you have a promiscuous character doesn't mean you, the author, are promiscuous—or even want to be. Yet people often will ask you if the character is you.)

Eighty percent of all blocks are of the inner variety. It's our inner voice talking to us and trying to scare us. How soon we get over the block depends on how well we can tune out those voices.

Being a professional writer means taking risks. It also means taking criticism. You must have a hard skin and be able to take rejections, because you'll probably have enough rejection slips to paper your walls before you see that first book published or first movie produced.

DEALING WITH WRITER'S BLOCK

If you find you are truly suffering a writing block—then professionals who deal with the problem have several suggestions.

1. Take an exercise break. Get the blood flowing to the brain. (I, myself, belong to a gym and work out for a couple of hours every other day. Just the drive to the facility often stimulates my mind, so by the time I've reached the gym, I can already jot down solutions to the problem.) Getting some distance from the problem by doing something else—anything else—also works.
2. Take a nap and ask yourself the question bothering you before you go sleep. Very often the answer will come to your subconscious while you are sleeping. Blanking your mind and meditating for 10–15 minutes often helps here as well.
3. The subconscious also works when you are using major muscles in such tasks, as housecleaning, gardening, hauling trash, moving furniture, or taking a walk. Just moving books or shuffling papers about sometimes helps.
4. Read some of the old material you have from the beginning of your story. Read other books, too. Read screenplays.
5. Go to the library and begin researching a new project. You might become so enthused for the new project that you'll put your current one in the drawer. That's all right. When the time is right, you'll return to it. The important thing is that you finish something. Of course, you'll find there are writing projects which you don't want to do and which you must finish. When that's the case, grit your teeth and do them as quickly, but as professionally as you can. Intersperse the dreary jobs and reward yourself with writing on that book you really want to do.

6. Send out query letters to editors about other ideas. Write to a friend. Keep a journal with your feelings and write in that. Sometimes just the process of writing will loosen you up. Write something and then tear it up. You need the freedom to know you can be bad and still be all right.

Being professional also means knowing yourself and setting reasonable goals. Don't say you'll have a play or book done in two weeks when you know that, because you also are working full-time, it will take close to six months. If you don't have a regular deadline for finishing something, then set your own deadline and divide your work up into small goals (say one chapter a week). At the summation of each goal, find something to reward yourself with—a new book, a walk, a movie. (Please don't use food as a reward. Too many writers have backside spread from sitting and you don't want that to happen to you.)

In that journal, keep a daily log of how much writing you've gotten done. It's pleasing at the end of the week, when we feel despair because we're not finished yet, to see just how very much we've accomplished. Get to know yourself and the best time for your own writing. I found I am a morning writer and work best very early in the morning with a cup of coffee by my side. But you may be a night person or find that midday is your most productive time.

Being professional means never being without pen and paper somewhere near. You never know when someone will say something or you will hear something, which will spark your curiosity and interest. Too often if it's not written down immediately, the spark will be lost. I keep paper and pen not only in my purse, but also in the car, near my bedside, and even in the washroom. (A great place for thinking!)

While you shouldn't waste time, you also must know when it's time to relax and to take time off from your work. After I've finished a book or a project, I usually need a week of just doing nothing to recuperate before going into my next project.

Of course, you want everything, which goes out under your name to be perfect, but too many writers have the "perfection agony." This means they'll agonize over every word, every sentence, tear up and try it over again. Probably they'll never even send their work out. There comes a time in the life of every project when you must either decide to dump it or send it on its merry way.

Because publishing houses are often understaffed and the editors and readers are underpaid, you want your work to reflect the best and to require from the editors as little revision as possible. In some houses, they'll not even give you a second chance if your work has too many errors. It's often difficult to see just where you are going wrong yourself, or whether a particular section of the book works. I've even had problems of inconsistency where my hero has blonde hair in chapter one and brown in chapter five. (One good reason to have someone else read your material before you send it out.)

With money tightening up, the less the editor has to do to fix your book, the more chance you have of a sale. This applies to screenplays as well. I send my own work out to a freelance editor, whom I pay to check for inconsistency, bad grammar, misplaced modifiers, poor transition, and the like. It's an investment, which pays off in the end. Having an agent isn't enough. Agents cannot sell material which isn't done right. They are not miracle workers nor are they there to critique your work. If you have an agent who does critique, you're very lucky. Most will just return the item and say they're too busy to handlc you.

Being professional means keeping yourself going on new projects. The more you do, the better you become. It would be nice to be paid for everything we did, but then, if that were the case, we should still be in our nine to five routine job where we could loaf and get the pay check. When one project is done and while that's making the rounds (it can sometimes take years for a project to sell), you should be working on something else.

Persistence . . . and faith . . . is the key. I just found out that a TV project I developed years ago has finally found its way into the right hands and is being considered as I write this.

When agents or managers are considering new clients, while they don't want to be overwhelmed with your projects, they do want to know you are more than just a one night stand.

If there is a formula to the work you are doing—if you are writing a genre piece or a teleplay—you must not think that because you are creative, you can ignore what the editors and producers have set up. This is especially true if you're writing in this category the first time. Rules are—as they say—made to be broken, but only when you have mastered those rules sufficiently can you dare to break them.

Some rules can never be broken. Manuscripts or scripts must be neatly typed—with as few typos as possible. If there are more than three to a page, the page must be reprinted. Good bond paper, not onion skin or correctable paper, is acceptable. (Yes, some writers still use typewriters and erasable paper, even today.)

On manuscripts, word count is a must. The average 8 x 11 sheet holds 260 words, but that varies with type style and chapter sections. The best way to find out word numbers—if you don't have a computer to do it—is count the first five pages, divide the number by five and you have your average page. Then multiply that number by the number of pages in your manuscript and you have the approximate count.

Proper format is necessary and each type of writing has its own format. Manuscripts should have a 1 1/2 inch margin on either side. Screenplays have one format, teleplays have another (and if you are doing a sitcom—you have to know if you are writing a single camera or multi–camera script), soaps have another format. Know them if you want to write for them. All demand that the author's last name and a tag line plus page number is at the top.

Even if you have an agent, it never hurts for you to be reading the trades. Publishing has different trades than screenwriting, but each gives valuable information for the field you are pursuing. If you don't have the money for all the magazines, then share with a friend or religiously read the ones the library gets. (Some good trade publications include Publisher's Weekly, Romantic Times is not, I don't believe, being published anymore, Variety, Hollywood Reporter, and newsletters from various professional groups, such as Romance Writers of America, Mystery Writers of America, Western Writers, etc.) Each field has its own set of guidelines and it's important for you to keep up and to keep a hold on your agent/or manager so that he is aware of your interest in a particular area.

Being professional also means keeping your taxes in a professional way. Make lists of your expenses. You'd be surprised at what can be taken off. They include materials for writing, Xerox copy receipts, book and magazine receipts, lunch receipts with other writers, class fees and even this book. I try to write checks whenever I can, since that serves as a ready–made record in case your accountant or the government wants to check up on you. And yes, even if you haven't sold yet, you can deduct expenses as a business starting out. (Check with your local accountant for the varying state rules.)

When sending out your own material, or sending material to your agent, the professional writer always includes an SASE. (Self addressed stamped envelope big enough for the return of your manuscript or indicates in their letter that the work does not have to be returned.)

Invest in a good printer even if it's slower than you want. What you do reflects not only on you, but on your agent as well.

Manuscripts are sent loose—not stapled or bound in any way, unlike scripts, which often are on hole punched paper and bound. Paper clips only are used. Large manuscripts are sent in boxes—return postage is a must if you want the work sent back.

Lastly, a professional is always willing to rewrite and revise. He meets any deadlines he has or calls well in advance to find out how much of an extension he can have. He allows his agent or lawyer to do the negotiations and doesn't banter names about. It means—as I said in the beginning—determination, desire, and devotion. Luck, of course, plays its hand. The more people you know and talk to, the more conferences you attend, and the more contacts you make, the better off you are. But when it comes down to it—it is the quality of your written work, which sells you or leaves you flat. You won't get anywhere being a prima donna—especially if you don't have a history of successful movies or books behind you. Even then, there's always someone else waiting for the place you vacate.

***

THE JOYS OF PUBLICITY: OR JIMMY FALLON HERE I COME

We'd all like to think our book—our baby—is the masterpiece of the literary world. Maybe to our spouses, parents, and friends, it is. But to the editors who see dozens of books each day, only the elite few become "leader" titles.

How does one become a "leader" title? And what makes a "leader"?

I wish I knew. Editors and houses have their own ways of deciding which books they will heavily promote and which will just be put out as "mid–list." (The mid–list has by now almost disappeared.) Chances are, if you've been selling with this publishing house for some time and have already made a name as a good seller, you will be promoted. There are those few authors—Jean Auel and ***CLAN OF THE CAVE BEAR***, for example—which hit the jackpot immediately. The majority of us—once we get over the ecstatic joy of having our book accepted—have to do publicity on our own.

The reason it makes the news when Mary Higgins Clark signs a new million dollar deal is because it is news. Most writers, as we have discussed before, are lucky to make a few thousand on their advances.

It's a vicious cycle. The publishing house wants to see if you can sell before they'll back you and help you sell. But the fact is—publicity does help sell books! How much or how little you do depends on the effort you want to expend and the amount of ready cash you have on hand. Publicity can be done without a huge expense, but it will take time.

Every writer needs to have a market plan for their book even before they start writing. You must know who your audience is and have plans on how you will reach them.

You can start with your area newspaper. They're always eager to learn about "local writer makes good." Your clubs—writing, mah johng, PTA, high school alumni association, newsletter from work, etc.—will all want to know what you've accomplished.

Today, social networks—often called the author's platform—are crucial for this sort of marketing—Facebook, Twitter, LinkedIn, and the rest. Some people start to advertise and give notice of their forthcoming work six months before the book or film is released. It takes that long, at times, to get the word of mouth moving toward your story. If you do not have a good network, it's time to develop one now.

Listen to your radio and TV shows. Which ones have authors on? Again, local shows are the best bet. Check with the Radio and TV Interview Report (RTIR.com) which has a program to help authors get interviews. (They work best with works of non–fiction, but at times can help novels.)

You'll want to make a list of questions they can ask you and indicate why your book is different from others of this type, why you, yourself, are different. It could be you're raising two children, working full-time, and accomplishing a spotless house at the same time; it could be you come from a strict Catholic family and the book deals with a heroine who has an abortion. In other words, anything which will make you stand out as different.

Speaking of standing out, it's good to have a style all your own. I, myself, have taken to wearing hats—usually those large brimmed romantic kinds with the veils or perhaps with feathers. In this day of more casual dress—especially in Los Angeles where I live—not many people wear hats any more. My doing this makes me stand out. It makes people remember me—even if they don't remember my book. In the music world "Boy George" with his crazy get up or Michael Jackson with his constant wearing of sunglasses are two examples. People might not like their music, but they remember them.

Hopefully, you'll have more than just the one book published. You are striving not only for sales for this book, but for name recognition. This is especially important when you're book is coming out in a field like the romance market, which is already crowded. Now that readers are buying according to the author's they favor, you want your name to be one they'll remember.

One reason people write under pseudonyms is because they think these names sound better than their own names. Sometimes they're right—and sometimes not.

You will, of course, want to get a professional photographer or perhaps a friend skilled in photography to take some photos of you. Most writers take photos at their typewriter or computer. My photos are taken either wearing a costume indicating the period I'm writing about, or in my romantic lace canopy bed with my black cat curled up on my lap.

A bio indicating not only a little about your background, but also how you've struggled for your writing and what kept you going is important. Your success probably hasn't come easily, but even if it has, the public doesn't want to know about it. The overnight success is very rare and mostly it takes people several years to become "an overnight success."

A list of local bookstores is also important. I subscribe to a number of romance and mystery oriented publications and one reason is to get lists of booksellers. Not only do I take out small ads in these trade journals, but three to four months before my book is out, I write letters to these bookstores, telling them about myself, about my book, the publisher, the ISBN number, and including a Xerox copy of the cover (if you have it). It's necessary to schedule this early because bookstores order six to three months ahead. Going into the store once your book is already out may be too late—especially in a market like romance, where books are turned about every month. When you write the letter telling the seller about your book, you might also want to ask them (if they're local or if you're going to be in that area) if they'd like you to autograph your books.

If you've been able to get any TV or radio time or newspaper space, be sure to mention the autographing date. If you haven't gotten the space, find out who does the "in city" column for the paper and ask them to mention it in their section.

Bookmarks are another good publicity trick. Any printer can make these easily. The common thing to do is list your published books and when they'll be out, perhaps with your photo or a copy of the cover on top. On a computer, you can center things directly and then just bring it over to the printer for photo stating. Otherwise, you'll probably pay a small fee for typesetting. Bookmarks should be put into the stores and given out just about the time your book is due out.

I also get stickers from those address places and have it say the title of the book, my name, and when the book will be out. These go on ALL my correspondence—even bills. Pens and pencils with the title imprinted on them is another gimmick used by many authors.

A publicist can, of course, be hired. If you are, however, a new author in a saturated field, there might not be much she can do other than take your money. Have an honest talk with her as to what she can and cannot accomplish. If she promises you *The Tonight Show* and *Good Morning America*, and if you believe her, I have (as the saying goes) a nice bridge in Brooklyn I'd like to sell you. Chances are slim a new author would get that far—unless your book is truly exceptional. Word of mouth and lots of social networking is what often gets us notice.

Publicity people are good if you are going to visit your aunt in Small Town, LA. (The Southern cities tend, as a rule, to be more romantic than Northern cities and more open to genre writers.) Your publicity person can then set up some newspapers, TV Shows, and bookstores there—and you deduct your trip to see auntie from taxes. (Yes, keep any receipts for any promotional work you do.)

It never hurts in the contract to ask if they will be doing any promoting for you, but don't be disappointed when they say your book is just going out as part of the line. Period. Most publishers do not have a budget for promotion these days, unless they deem the story an exceptional one.

Even if you're the original shy person, you'll have to develop a set of answers because you'll probably be asked to speak to your local groups—especially if there aren't many writers published in your area. The more you get out there, the more your name gets out there, and the more you sell.

You will, of course, want to order at the 40% author discount a good stock of your title (I get a minimum of 100 per title), which I sell when I speak. People love to have autographed copies. Don't feel bad that you're charging them the printed price instead of your price. Chances are at least half that box of 100 will be given away in promotion to those TV shows and newspapers. So you need to make up the costs somehow.

Since TV and newspapers are not known for their affection for authors of the romance or mystery genre, be prepared for reporters who hate your book, who have not read your book, and who are doing this only because they have to. Don't be put off. For every one of them, there are ten readers who will love you. You developed a hard shell taking tons of rejections to get where you are. Don't stop now.

Last of all, once your book comes out, go into those stores you checked with before and even ones you didn't. Find out if they have your book, and if not, why not? If they have your book, push it up front. Make sure that cover shows. Tell them how glad you are they have your book and ask, since you are a local person, whether they wouldn't mind ordering a few extra. I often give free copies of my book to the clerks to insure that added assistance in keeping my book up front.

EXERCISE:

1. List three major papers in the local area—include their address, name of the city columnist, name of the book editor and address.
2. List two more papers in towns or cities neighboring.
3. List all the schools you have ever been to. (Their alumni association will probably have a newsletter.) Offer to speak at the schools about how it was

for you to be a writer and succeed. High schools, especially, welcome outside speakers to classes.

4. List all the clubs—writing and otherwise—you belong to and their addresses. Again they have newsletters.
5. List at least three local TV shows and radio shows that do author interviews. The library should have a list of addresses and programs in the publicity files. Books cover different areas of the country for shows, newspapers, etc.
6. Investigate printers' prices for doing up bookmarks. You might just choose to do it via Xerox. While not as nice, it is cheaper.
7. Make arrangement for a good black and white photo. Have some 8 x 10 glossies always on hand.
8. Write a short bio on yourself. Make up a list of questions for the reporters to ask you.
9. List bookstores likely to carry your book, the name of the manager, and if you've contacted him or her. Schedule visits to these bookstores in your calendar.
10. List relatives in out–of–the–way places that you might want to visit and write off as a tax deduction. Arrange for a tour of that area from your promoter or do it yourself. It takes a bit more time if you do it on your own but the experience is great.
11. Have you been promoting your book on your social networks for even as far back as six month before the release date? Do you have an active Facebook, Linked in, Twitter and Pinterest account.

One author I know went on Barnes and Nobel and Amazon sites, and under a different name, gave herself stars on her book. It may not have been ethical, but it did get her notice.

Be sure you contact your publisher so that books are in the stores when you're on the air. Nothing is more frustrating than to arrange an autographing and find no books!

It's not easy promoting yourself, but the more you do it, the more fun it becomes. Remember this is a business. We need to take our heads away from the computers and put our business caps on.

***

DEALING WITH REJECTION

While it's nice to think that everything we write will be accepted, realistically we know that's not so. In fact, it is said the readers look for reasons to reject your project. As I have previously stated, everyone in the Los Angeles area believes himself to be either a fabulous writer or an award winning actor. Few of these people ever make it.

We talked a little about rejection under the rewrite chapter, but here's more.

The advantage of being a writer over being an actor is that you do not have to be physically present while you (your work which is the extension of you) are considered by the money people. But you do have to have a product worthy of selling. Even then small obstacles can get in the way of your selling . . . sometimes it's not even you or your writing. Maybe they already have a story similar, maybe they promised the assignment to their brother (nepotism is rampart here . . . that and who you know is crucial), maybe they became upset because your format was not correct. (When I did my first Cagney and Lacey, the producer in charge of story assignments was upset that my script was being considered, since I had not come up through the ranks as he had. He made it clear that if I could not write it in the proper format then obviously I didn't know how to write a script!)

Those writers who have their first story accepted are few and far between. Sometimes a writer will say this is her first story when in fact she's done several things already, which are sitting on her shelf.

As I said, I myself wrote seven novels before my "first" one was published. And just like book writing, script writing requires an apprenticeship. You must study the masters. Read scripts, read plays, and watch movies. Analyze everything. Why does this work or not work for me?

Although I had been writing since my childhood, I didn't start writing with the hopes of getting published until 1971. My first published novel did not sell until 1980. My first screenplay did not get optioned until 1988.

Would I have kept at it so persistently had I known it would take so long? Maybe not, but probably yes. One of my teachers said, "If it's (writing) part of you, if it's in your blood, you'll keep at it, no matter how long it takes. If you don't have the obsession, then give it up."

Persistence is the key, and as hard as it sometimes seems, having faith in yourself. Of course, it helps if you have supportive family or a spouse who'll stand by your side. But success can come without that support as long as you are willing to keep trying new avenues and new ventures. Sometimes a story has to sit in a drawer until the time is right. My problem young adult book, ***AGAINST HER WILL***, which I wrote the chapters and synopsis for over ten years ago, is just now seeing the light of day because problem books are back in vogue.

Knowing that your story is good, holding your head up and pushing forward is sometimes just a process of gritting you teeth, watching and waiting. Sometimes, it means working on other things until your first story sells.

The young adult mystery (***A GATHERING STORM***), which I sold to Silhouette First Love, was first written four years earlier on a trip to Cape Cod. I can't tell you how many places that manuscript and the copies traveled to! "Good writing, but we're not doing mystery now," or "Sorry, not for us," or "Too gothicy," etc. These were some of the remarks I gathered. One publisher even kept it over ten months and then rejected it, saying her line was full, but if I didn't sell in a year, I should reconsider her. Then, on a fluke, I called up Nancy Jackson (then the First Love editor). "Was she doing mystery?" I asked. I knew that First Love was not (then) a line, which did mystery, but I thought she might be interested in something different, as she had liked my writing before.

Nancy told me to send it along and a few weeks later called to say she was glad she could make an offer, because she had spilled coffee on it when reading!

This book was later optioned four times from various producers, although it has yet to be made as a movie.

My gothic, ***SHRIEKING SHADOWS OF PENPORTH ISLAND,*** was the second of that famous first seven stories I had written, but not yet accepted. I wrote it while living in England and associated with the Romantic Novelists (UK). But it was my fourth story accepted. Why? The market wasn't right.

I had cut my reading eye–teeth on Mary Stewart, Norah Lofts, Victoria Holt, and Helen McInnes. But gothics and romantic suspense had ceased publication—though they were still being sold. (At that time, I wasn't aware that what was on the stands was not what the editors currently wanted. What's on the stands or in the movies is usually a year behind what is being sought for.) I was later able to turn this story into both a screenplay and a radio mystery play.

The same publishers must have rejected that manuscript twenty times, and several times, at various stages, they rejected it again (with different titles.) But I liked the story. I knew it was a good story—if a bit unorthodox. (It had sex, which most gothics at that time did not.) Finally, I heard that Zebra was looking for gothics again and sent it out. It wasn't quite the right time. A few months later, I sent it back to them—hearing once more that they wanted gothics. This time, they bought it. Of course, the story had to be revised slightly and rewritten since they wanted first person and since my writing style had improved (I hoped) from the first draft.

THE BLOODSTONE INHERITANCE, my fifth story of the seven, was part of the third novel I published. That had been a reincarnation love novel which received good reviews from agents and editors alike, but which, I was told, didn't fall into any category. Taking apart the story, I realized I could make several novels of this and still succeed. So I did that. In a way, it hurt me to pull apart the story because I really wanted to write that novel as it was. However, I learned that in writing you must be flexible. It's very possible that at a later date I'll be able to make use of my original story. Meanwhile, I'm planning another gothic as an offshoot from that first story.

HEATHEN HEART—a historical about Boudicea's British rebellion from Rome in 45 AD (Maxim) also took me almost five years to sell. Everyone liked the writing, but no one wanted to take a chance on that time period. Finally, after having some success in the publishing world, I found someone who would gamble on it.

So rejection doesn't always come because you're a terrible writer. Those of us trying to make our living at writing are more closely identified with our writing and we feel rejection more keenly because our writing represents our essence and self–esteem. We writers are sensitive souls, and it's difficult to tolerate rejection.

I've learned that one must be like an "Israeli sabra"—a hard cactus on the outside and softly mellow on the inside. Difficult as it is, you have to know that rejections should not be taken personally. If the story feels right to you, then possibly it is right and you should continue listening, reading the trades for hints of trend changes. If you think you might have something, which fits a publishing house, jump in as soon as possible. (This is one reason why I read PUBLISHER'S WEEKLY religiously.)

Even if you have an agent, that person cannot be expected to know all that you might have on your shelf, or know what all your interests are, even if she's a personal friend. In the final analysis, you are responsible for yourself. Which is why, even when I use an agent, I tell her, "I'd like to see this material going to this publisher."

Of course, just because you think a story is right, doesn't necessarily mean it will sell. Many famous writers indicate stories, which they adore, that have rested on their shelves for years on end, and probably will never see the light of publishing because their style—as it stands now—does not fit the mold of the readership.

Each time your story comes back, you must look at it carefully and say, "How do I feel about this? Will making the changes this editor or reader suggests improve my story? What if I started someplace else? What if I told the story from another viewpoint?" Because writing is a growth process, you have to constantly analyze where you are.

Another myth about persistence and rejection is that once you've made one sale, the others flow in automatically. I wish that were so. It took two years after my first sale before my second story was bought. I think part of that reason was historicals had ceased being bought for a while and that's what I enjoyed doing.

Only when I was able to be flexible and switch to doing a young adult story, did I make my sale. Since then my sales have been steady, but it's still rather like going to the dentist and having teeth pulled. I still get my share of rejections—usually because I've misjudged what the editor wants.

Persistence also means attending conferences and meeting with the editors, listening to what they want. I fully believe that the editors who know you personally are more willing to work with you and help you, though that doesn't guarantee a sale. And I've made many a sale to editors whom I knew only over the phone, after they bought my manuscripts.

Whatever happens, if you want to be a writer, you will be. If you stick at it long enough, have enough wisdom to learn to write to SELL, and the self–discipline to edit and re–edit your precious words, it will happen for you. If you don't have the stamina, if you wanted something easy and quick, then you're in the wrong field. (I know several students who took my classes because they thought that romances, etc. were so easy to write. They fell apart after two rejections.) Have faith in yourself, because if you truly want it, and if you continue to study the market and take classes from other writers, you'll succeed.

I recall vividly the two words sacrifice and commitment, which were brought up several years ago when I took the EST training. I can complain about how much I'm sacrificing for my writing career by working at it all the time and giving up dates, and other activities. Or I can say I'm so committed to my writing that I'm willing to give up dates, and free time. The actions are the same, but the attitude is what matters. Be committed to your writing.

Hillel, the Hebrew sage, said, "If I am not for myself, who is for me. If I am for myself only, who am I." Be for yourself and others will be for you. Help others—in writing groups and at conferences—and you, in turn will get the help you need.

EXERCISE:

VISUALIZE YOURSELF AS A SUCCESS. SEE THAT MANUSCRIPT AS A STORY. SEE THE COVER. SEE IT ON THE New York Times BEST SELLER LIST. (Go for the top!)

GO TO THE BOOKSTORE AND SPEND SOME TIME LOOKING AT THE TITLES. WHICH PUBLISHER IS DOING STORIES SIMILAR TO YOURS—HISTORICALS, SCI–FI, WESTERN, ROMANCE, MYSTERY, ETC. LOOK THEM UP IN WRITER'S MARKET, OR LITERARY MARKET PLACE. WRITE (with a SASE) FOR GUIDELINES, IF THEY HAVE THEM.

READ THE TRADES—PUBLISHER'S WEEKLY, VARIETY, HOLLYWOOD REPORTER (they can be found at the library.)

LIST THOSE PUBLISHERS OR PRODUCERS YOU THINK MIGHT WANT YOUR STORY. THEN SEND IT TO THE FIRST ON THE LIST. NOTE DATE SENT, POSTAGE USED, AND EDITOR'S NAME. (If one editor rejects the story and then changes to a different house, you might want to resubmit.) ARE YOU SURE YOU SENT ONLY WHAT THEY ASKED FOR—BE IT QUERY, PARTIAL, OR FULL MANUSCRIPT. BE SURE YOU SEND RETURN POSTAGE IF YOU WANT IT BACK.

IF YOU GET THE MANUSCRIPT BACK, LOOK IT OVER. IS IT CLEAN? ARE THERE ANY COMMENTS ON THE LETTER, WHICH YOU MIGHT WANT TO INCORPORATE INTO A REWRITE? IF IT SEEMS FINE TO YOU, SEND IT OUT TO THE SECOND PERSON ON YOUR LIST.

REPEAT PROCESS UNTIL SALE, UNTIL REWRITE, OR UNTIL YOU'VE USED UP EVERYONE ON LIST. THEN, GO BACK AND SEE IF THE MARKET HAS CHANGED ANYWHERE, OR IF ANY OF THE EDITORS HAVE CHANGED.

KEEP THE FAITH.

***

SELF-PUBLISHING

I recall watching an episode of *The Waltons*, where John Boy had a book of poetry that he wanted to publish. Being a novice, he sent his book to a vanity publisher and was thrilled when they wanted to publish his book. He wasn't so thrilled when the book arrived and the bill for the printing along with it.

It's a great feeling to see your name in print and know that millions . . . well, maybe thousands are reading the words you created. But often what we write is not for the thousands and millions of readers. What you have to say may be pertinent to only a select few. You've probably sent your book around the editorial merry–go–round feeling sure each time that an editor would call and say how wonderful it was, and offer you a huge advance. And each time it would come back.

I've often thought that if a book is good, it will find a publishing home, and that to waste money on self–publishing is pure vanity—hence the name Vanity Press. You, the writer, need to decide if you have a market, if this book means that much to you, or if you're willing to wait. Perhaps your mother's dying and her only wish is to see you in print. Maybe that's a good enough reason for you to go with Vanity Press.

These days more and more people are self–publishing through Amazon's Kindle, Book Baby, and a variety of companies now prepared to help you. It's easier than it ever was before.

Just remember that the responsibility for this book doesn't end with The End typed on your last page. While there used to be a lot of prejudice against self–publishing that is waning, one still gets more respect if you are published with a major publisher. Most authors whom self–publish for any audience bigger than their family members are usually looked down upon. So, even more urgent is doing things a professional way.

Self–publishing is not just writing, it's a business. The person who self –publishes must wear a variety of hats, from author to agent, to copy/proof editor, to distributor, and finally publicist. It can be a headache and a big time investment. Many, I know, who have done it once, vow not to do it again. On the other hand, you, the author, retains control of the book. You can dictate when it will come out and what it will look like and even who will read your story. In cases like these, a marketing plan is even more crucial.

Let's consider why you haven't sold. Maybe you've chosen the wrong market or maybe the timing isn't right? That certainly was the case with my gothics and I would have been foolish, especially since I didn't have the distribution, to try and self–publish those books myself. They remained on the shelf until the moment was right for them.

However, my workbook, which I did self–publish for a time, is another matter entirely. While there are other writing books out there, I think mine is unique. Until recently, the editors didn't agree. There is, I know, a ready–made audience for me in the form of my students and former students, not to mention all the conferences where I've spoken.

Because my classes are often short—four to six weeks—and we often have to speed along in the material, certain information I know must, as a matter of time, be left out. My students will then be provided with my words on paper, so they don't have to get writer's cramp and they can concentrate on their writing.

But let's go through the steps I have to do now in order to self–publish.

1. I write the book. There's no selling on a partial when you're self–publishing.
2. I have it edited and proofread.
3. I get quotes from various vanity houses. I tell them the pages in the book, if they will have to typeset it (that costs extra or you can chose as I am to have it typewriter style), if the cover will need more than two colors, if the cover

will be laminated, and how big the book will be. (8 x11, 7x10, or 5x6). Read whatever contract they give you VERY carefully. You don't want to be stuck with an extra fee.

4. If I want a drawing on the cover, or any type of artwork, I must hire the artist.
5. If I want quotes from people in the industry, I must send the copies around to those who can give me back cover quotes. I must have this before I can send the book to the publisher.
6. I must determine what the final cost of the book will be. That takes into account not only what the book will cost me to produce, but also the shipping costs from the publisher, the shipping costs to the individuals—envelopes, stamps, boxes, labels, what it will cost me to advertise, and state tax which must be paid. And then you want to see at least a small profit for the work and effort you've put in. But the price still has to be one that is palatable and competitive with other books on the market.
7. Don't forget to copyright the book with Washington, as well.
8. I make a list of places where I will advertise and send them copy material well ahead of the deadline.
9. I contact various bookstore owners to see if I can sell my books in their store and how much percent they will want for that. That cost also must be included in the price.

Is it worth all the hassle? That totally depends on how badly you believe in this and how much you want to see it out. If you think the market may change, and you can wait, then do so. Receiving a $2,000 advance—small as it might seem—is always better than paying out that money. But, if you don't feel there's any hope for the book to be picked up, and you feel the burning need to see it in print now, then investigate the idea of self–publishing.

With the buying up of various publishing houses, many authors determined to be published and to have control of how their work is shown, have gone to self–publishing. In fact, there are several web groups devoted to that, but it is hard work.

If you do self–publish, remember that the cover and especially the spine is the first thing the reader will see on the shelf, and you want that to look professional. You want the spine and cover to be cohesive in design and hint somehow at the genre of the book. Color is important. Nothing too gaudy. Different colors mean different things to people. Contrasting colors are best. It helps your book stand out. Make it interesting, but not overwhelming. Fonts for the spine are also an important consideration. The larger block fonts stand out better than the cursive and fancy ones. Next time you are in the bookstore, walk down the aisles and see what stands out to you.

The font that you choose for your book is more important than you think. It contributes to creating a more compelling book that readers are drawn to. Your choice also says a lot about you as an author. Different fonts can look more credible and professional, while others look tacky and overused. Sans serif fonts, like Times Roman and Helvetica, are easier to read than Comic Sans MS, which looks unprofessional. Some fonts to avoid are Ariel, Copperplate, Curlz, Brush Script, Papyrus, and Courier New (it's supposed to look like old type, but it can bother the eye.)

A list of some of the places that help writers self–publish will be in the appendix.

***

WRITING FOR THE YOUNG ADULT MARKET

Kids are people and people are kids. Writing for the children's or young adult market is essentially no different than writing for the adult market. Whatever you are writing has to be your best. You have to know your reader, his likes and dislikes, and how to help him identify with your characters.

Writing for children might, perhaps, be even more difficult than writing for adults, since you, the writer, must identify with a world that is no longer yours. Of course, we were all kids—once. But in my teen world, I was worried about kissing a boy goodnight on a first date. The drug scene was only beginning to mushroom, and I, being the innocent I was—knew nothing at all about it. In the world teens inhabit today, they're more concerned about whether they should go to bed with a boy, or if they should take drugs. But they also have the same worries that I did—if they'll pass the exams and get into college, if they'll finish the term paper on time, if they should turn in the person they know is cheating, if the new boy will notice them, if they'll have a new dress for the prom—or if they'll even be asked.

As with historicals, regencies, westerns, and sci–fi, if you are writing for a young adult market, then you must know your settings and your characters as if they were your own. That means research. If you happen to work with children on a daily basis, or have children of your own, you have a ready–made lab. If you're single and in a profession where you have little or no contact with kids—you have to investigate and talk to parents, talk to children, and make your story as lifelike as possible.

Most writers seem to see writing for children as a stepping–stone to writing for adults. Actually, it's a world of its own. Books that children read affect them far more than books adults read. In fact, I became a nurse because of reading the Cherry Ames nurse mystery series. (For those of you who do not know these books, she was a nurse type Nancy Drew—solving crimes while being a nurse.)

In order to write for children—as with any genre—you must respect the reader, you must respect the child.

Do you recall what it was like to be a child—your fears, your pain, your hopes, dealing with adults and other children? Do you believe that everything is possible—as a child does?

In the young adult market, there are basically two kinds of books. The sweet young adult romance, which usually takes place in the high school setting, and where the heroine never uses drugs or even considers going to bed with the boy. (The hero would never ask her anyway.) This was put out in lines like Bantam's Sweet Dreams and Silhouette's First Love.

They are, like the adult contemporary romances, following a formula. The second type of book—the problem novel—deals with the nitty-gritty of teen life: dealing with anorexia nervosa, divorcing parents, abortion, psychiatric hospitals, etc. These are stronger characters who might use drugs, or have sex, but who in the end realize they must make the decisions regarding their lives and they must be the ones in control. A romance, if it occurs in these books, is usually secondary.

For a long while, the problem novel was out of vogue, but now it has come back into its own. (I'm glad to say, especially since I have one that I wrote many years ago—***AGAINST HER WILL,*** which can now make a debut.)

The supernatural love stories with vampires and werewolves are now disappearing from the shelves. That doesn't mean an exceptional one might not make an appearance, but they won't be the norm, at least not next year.

Emotionally, the latter books are stronger and can deal with children at any age, whereas the young adult romances must be teens of fifteen to sixteen years of age (heroine) and seventeen to eighteen years of age (hero).

Now there is the new adult fiction where the heroine is no older than twenty -two years of age, but can still relate to the teens in her life.

For your ideas, you'll want to consider what problems children of different ages might experience. Any problem must be endemic to the life of that child. A ten–year–old isn't going to care about the hostage crisis as much as the disappearance of his neighbor's dog. A teen might care about the hostages, but isn't going to be able to do much about them and will probably be more concerned with being able to run the marathon, or if his dad is losing his job. (Now if you can tie that in with the hostage crisis—that's fine—but don't make it artificial. You can certainly tie it into the government shutdown!)

The character is usually only a few years older than the reader—and the reader must be able to identify with the character. The character must have a lifestyle the reader can respect and look up to.

Children and teenagers are smarter than we think. They will know when the author is writing down to them, and when the story doesn't flow naturally. They will also know if you're trying to force your theme down their throat. Medicine always tastes better when it's sugar coated. Any theme should be interwoven with the story.

The reader must come to the decision of the story's value for himself. He shouldn't be told the theme by some understanding character adult and then immediately agrees. Showing and not telling is crucial here.

Of course, teen stories can be mixed with any other genre. I mixed mystery with my teen romance in ***A GATHERING STORM.***

CHARACTERIZATION

To make your characters come alive, you do a character chart not unlike one you would do for an adult, but additional questions you might ask would be:

1. What does he like/dislike about school? Favorite subjects? Favorite teachers? Why?
2. Favorite foods? Favorite TV Shows. (Be careful about mentioning exact shows or popular bands, since that will date your book.)

3. What clothes does he like/want/need? Does he fit in with the crowd?
4. Does he get along with other family members? Other children? Adults? Or is he a loner? Is he insecure? Does he like physical sports or mental ones?
5. How does he react when teased? (And we all know how children tease.)
6. How would your eight, twelve, or fifteen-year-old view the crimson sofa? (Most likely they would just call it red, though we adults would name it several possible colors. Remember the thoughts, feelings must be in that character's voice. A kid doesn't think of his heart pounding or of the relief he'll feel when someone moves. He thinks in much more basic terms.)

While dialogue should be snappy, be careful of using slang that will date your book. Rather than concentrating on a theme, concentrate on the conflict and emotion, and how the character struggles with his/her problem.

As with the other genres, you should be reading young adult books by authors like Judy Blume, and Beverly Cleary—analyze and study them.

Above all, become your character—feel what she's feeling, fear what she fears, and your reader will, too.

EXERCISE:

CLOSE YOUR EYES AND TAKE SOME DEEP BREATHS.

NOW, THINK BACK TO WHEN YOU WERE A CHILD, OR A TEEN.

WHAT ARE SOME OF THE MOST EMBARRASSING MOMENTS YOU HAD?

WHAT WERE THE BEST?

WHAT DID YOU FEEL ABOUT SCHOOL?

WHO WAS YOUR BEST FRIEND?

DID YOU HAVE MANY FRIENDS?

DID YOU EVER FEEL LONELY?

WHAT WAS THAT LIKE?

HOW DID YOU GET ALONG WITH YOUR BROTHERS AND SISTERS?

If YOU WERE AN ONLY CHILD, How DID YOU FEEL ABOUT THAT?

HOW DID YOU FEEL ABOUT YOUR FOLKS?

WHAT DID THEY DO WHICH IRRITATED YOU?

WHAT DID THEY DO TO EMBARRASS YOU?

WHAT WERE SOME OF YOUR DREAMS?

HOW OLD WERE YOU ON YOUR FIRST DATE?

WHAT WAS IT LIKE?

WHEN WERE YOU FIRST KISSED? WHAT WAS THAT LIKE?

WHO WAS YOUR FIRST "LOVE AFFAIR" WITH?

WRITE YOUR FEELINGS DOWN, NO MATTER HOW HORRID OR STRANGE THEY MIGHT SEEM. MANY OF THESE FEELINGS AND ACTIONS ARE WHAT TEENS TODAY GO THROUGH.

WRITING SHORT STORIES

The good news? As other publication opportunities keep shrinking, what many are calling the Second Golden Age of short mystery fiction continues to flourish. The bad news? Writing short demands entirely different skills than writing novels. If you want to create publishable short stories, it's a good idea to brush up on those requirements.

Where do you start? The best place is with the idea. How do you know when a plot better suits a story, rather than a novel? Stories work best with "short" or "small" ideas, especially in the short–short (up to 1,500 words) or mid–length (up to 4,000 words) range. In "small" ideas, the action is played out over a short arc and can usually be summarized quickly.

If the concept comes to you whole, especially when coupled with a twist ending, or if you hit on a clever title first that relates to an ironical element in the plot, or if it cries out for a black humor tone—it's a good bet that's a short story idea.

Longer stories (4,000–5,000 or more words) will sometimes employ an idea that could be developed to novel length, but the idea will be treated more narrowly, with fewer complications.

An easily remembered formula that can be used for any length story is A–B–D–C–E:

A = Action. Hook the reader with a burst of action or an intriguing concept.

B = Background. Provide some background or explanation of the initial action/hook.

D = Development. Further develop the action of the story.

C = Climax. Bring the elements together in a confrontation.

E = Ending. Wrap–up.

In a longer story, the "development" portion of the story can be played out longer. Provide more ups–and–downs for your characters at this length, but don't pad it.

Other points to remember when writing short stories:

- Start fast. It's essential that you hook the reader's interest quickly. Characterization, setting, and conflict must be established early, as well as the crime or the potential for the crime.
- Eliminate the unnecessary. The form demands economical writing. That doesn't just mean writing tightly—it means, whenever possible, elements must achieve multiple purposes. Learn to say more with less.
- Keep it in scale. Every element should be in proportion to the length of the story. That includes both the development and the number of characters, as well as setting, action, and all other elements.
- Dialogue must be direct. And just as the structure is more streamlined than a novel, the resolution should be quicker than in a novel.
- Eliminate most transitions. A story just jumps from one scene to the next.
- Limit scene changes. Many short stories take place in a single scene. While scene changes are permissible when required, limit the scope of place.
- Write to a single theme. While a novel may explore many ideas, a short story should be sharply focused.

Generally, a short story reflects a single point of view, but not always. A technique that's sometimes effective is to create two viewpoints that appear almost parallel, but which will actually intersect in the climax. It can be a powerful device, especially if the reader doesn't anticipate where the two forces will collide.

Similarly, while most stories employ a linear chronology, shifting between the past and the present until the times converge in the climax is also an option. Both techniques require some skill, however, so they might not be an ideal choice for a first story.

Short stories in the crime genre aren't burdened by as many rules as novels. They can be mystery, suspense, or whodunits, traditional or totally groundbreaking. They can be written from the detective's viewpoint, as novels generally are, or from the killer's, or even the victim's—the only limit is your imagination. Some editors do want to see the villains suffer the consequences of their choices, while most just want a good story. Short stories allow writers to create characters that might become tedious at novel length, but which can be deliciously fun for a short time. Writing stories can provide a writing workout, allowing writers to try new techniques and flex particular muscles, as well as providing a faster sense of accomplishment. Publishing short stories provides professional credentials; most writing associations consider published short stories as sufficient conditions for membership.

In an age when no one seems to have enough time, there has never been a better time to read and write short.

Writing and producing a short script is also good training. The script can be as limited as four to five pages or as long as twenty pages.

Often, if you can't get your script writing career off the ground, having a short produced is a good calling card for what you can do. There are numerous opportunities for short scripts. These, however, do not make a lot of money—if they make any at all. My own short script, which I produced, ***THE UNBORN,*** was bought by Shorts International. I have been able to use it to show people my writing skills and have been asked to expand it into a feature.

NOVELIZATIONS, SCREENPLAYS, AND BEYOND

Each story has its best medium to be told in. For some tales, that is the novel, for others a play, and still others are best as screenplays. Some things, not all, can be done in more than one style.

In a play, the actors tell the story; in a novel, writers tell the story; and in the script, the camera, actions, and visuals tell the story. The roots of cinema are visual. Movies originated from pictures, whereas TV originated from radio. Hence, more dialogue is used in TV scripts.

Consider all the silent movies—mainly action with very little subtitled dialogue. Look at the recent success of ***THE ARTIST,*** and how the action is told in the characters reactions, expressions, actions, and then the camera angles. For this reason, the contrast between the characters, their relationships, and environment is more crucial than in the novel.

For every screenplay that is produced, there are dozens or more that have been commissioned, which just sit in their boxes untouched. Many screenwriters, in fact, much to their chagrin, make a living at just doing assignments and getting optioned, but it's a fact of Hollywood life. There are great scripts that languish for lack of production funds or interest—some of these are revived years later when the cycle turns.

Those who write screenplays will be the first to tell you that writing a screenplay is totally different from writing a novel. The structure is similar, but many other things are different.

A film, by its very nature, is visual. Most new screenwriters believe that a scene should compose of people talking, when, in fact, while that might be good for television scripts, it is not good for feature scripts. You need to learn to write dramatically cinematic scenes.

A scene, which needs to be kept short—no more than two–three pages—like a mini short story on its own, has a beginning, middle, and end within the concept of the larger story.

When writing a scene ask yourself:

- Who is the protagonist? Who has the most dramatic need here? Who is the antagonist that opposes the need? This should create conflict. They each want the same thing and it creates the conflict.
- Who are the other pivotal characters in the scene and are they necessary? How do they push the conflict forward?
- In dialogue, how do the characters communicate best with each other. Is there plenty of non–verbal communication? Can a character say "I love you," then turn their back, and by her expression let the audience know that she is lying?
- Why is each character in the scene? What is the driving motivation behind it?
- What subtextual emotional bubble is beneath the scene? What is it really about?
- How does the scene relate to that which came before and that which goes after it? Does it have the same suspense or comedic tone as the rest of the story?
- Can you write the scene using only non–verbal action and reactions?

The fact is that most writers who specialize in screenplays cannot write novels, can't describe their visions as they want to, and don't have the capacity to sustain detailed description and narrative. They must rely on the interpretation of others—directors, camera crew, and actors to get their message across. Many have told me that they are jealous of those who write novels—and rightly so. It takes far more effort with words, and more patience, not to mention more time, to do a good novel. But you also have to be in a different frame of mind.

A novelist can talk about the inner feelings of her characters, what they are thinking, what they are going through as they trek through the rain forests, as they climb the dusty attic stairs, or as they make passionate love. We novelists draw pictures with our words so that our readers envision scenes on private screens of their own. Pages upon pages can be devoted to descriptions. Not so with the screenplay.

The screenwriter can only hint at what the character is thinking and feeling. Everything must come out through dialogue and limited VISUAL description. In your description (for a screenplay) you can't say, "She thought he was going to turn away." You merely have him turn away and what she thinks or doesn't think has to be portrayed either in dialogue, or better yet, in the facial expression of the actor portraying the character.

While in some ways writing a screenplay is fewer pages, it's also harder since the screenwriter must convey in fewer words the essence, feeling, and subplot that she wants the director and actor to convey on screen. The subtext, or what the character is saying and thinking beneath the words, must also be conveyed in the few words of dialogue or description allowed, so the actor will know how to play the part.

The other big difference, of course, is that whereas the novel can be of any length appropriate to the story—from 100 pages to 1,000, the screenplay is limited to a definite length. A two–hour movie (any longer and you may lose your audience) runs no more than 120 scripted pages. Actually, most scripts these days are running 95–110.

Acts are set and more formalized than in a novel and the story is (usually) more linear. Flashbacks are seldom done in a movie because they can be more confusing than in books.

In addition, point of view (POV) changes more with a novel, especially when you have an omniscient story and several views. A film cannot have this happening. Scenes are all controlled and each scene must relate to the one before, without meandering, as a cause and effect fashion.

Each scene must have a good beginning, middle, and end. You must learn to jump in late to a scene and get out quickly. This is, of course, the same for a novel. But in a novel, one can skip around. In a screenplay, one seldom does. Action in scenes should be started in the midst of the problem. The novel scenes can run a half page, but in a screenplay, they can run no longer than five pages without a break.

If you are at all interested in screenplays, then, as with any genre, you need to study them. This is easier said than done, since screenplays are hard to come by.

The stores in Hollywood, which sell them, charge exorbitant rates. And the only other option is to spend time reading at the Academy of Motion Pictures Library (which is open to anyone, but material must be read there) or the Writer's Guild (which has the same rules) and American Film Institute—again in Hollywood. Places that sell scripts charge anywhere from $10 to $25 for them (more than it costs to Xerox them), but the market pays it. Barring that, read books on screenplays like Syd Field's book, ***WRITING THE SCREENPLAY. SAVE THE CAT*** series is another good text for screenwriters. You can also find scripts online at Script O' Rama and Scriptshack.

In addition, The Writer's Store in Burbank has a huge selection of books on writing.

Kevin Spacey, the actor, also has a production company website, www.triggerstreet.com, in which you can read screenplays of other writers and critique them. By seeing what they are doing wrong and reading some of the reviews, you can learn.

Www.Talentville.com is another place you can read scripts—some good, some not so good.

Form is crucial in the screenplay. For that you want to read ***THE HOLLYWOOD STANDARD (2ND ED).*** If your format is off, it may be an automatic toss.

You may have the best story, but you still have to do research. You still have to do character bios, space and time lines, with a tight beginning, middle, and end. And you still need to have all the plot lines tied together at the final moment. At the same time, if your form is off, you are marked as an amateur and won't get past the first reader. The more screenplays you can read, the better. If you want to write for a certain television show, a difficult feat at best since, most work is staff written and those not done by staff are done by writers they know, it's best to study scripts from that show. Each show has its own peculiarities of form.

Things, which mark you as an amateur, are numbering scenes and assigning times (something I only learned recently). These are done at the typing of the final draft (usually done by the staff writers and not by you). Using camera angles or shots in your story is also a no–no.

In general, tabs would be set at:

17--Left margin (this allows for three hole punching, since that's how scripts are bound) to 75 for right margin. 72 are the page number.

28--Dialogue.

35--Parenthetical directions.

43--Character's name—above dialogue.

66--Transitions such as CUT TO: or DISSOLVE TO:

It might look something like this:

FADE IN:

(Double space here)

INT. PLACE — SPECIFIC LOCATION — DAY (OR NIGHT)

Skip two lines and add more about description here and any immediate action needed. CHARACTERS names are capitalized when they first come on, as SOUNDS like the bang of a gun that are heard off stage . . .

(Single space narrative)

NAME

(Shrugging)

Despite what many newbies do, actions do not occur in the parenthetical.

The fewer you have of these, the better. What she says goes here and stays within this limit, since actors don't like to memorize. Keep it under five lines, if possible.

NAME #2

More dialogue

NAME #3 enters the room and pours coffee. Brings it over.

Karen sits by the corner table.

However, these days many writers leave out the stage directions and simply focus on the characters. And in interest of saving space, CUT TO is often not used either these days.

KIM

Eats her bagel

Do you see how that focuses the action without making the director think you are trying to take over his job? They also leave out CUT and FADE TO—except at the very end.

It's impossible for me to give you everything here, so you'll just have to read other scripts to see how it's done, but this should help as a starter.

Good investments, if you want to do screenplays, are the programs Movie Magic Screenwriter and Final Draft. A lot of people in Hollywood use the later, but Movie Magic is popular too. I like that one because they don't charge for updates or tech support as Final Draft does.

Before writing your screenplay, as before writing the novel, you should have a step outline of where each scene will lead you and what events will happen.

Of course, there are writers who prefer to write without an outline. But as I've said before, it's my experience that you cannot really start to write without knowing where the end will be, unless you know what will be happening to your characters. The step outline often follows and is more expanded than the treatment.

The treatment, like the synopsis, is written before the story. It can be as short as one page or fleshed out to be as long as forty. The treatment must have the premise of the story as well as the logline. This is a unique part of the story which you would pitch to an executive in eighteen seconds—which is sometimes as long as you have). It should have something about the characters (not a lot), but hint at their motives and obstacles. Touch on the conflict they will face.

It is done double spaced with concrete verbs and usually in present tense. Unlike in the synopsis, every scene is included, and it must be written in catching prose. Prose, which can translate to visual film, not long winded narrative. Describe here what we will be seeing. A short treatment will be seen at the appendix.

Some terms, which you'll be using, are VO (Voice Over), POV. (Point of View), DISSOLVE TO: (a slow fade), CUT TO: (A sharp cut), MATCH CUT: (where one scene relates to the other by means of an object or a word), O. S. (Off stage—sounds heard, but not seen), INSERT (close up of something).

For each scene you must ask yourself, if it is really necessary and how can you make it more visual. Can you cut out some of the dialogue and show the characters doing something instead of talking it.

Subtext is crucial in writing the dialogue. "On the nose" words—that is saying what the character is really thinking—is limited, at best.

EXERCISE:

WRITE A SCENE IN SCRIPT FORMAT USING THE ABOVE TERMS, BUT NO CAMERA ACTION.

DOES EACH SCENE RELATE TO YOUR STORY LINE? HOW?

As with novels, but more so with script, dialogue should create conflict and push the story forward. Don't have your exposition sounding like a lecture. Dialogue should be no longer than four lines—max! (If they are longer, cut them with action.)

Scenes are anywhere from one half a page to five pages. Any scene, which seems to be more than this should be broken up.

The screenplay pages must look pretty, too. Seems odd? It's not. Most producers do not like to read and the way a page is laid out affects them. Therefore, you don't want to have too many sections of dialogue without having a line of action to break it with.

One reader I know flips the script and thumbs through it to make sure there is an equal balance of dialogue and narrative, and that there is plenty of white space. They will also glance at the page count. If it's more than 120, some will directly trash it.

Many readers will give you, at most, ten pages or less to hook them. Some give you only the first few.

Each scene should be started in the middle of the action. Each scene must relate to the story line.

WRITE AN EXPOSITORY DIALOGUE WITHOUT LETTING PEOPLE KNOW THEY ARE BEING GIVEN INFORMATION. DO IT IN SCRIPT FORM. MAKE EACH SPEECH DIFFERENT FOR EACH CHARACTER. DO NOT WRITE IT "ON-THE-NOSE."

Sub-text is shown through the feelings of the characters, and the actors should understand the underlying emotion so they can let it show in their face, in their actions.

What is the sub–text here? Since the characters cannot betray their internal thoughts as they can in a novel, it's important that they have a way of getting their real feelings across. WATCH THE SOAPS. They're a good example of sub–text, where they are saying, "I love you," all the while holding a gun on someone.

WRITE DIALOGUE WHERE THE PERSON IS TALKING ABOUT DINNER OR SOMETHING ELSE TRIVIAL, AND REALLY MEANING SOMETHING ELSE?

Novelists are at the mercy of their editors. Screenwriters are at the mercy of actors, directors, producers, studios, and—more often than not—the original story they wrote is rewritten and rewritten so that it appears on screen looking nothing at all like their first concept of it.

Because the scope and audience all differ, not every screenplay or television show makes a successful novel. The A–Team novels bombed out because those who watched that show are not the type who read. Those folks watch the "boob tube" for their mindless escape. Whereas the viewers of Cagney and Lacey are, we hope, the type who will read and want to know what happened to their characters before the start of the show. (Hence, the book on ***CAGNEY AND LACEY*** that I was hired by Dell to write.)

Technically, a novelization is the transference of a script to novel form using much (but not all) of the original dialogue. Usually, the film has not yet been done, or is only in rough–cut, and so the writer of the novelization must visualize what she thinks the screenwriter was trying to say. Last minute changes in films are not unheard of and therefore the novel can seem vastly different than the film.

Often—as with ***THE STUFF***—the novelization I did for New World Pictures based on the film of the same name, the screenwriter had not done a character history, had not done an in–depth study of the relationships in the story. In order to do the book, I had to write this for myself and get a feel of the characters.

In writing the novelization of ***DAYS OF OUR LIVES*** (the soap), I had to know the show and the background of all the characters by talking to people who had watched those episodes (years and years ago) and by reading as much as I could about their world from Soap Opera Digest and Soap World.

You must remember that these are not your characters you are working with. These are characters created by someone else and you are merely a worker for hire. You must, therefore, stay true to whom these characters are and have been established as being.

With the ***CAGNEY AND LACEY*** book, this was even more difficult, since this was not a novelization, but a new novel of my own design based on material given me by the studio—a line here, a line there—indicating what the lives of the two women would have been like before they went into police work. Believe me, it's not easy getting into the heads of characters that are not your own.

Getting into novelizations is fun, but financially is not as rewarding as doing your own work, since mostly the books are work for hire. That means the studio or the publisher planning on the novel hires you and you sign over a good deal of your rights merely to have your name on the cover. Is it worth it? Sometimes, yes; sometimes, no. It all depends on where you are and where you want your career to go. In my case, the novelization for Cagney and Lacey opened several new doors for me, which would otherwise have remained closed far longer.

To do novelizations, you need to have an established bio and be able to show publishers not only your writing style, but that you can write fast. You need to prove to them that you can perform, since often the studios will come to the publisher with only a few months to spare before the movie is released. However, you do receive your checks within weeks after the finished product. (Unlike publishers, who sometimes wait for months before sending out funds.) Except for the fact that they are both creative, the two industries are very far apart in policies and in timing.)

If novelizations are something which interest you, contact the publishers who do these books and send them your material. Be a fan of the show you want to novelize. I entered through a back door. Wanting to expand, not really knowing what was involved, I asked my manager to investigate and she did. Within a few weeks of my initial request, we had appointments with all the major studios. Each one told us they liked my style, but had to talk with the publishers with whom they had already contracted.

In most cases, the publisher had already chosen a writer for the project, but we soon came to Cagney and Lacey. They had just decided that they wanted a book, and liking my style, told Dell they wanted me. Period. In this business, more so than novels, timing—and who you know—is crucial.

Whether you stay with writing novels, go to novelizations, or do screenplays, remember the more visual you can make your words, the better your writing will be.

EXERCISE:

READ SEVERAL PLAYS OR SCRIPTS. NOW TRY TO FIT YOUR CHAPTER INTO SCRIPT FORM. REMEMBER NO INTERNAL MONOLOGUES!!

An example of a screen scene follows.

FINAL QUESTIONS FOR YOUR SCREENPLAY

1. Is the genre clear in the first ten pages? If this is a romantic comedy, we need to know that, if; it's slapstick, we need that.
2. Have you opened with action? Better to set the mood and give latecomers a moment to get into their seats.
3. How long does your set–up last? It should only be ten pages. The first plot point should come between 25–35 pages and the second between 75–85, with the climax being 110–115. If you deviate from this formula, you'll have difficulty.
4. Does the set up introduce the main characters, location, and situation?
5. What is the catalyst that makes things work? Best catalyst is some form of action.
6. Does your first plot point build character and suddenly become something different? (Is a girl shot at just as she thinks she's safe?) Does PPI (plot

point one) turn your story into a different direction? Do two characters come together?

7. Reversal is the strongest type of plot point (i. e., going from the absolute pits to being in love). Are your plot point's reversals?
8. In a good screenplay, the character increases his capacity to love in the end—does yours? They grow or change in some form. This is called the character arc. Novels should have this, too, but screenplays even more so.
9. To prevent Act 2 sags, have mini–stories—a story within a story—in seven–minute sequence with complete beginning, middle and end. (Like the burning of Atlanta in ***GONE WITH THE WIND.*** How many mini–stories do you have?
10. Subplots 3 & 4 fill in the slack. While the first major subplot is the romantic entanglement and has several scenes, the 3rd and 4th should only be three beats each. They should show parallel conflict and have a beginning, middle, and end, being mentioned three times.
11. Main plot should be concerned with life and death—a murder, finding out something, a mission, a crucial problem to solve, a definite quest. (Death can be mental as well as physical—as in losing your best friend.)What is your main plot?
12. Sub and main plots should peak at different times to keep up interest, but must intersect at a crucial point. Do yours?
13. Does each scene advance the story and build character?
14. Something should be happening every ten minutes—does yours?
15. Is it commercial—do you have topical themes? What are you feeling different? What trendy things are affecting you?
16. What myth, or fairy tale—the hero tale is of a journey that comes near death. In the healing myth, the character is broken and separates to understand another's world (he must leave home to be healed), inner conflict (which doesn't work as well in novels), in Pandora's box, she wants a treasure—are you using these?

17. How many characters—seven are the most people can keep track of. Minor characters should do double roles (be a confident) and even be a catalyst.
18. What is transformed and healed?
19. Each character must have a mutual escalation of the goal.
20. Do you have a teaser scene—like in ***SPLASH***, which hooks us into the story?
21. Why are we sympathetic to this lead character? How is she/he dumped on? What underserved misfortune comes her way?
22. Characters do not think, they act. What actions do you show from the characters thoughts?
23. Is the movie for both sexes? Or are you concentrating on one quadrant of the audience? What are the markets for this? (Movie audiences are divided into four quadrants—young adult—usually boys; chick flicks, older adults, and kids or family. It's a rare film that can appeal to all four areas.)
24. How does the character change in the movie? The character must evolve both physically and emotionally.
25. Do you give away the climax too early?
26. Where is the final arena of the climax?
27. What is your page ten hook? Do you have resolutions for all three plot lines?
28. Does PP1 (plot point one) turn the story around in a different direction?
29. Does your second subplot complicate the main story—like in ***ROMANCING THE STONE,*** where the authorities are chasing both her and the bad guys.
30. Does the set-up show the main character at work, play, and home?
31. Is there urgency and reason for the main character to jump into PP1?
32. Is your form correct? Do you have the dialogue and action in right proportion?
33. Is there plenty of white space on your pages?
34. Are your scripts three hole punched, with nice, plain white—not expensive covers? (You don't always get the scripts back and most producers think its

a bad sign when they show up with zebra embossed covers! It's as if you're trying to impress them with the cover because the inside is no good.)

35. Now that this one is out and making the rounds, are you working on another?

Once you've written FADE OUT you're almost there, but not quite. You don't want to send along anything that isn't completely right. For that reason, I often pay consultants to read my material and give me development notes. The Writer's Bookstore is one such place where you can get this service and there are many independent consultants out there. Prices can vary from a few hundred to over a thousand. Many advertise in writer's magazines.

Check out their credibility. Have they, themselves, produced anything? Some people are good at teaching and breaking down other's materials, but have never themselves succeeded in the process. You do get what you pay for, so make sure you are paying for what you really want—just coverage or development notes. (See definitions of them in the front section.)

As my friend, Marc Zicree, of the Supermentor fame, says, you are judged by the people you are associated with. And if you associate yourself with someone well known in the screenwriting world, it's better for you.

TV is even harder to break into. You have to do not only original pilots and stories, which you probably won't control because the networks want established showrunners for their programs, but they look for spec scripts (scripts written without pay) based on current TV shows. Most writers who break into TV do so by becoming writer's assistants and then becoming part of the writing staff. Again, you need both specs of existing shows and original pilots to show people that you are as talented as you say you are. One advisor suggested that if you wanted to keep control of your TV idea, it is best to do it as a webisode and put it up on You Tube. There, if you are lucky, it will be discovered. And even if not, you will get your work out to the audience.

Because it is so hard to break into show business, many of us have begun doing our own productions. As Marc says, be proactive. Therefore, I shot my own short ***THE UNBORN*** (the script and story are in the appendix), and have been showing that around. And now have been asked to write the feature version of the story. So being proactive does work. More so than ever, persistence and having definite goals is the key here.

GETTING TO PRODUCERS

All us scriptwriters want to see our scripts on the desk of the major studios, but times have changed. The bigger studios are developing less and less and producing less on their own. They are taking material from independent producers and distributing them.

Most indie producers do not have monies to option material and have to find financing on their own. (Hence programs like Kickstarter and Indigogo.) Nevertheless, getting your stories to them is still a challenge. You need to have an agent, a manager, or an entertainment lawyer to send your material out. That doesn't mean you can't meet them on your own. A book called, ***THE HOLLYWOOD DIRECTORY*** (published yearly by the Writer's Store) lists producers and what they are looking for. You can query these independents, but if they ask for the script, you will probably need to sign an NDA (non–disclosure agreement) that says you will not sue them if they produce something similar to your story. (This is one benefit of having the agent as an intermediary.)

It always helps in selling your script if you have someone attached. That is a well known director or actor who has not only expressed interest in your story, but is willing to give you a letter of intent.

Networking, networking, and more networking, especially if you live in Los Angeles, is the way to meet people. Befriend everyone. Let people know you are a writer. You never know if the person you are standing in line with at the buffet could possibly know an actor, director, or producer looking for a script.

As writers it is difficult for us to attach well known people, because they often want to know if there is money behind the script yet. Agents will not give their actors or directors your script unless you can make a firm offer for them. If somehow you can meet someone who knows them and who can get the script to them, you are far better off than trying to go through the agent or manager. Again, networking here pays off.

For those living in the Los Angeles area, belong to groups like Women In Film, Breaking Into Hollywood, Hollywood Networking Breakfast, and others. It is possible to succeed and sell your script without being in L.A. Listing your work on InkTip, Virtual Pitch, and the Black List are ways to get your material around. They are small investments, but can be worth it. Getting to know people on LinkedIn, Twitter, and Facebook also helps.

ADAPTING NOVELS TO SCREENPLAYS

It's not easy to compress 200+ pages into 100 pages of script. And if the book is popular, you have an even harder road ahead of you. People have images and ideas already in their head of what they want the film to look like.

More so than in books, the audience has to be kept at the edge of their seats.

Here are some hints in translating your novel to a script. Every novel or story is about a character so—

1. Read the novel. Determine what the spine of the story is.
2. Write down everything you know about the various characters; their arc, their goals, and how far they are willing to go to get them.
    a. Determine POV.
    b. Who is the protagonist.
    c. Who is antagonist.
    d. Who are the others.
    e. What are the relationships of the characters to each other.
3. What happens if the character fails at his quest?
4. Determine what the theme is.
5. Which scenes mesh with the theme and which don't? Add scenes to make

the story more cinematic or to add conflict. Support the visual story and increase tension.

6. Most novelists, even if they are good writers, are too verbose in their descriptions and narrative. Tighten that and cut it back. (When I was first adapting, I had the "novel problem" of making my descriptive passages too novel–like. It was a habit I had to break.)
7. Consider changing the ending. Don't change it just to make changes, but realize that you are painting the canvas and your priority is to tell a great story. Avoid the predictable ending even if it is in the book. Take this work and make it your own.

You can take the book verbatim and translate it, but often the characters in the book have to be compressed and scenes have to be changed. So this is not often the best idea, but it is a start.

Divide the book up into eight sections (i.e., 24 chapters/8 = 3 chapters) as approximate sections, but this is very artificial.

Do a character analysis of the hero. What do they want, need, or desire? How does he change? What does he say first when he is introduced? If he talks about himself, the audience will not like him.

Avoid the predictable ending even if it is in the book? Take this work and make it your own.

List the obstacles for obtaining his goal.

What is the log line of this story?

List the plot points. A few sentences for back story. What is ordinary and yet unique about him in the first three chapters, and how is he pushed to change?

2nd—What has happened to him to gear him into action? (This is the initiating incident or plot point 1.) Hero denies the call. Gradually being locked into the conflict brought in by this call. Tries to solve the problems himself, but fails. Can we raise the stakes at all?

3rd—Beginning of act 1–the hero is spurned into action by something propelling him forth.

Hero's first attempt to solve the problem. The first things that anyone would do in a situation like this. Routine appeal to outside help. One by one the doors close to her. Ends when these avenues are all shut down to the hero. Shows why character is the only one who can solve the problem.

4th—Plot point 2–what does the antagonist do to combat the hero? All is not what it seems. With all ordinary means exhausted, Hero spawns a more grandiose, more extreme plan. He prepares for it Gathers what he needs, allies, puts the plan into action, but it all goes wrong. The plan goes to shit due to missing certain vital information that the hero lacked about the antagonist . . .

What keeps the hero from giving up on his quest?

5th—Mid point—Having created the plan without changing, he knows now that he needs to change. He is forced to look at his own world and to change. Problem he is having is to some degree his own fault. What has he done wrong? What has held him back? Driven by antagonist to change or die, he retreats to lick his wounds.

Hero must examine his flaws. He confronts his flaws. He created a plan to succeed without change. Now he needs to change. Plans went wrong because he was not willing to change. His eyes are open to his own weakness. Driven by the antagonist, he must change or die. From here on life changes completely. No going back. Everything is going worse and beyond that even more horrible.

6th—A new plan forms again and he is ready to change,. True depth of the villain comes to light. It looks like things will go wrong again.

Act Three

7th—Begin to turn the tables. Rejoins the battle and sees victory new fervor. And then the tables turn one more time . . . In tragedy, hero looks like he has lost everything. Hero realizes key that is missing. Fear needs to eclipse the hope. There is tension here. Chris Soth says "fear+hope = tension." What do they hope for? What do they fear? How will they get out of this?

8th—Intensity is higher. Main tension is resolved/they went further than they hoped. A bit worse for the wear. Wrap up all of the subplots. More tension. Things go from hope to fear. Villain grabs him by throat. A twisted point as. Hero puts down the antagonist last attempt to defeat him. Story and subplots wrap up.

Do a beat sheet and put your scenes in order. Think about the order and the pattern to create meaning.

Remember that only things seen and experienced can be written about–no emotions. No feelings. Always ask yourself, how I will show it? Any time you can replace dialogue by action, do so. End your scenes early. Take the last line of the scene and see if it can be cut. See how it sounds without that.

Now go back and read more scripts.

WHAT MAKES A WRITER?

1. First put pen to paper/fingers to keyboard.
2. Finish a manuscript.
3. Actually submit a manuscript to an agent/publisher.
4. Place or final in a contest.
5. Sign with an agent/publisher.
6. Have a piece published that others must buy to read.
7. Receive money for something published.
8. Have SEVERAL things published.

Anyone of these or combination thereof can define you as a writer. All elements are not necessary for you to call yourself a writer. If you will it, you are.

NON-FICTION, MEMOIRS AND BLOGS

According to recent sources, non–fiction books outsell fiction by half. That is for every novel that sells, two non–fiction books sell. One reason for this is because people are eager to learn new things, and at times, it's easier to pause in the midst of a book on "How To—" than it is a hot and steamy work of fiction. Nevertheless, both are our creative babies and we want them all to see the light of day.

As you have heard in journalism (and in the chapter on beginnings), the Who, What, Where, When, and Why is crucial to be established up front. We need to know who the main character is, where it is taking place, what is happening, the time period, and if possible, the motivation for the event.

Like we said before, it is best to write in details and specifics. It makes your work stand alive.

Showing and not telling is just as important here as it is in fiction. Don't give too much backstory (story that happens before the main event or the scene starting), but plunge right into the event. Get the reader engaged sooner than later. Imagine the scenes as they occurred, and then get us into the mood and the sense of the moment.

As both a journalist and non–fiction writer (***THE BOOK OF POISONS*** and ***THE FORENSIC NURSE***), I have found that people learn best from examples and vignettes. Despite the fact that it is non–fiction, I will use all my senses, and taking the facts, will construct a story around the material I have—sometimes even giving voice to dialogue from the participants, if I have that available. I try not to make up things unless, as in the case of ***FORENSIC NURSE***, I needed to do it to hide the identity of the clients we were talking about.

To sell a non–fiction book, you need at least two chapters and an outline of where the book will be going. Sometimes the publisher will insist on the whole book, but often you can sell on a partial manuscript. This later is especially true if you are an expert in the field you are writing about. Be sure you mention your credentials when writing the query letter.

Book contracts go to those who have mastered their subject, not someone who says once you pay me, I will finish my research and interviews. Don't write your book with an axe to grind. Write it because you have something informative to say that has not yet been said by the competition.

In your proposal you must answer—Why is there a demand for my book? Why am I the best person to write it? If you are not already a recognized authority on the subject, you should be partnering with someone who is. Patience is paramount here. It took me nearly four years before St. Martin's Press agreed to publish ***THE FORENSIC NURSE,*** because although I have training in the field, I am not an expert. I did, however, have the backing of the IAFN (International Association of Forensic Nurses) and many of my colleagues were willing to be interviewed for the book.

Let's say you have a great new diet you want to write about. Go to the bookstore and look at the publishers who do diet books and other health related material. These are the ones you should be targeting. If you don't already have ***THE WRITER'S MARKET PLACE***, which is put out every year, get it and find up – to–date information on what each publisher is looking for, what their submission guidelines are, and sometimes they will even list editorial names.

If you can direct your query to a specific editor, all the better. (Just make sure you spell their name correctly. Sometimes, I will call the publisher to make sure that editor is still on staff, because people do move around and the book might have been correct when it was printed, but changes can happen.)

Blogs and memoirs too, are not only our babies, but they are the stories of our lives. These fall halfway between non–fiction, since they are telling scenes, experiences, or thoughts of our lives, to fiction, since for the scenes to come alive, we have to use touches of our fiction training. Blogs are a safe place for the writer to express his or her honest feelings and talk about events in their lives, but remember that you are putting it out for the world to see.

Memoirs, in fact, are becoming a popular literary form. You don't have to have robbed a bank or climbed a mountain to be unique enough to write a memoir. Each one of us is special in our own way. A memoir brings back lost time periods to us and to others who are reading them. It helps us understand ourselves and others in a way that we might not have before.

While I have not attempted this myself, yet, I find that keeping a journal is a great way to keep track of the stories of my life. It also keeps my writing fresh. When I am looking for how I felt when the boy I liked refused to take me to the prom, all I have to do is look at my teen diary. The emotion comes flooding back to me.

According to Galleycat.com (part of media bistro), publishers are looking for interesting blogs to expand into books. If this is your interest, then find out what publishers are seeking your topic—maybe you have just recovered from cancer, maybe you're an immigrant and have tips about settling in—and after putting a couple of your essays together, send them off with an outline of where you might be going in your book.

When doing a non–fiction, blog, or memoir, you have to decide what is your goal for this?

What makes your story different than anyone else's? How are you unique?

The agent or publisher wants to know you have a deep passion for your subject and that you have an authentic and original writing style, not a dry, academic style. You need to have a grasp of the competition. Know what books are out there and how your book differs. Chapter summaries must be compelling and convey something about the unique material your book plans on getting across.

Your query can be done in three to four paragraphs, highlighting your credentials and expertise. A good proposal, with outline, can be done in four to five pages.

If you are telling the story of your own personal journey, why will people (unless you are a star and this is a "Tell–all" book) be interested?

Who will the market be? Are you just doing it for family? Then maybe self–publishing might be best for you.

Are you trying to reach a larger audience? If so, do you have plans on how to do that?

As we discussed in outlines, the book proposal must also have your target audience and marketing plan listed. A writer needs to understand their audience and how to reach them. The publisher will ask about your author platform, as well—i.e., how much social networking you do. How will you, the writer, use your connections to help sell the book?

We talked a bit about publicity already, but, for the most part, you can do what most publicists can do. The only group I would recommend is the Radio and TV Report (RTIR), which helps to book you interviews on various shows around the country. This is especially good for non–fiction. Just remember that you are the best publicist there is for your own work.

POSSIBLE CHARACTER GOALS

ENEMIES

Locate an enemy.

Expose an enemy.

Destroy an enemy.

Capture an enemy.

Get an enemy out of your life.

Deal an enemy a serious blow/wound.

Okay, enough with the enemies already.

Get an item or person.

Having gotten an object or person bring it to where you need to take him/her/it.

Close Pandora's Box.

Save the group or get the group to safety.

Escape.

Make your way home (or someplace else).

Triumph over a harsh situation.

Get a second chance.

Get recognition/make something of himself or herself.

Leave his or her mark.

Get others to accept your character.

Get the girl or guy.

Learn the truth.

Expose the truth.

Getaway with mischief.

Get revenge.

Right a wrong.

To prove one's own innocence.

To prove the innocence of another.

To further a cause.

To learn one's true identity.

To save a business.

To commit a crime.

To run for political office.

To escape the past.

To search for treasure.

QUIRKS AND ECCENTRICITIES

Localized trait reversals—if the traits you picked were reversed how would we see them in your character?

Opinions that he especially holds important? Is he Republican or Democrat? Pro or Anti Abortion?

Philosophies of your character—

Beliefs and passions?

What kind of member of the opposite sex are they attracted to and why?

What's most fascinating or memorable about your character?

Anything unique about the way your character that you can write down?

His behavior under alcohol?

What does he do or where does he go when he is happy or sad?

How does he respond to or give criticism and praise?

How does he decorate his living quarters? Neat or sloppy? Style? Why?

Taste in music? Favorite recording artists or type of music?

Taste in entertainment? Favorite movies or books?

Nicknames when younger or now? How did he get those?

Does he have any special way of talking? Any verbal traits or mannerisms as with Valley girls who always say, "Cool, Dude."

Ways to make us care about the protagonist or rooting interest techniques.

- Another character says or tells something sympathetic and others like and admire him.
- Conspiracy against him.
- Courage.
- Defies the masses, goes own way, follows no one, own slant on life–Bogart, Ace Ventura.
- Easy and authentically warm, genuine.
- Everyman.
- Fighting for any just cause.
- Fun, playful.
- Have others be worse—*The Godfather, The Unforgiven.*
- He chases a higher goal or vision, spiritual values.
- He feels pain and/or hides pain. (He looks around at the couples in the park.)
- He gets up by his bootstraps as in Rocky.
- He has a generous heart /does good acts.
- He relates to kids and loving toward family.
- He solves own problems, doesn't have or count on someone else coming to his rescue.
- He takes responsibility for his own actions and is ethical.
- He's funny, witty, clever.

- He's thoughtful and intelligent=Denzel Washington in Philadelphia.
- Helping the unfortunate or helpless.
- He's an excluded outsider.
- Insecurities or emotional problems.
- Is there anything about the character that he or she is trying to change about him or herself?
- Loves himself or herself.
- Loyalty to a friend or coming to their aid–TALE OF TWO CITIES—(Either of these two might involve self–sacrifice.)
- She's a crazy woman/man in a crazier world–Forest Gump.
- The Stakes get higher.
- Touching endearing habits, traits, and eccentricities.
- Underdog.
- Undeserved misfortune.

CHARACTER CHART

Name: ______________________________

Nicknames: __________________________

(Nicknames and how they got these names tell us a lot about the person.)

Age: _____ Height:___________ Weight: __________

Hair: ____________ Eyes: __________

Birth date: ____________ Birthplace: ____________

(Zodiac sign: sun, moon, and ascendant, Venus)

Profession:_______________ Rank in his profession:________________
Does he like what he is doing? What would he prefer doing if not this? How did he get into this profession?

Where was he raised? _______________________ What class was he brought up in? _______________What class is he in now—poor to wealth? Or visa versa.

What, if anything, does his character think would make his life better . . . often he is wrong about this.

What is his emotional state at the start of the story?

Is there anything about the character that he or she is trying to change about him or herself or someone else? Often the character is unaware of his need to change but might have an unconscious block, fear, or limitation that he cannot express, which by the end of the story he will not only be able to face but will overcome. The story will contain different phases of emotional struggle and inner conflict for your character.

What in the character's life is simple?

What in the character's life is complex?

(Often work situations and relationships fit here.) Does the character have any relationships, which are complex?

If so, picture this in terms of layers and describe each layer of feeling.

What are his physical, mental, or emotional scars or handicaps? (Some major conflicts can come from this part of the character.)

Educational background: what does he most recall about school?

What did he like most?

Who influenced him the most?

What stands out most from childhood?

What was grammar school like?

High school?

Was he shy or outgoing? Popular or a loner?

Sports or clubs?

Any childhood diseases?

Playmates?

Trips alone and with family?

Did he have everything he wanted?

A loving family or dysfunctional? If the later, then in what way?

If he lacked—what was that lack?

What would he change about childhood, if he could?

What type of neighborhood did he grow up in and how did that influence him?

What activities before and after school?

Did he go to church/synagogue? What was the religion in home? Was it because he wanted to or felt he had to?

What does he know of ancestors? Has it influenced him?

Any past lives? If any, and karma—that might be reflected in the story.

Work experience, or training for it?

How did he decide on his job? What led him to that? What promotions? What other companies did he work for? Does he want to have his own business? What is his relationship with his boss? Relationship with co-workers? Does he socialize after work?

Best friend and why is this person the best friend?

Other friends?

Enemies and why?

Parents and how they related?

If parents didn't shape life, who did? How?

What does the character feel about the rest of the family? Brothers? Sisters? Grandparents?

Are any of his siblings married, divorced? Have children?

If an only child, how did he feel about this?

Illness in family?

Family sayings?

What are special holidays celebrated? Which are the most important to him? Why?

Psychologists say the first four years of our lives are the most formative in shaping our relationships with EVERYONE and our survival traits. What survival traits does this character have? Is he amenable to authority? Does he rebel? How much? Why?

What does he think about courtship and love?

If married, how does he meet spouse? How was the question popped? Was it a big wedding? Did they elope? Relations with in–laws? Where was first home? Could they make ends meet? How did love grow? Does it stop growing? How? What are the joys and sorrows of married life?

What type of parties attended? Does he like parties?

Is he politically involved? If so, how? What clubs or functions does he now belong to? Why?

What is the present problem?

What does he need to solve this problem?

What does he want?

Is what he wants the same as what he needs?

How will the problem change within the story?

How will it get worse?

How does coping with the problem change or not change him? Show the ways he changes in scenes. (This is very important, especially if you're doing a bigger book.)

What is his strongest trait?

What trait will make this character come alive?

What is the weakest trait?

How does the character see himself? What is his attitude—negative, positive, and cynical?

How do others see him?

Sense of humor? Dry wit, practical joker? What other kind . . .

Basic nature? (suggest book ***YOU ARE YOUR FIRST NAME:*** Ellen Dodge Young, Long Shadow.)

What are private moments like? What does he do alone?

What are his fantasies? What was his favorite fairy tale—if had one?

Ambition: What does the character need?

What are motives for this need?

How much does he need this?

How far is he willing to go for this? (Will he lie, cheat, steal, and murder?)

Philosophy of life: What does he see as the future?

What does he see as his future?

What would he change, if he could?

What point of view does he have—pro–life, pro–choice, vegetarian, or a hunter?

Does he believe you can't fight city hall or believe the opposite? (Whatever he believes, the antagonist should believe the opposite to make for conflict.)

What world events happening now are shaping his view of life? (Especially important if doing a historical.)

What does he do with free time? Hobbies? What kind of music, art, and reading material preferred.

Favorite ways of dressing? Favorite colors?

Where does he live? Why has he chosen the housing he has?

What is home like? (Not just physical, but mental and emotional atmosphere as well.) Why has he chosen this area of town?

What is the most important thing to know about character?

Do you like the character? Why?

How do other characters feel about this character? Why?

How does he feel about them? Why?

Has he ever been in love before?

What happened?

What role models are in his life?

How does the character believe men and women should be in a relationship?

If married now, does it differ from the relationship he sees as being perfect?

What would she do if she found a treasure—and no one else knew it?

How does the character deal with money?

How does he react when angry? Swear words he uses commonly? Does he hold anger in or explode?

Characters most remembered are those who are strong in some way—saints, sinners, or combinations of both. Why will this character be remembered?

What would be a perfect day or afternoon for the character? If she could change anything about herself, what would that be?

Any pets? How does she feel about animals? About children? Does she want children?

How does the character believe he/she fits into the larger scheme of things?

How spiritually aware is he/she?

Does she follow astrology or think its bunk?

If there is a theme to your novel, how is the heroine actively involved in portraying that theme? (Make sure she is active not passive.)

If it is a hero personifying your theme, what does he do action–wise that contributes to the story?

Who is your main character? Whose story is it? (The person who is most active is usually your viewpoint character. The one that wins in the end (or dies trying) is the main character. It's important to know what you are focusing on.)

Any special way of talking? Accent? Favorite words? Favorite phrases?

What do the heroine and hero find in each other that the other lacks?

When he has a crucial decision to make, how does he go about it? Flip a coin, study pros and cons, intuition? The why of decisions is very important.

ONE LINE CHARACTERIZATION (CRUCIAL)

How different or similar is she from other characters in the story?

If he could say one thing about his life, what would that be and how would he say it?

What would he say he learned about his life?

How has he changed?

What would his epitaph read?

Choose an animal that reminds you of the character. Why?

Choose a flower or vegetable that reminds you of this character. Why?

Use these two for metaphors relating to the character.

He or she is as pretty as . . . / as ugly as . . . / as sweet as . . . / as sensual as . . .

Some of these traits and questions come from David Freeman's ***BEYOND STRUCTURE***

EXERCISE:

MAKE A LIST OF CHARACTERS. WHO ARE THEY? HOW DO THEY RELATE TO ONE ANOTHER?

WHAT DO EACH OF THE CHARACTERS FEELS TOWARDS ONE ANOTHER?

WHAT IS THE READER EXPECTED TO FEEL TOWARDS THEM?

WRITE A CHARACTER HISTORY. Work up an astrology chart too, if you want.

Choose three traits from the list that best fits the person. They can be two bad and one good (making him more of a villain), or they can be two good and one bad (making him more of a hero), or you can have a neutral trait instead of the opposite one. But please don't make someone all good or all bad unless he really is . . . and few people are that.

DESCRIBE THEIR ROOM FROM THEIR POINT OF VIEW. This process should tell us something about them as a person. DESCRIBE A FRIEND'S ROOM FROM THE CHARACTER'S VIEW. What they first see tells about them as well as the friend.

GET A FASHION MAGAZINE AND CHOOSE AN OUTFIT THEY MIGHT WEAR. DESCRIBE THEM WEARING IT—USING THE SENSES.

TWO CHARACTERS ASKING QUESTIONS OF EACH OTHER. DETERMINE HOW EACH CHARACTER'S VOICE DIFFERS? (ROLE–PLAY WITH ANOTHER PERSON.)

CREATE A SCENE WHERE THE CHARACTER IS IN DANGER AND HAVE US CARE ABOUT THE CHARACTER.

WHY DID YOU CHOOSE THE NAME YOU DID FOR THE CHARACTER? WHAT SIGNIFICANCE DOES THAT HAVE TO THE CHARACTER'S LIFE? IS IT CORRECT FOR THE TIME PERIOD? FOR THE PERSON YOU HAVE?

PICK A MAGAZINE PICTURE THAT REMINDS YOU OF YOUR CHARACTER AND PUT IT UP ON THE WALL WHILE YOU ARE WRITING.

MEDITATION: Close your eyes and take several deep breaths. See your character in your mind's eye. Repeat several times: I AM . . . (name of character); I FEEL LIKE . . . I REACT LIKE . . . THE PAIN SHE FEELS, I FEEL THE LOVE SHE FEELS, I FEEL I AM . . . HER THOUGHTS ARE MY THOUGHTS WHILE I AM WRITING THIS BOOK.

TIME LINE CHART FOR A STORY IN 1492

	day 1	1492	1493
Isabella	She refuses.	She gives in with the promise that he will convert the Indians.	She knights him.
Columbus	He begs for money.	He sails. There is a mutiny.	He returns in chains.
Fernando	He wants money for war.	He takes over Andulasia.	Starts the first inquisition.
Love interest	She doesn't believe Columbus.	She begs to go with.	She falls in love with one of the Indians.
Torquemada	Wants to kill all the Jews.	Gets permission of the King.	The first auto de fe.

- ***USE A TIME CHART, AS ABOVE, AND INDICATE THE DEVELOPMENT IN EACH OF YOUR CHARACTERS LIVES AND HOW WORLD EVENTS HAVE AFFECTED THAT DEVELOPMENT. What I have above is not from any real story, but I have used some world events and mixed them with the events from the story, so that we know where each person is at each time in the story. You can divide it by days, hours, weeks, or years, as you see fit.***

A MYSTERY CHART

Imperiled protagonist.	
Protagonists memorable trait.	
Suspect.	
Suspect's memorable trait.	
Relationship of S to P.	
That burning question	
Decoy suspects. Lethal weapon. Homicidal refinements. Raunchy repartee. Whodunit.	

APTITUDE QUOTIENT EVALUATION QUIZ

How observant are you? This is a test for you to see what you leave out when you read things.

DIRECTIONS: Read each question carefully, then fill in the blank space with the correct response.

1. If you went to bed at 8:00 P. M. and set the alarm to get up at 9:00 A. M., how many hours would you sleep?
2. Do they have a 4th of July in England?
3. How many birthdays does the average man in the U. S. have?
4. Why can't a man, living in Winston Salem, North Carolina be buried west of the Mississippi?
5. If you had on a match and entered a room in which there was a kerosene lamp, an oil lamp, and a wood stove, which would you light first?
6. Some months have thirty-one days, some have thirty. How many have twenty-eight?
7. If a doctor gives ***you*** three pills, one to be taken every half hour, how long would the pills last?
8. In my hand I have two U. S. coins totaling fifty-five cents. One of the coins is not a nickel. What are the two coins?
9. A framer had seventeen sheep. All but nine of them died. How many of them were left alive?
10. Two men are playing checkers. They played five games and each of them won the same number of games. Explain this:
11. If you take two apples from three apples, how many do you have?
12. A woman gave a beggar fifty cents. The woman is the beggar's sister but

the beggar is not the woman's brother. Why?

13. How many animals of each species did Moses take on the ark?
14. Why can't they hang a man with a wooden leg in Tennessee?
15. Why do birds fly south in the winter?

DO NOT PEEK UNTIL YOU ARE DONE! ANSWERS

1. Thirteen hours.
2. Yes, they have the 4th, but don't celebrate.
3. One.
4. Because Winston Salem is on the east of the Mississippi.
5. The match.
6. All have 28.
7. One hour.
8. Fifty cent and five cent coins.
9. Nine.
10. They played someone else.
11. Two.
12. It's her sister.
13. None. Noah took them not Moses.
14. You need a rope to hang a man; you can't hang with a wooden leg.
15. It's warmer there.

***

INTERACTIVE WRITERS' GUIDE TO OUTLINING, CRITIQUING, AND EDITING

You can customize this chart by adding and removing rows and columns as you wish. You can also add your comments right in the boxes and they will expand.

Name of Story: ______________________________

Author: ______________________________

YN	General Info For Writers. Check the "Yes" or "No" box for the following questions.
☐☐	Have you decided what genre your story will be? Mystery, sci–fi, fantasy, horror, etc.
☐☐	Have you decided who your target audience will be? Men, women, children, teens, etc.
☐☐	Have you decided whether your story will be literary or mainstream?
☐☐	Have you researched publishers to find out if there is a market for this type of story?
☐☐	Have you obtained guidelines from each publisher you plan to submit to?
☐☐	Have you decided whether this story will be a stand alone, part of a trilogy, or part of a continuing series?

OUTLINING YOUR STORY

Have you included all of the required elements in your story?

YN	Question
☐☐	Decide on a title for your story! Sometimes choosing a title before you begin can give you a hint of what the story will be about and what direction it should go.
☐☐	Decide the approximate length you want your story to be.
☐☐	Have you written a short description of what your story is about?
☐☐	Have you decided how your story will end?
☐☐	Have you decided how and where you will use surprises and twists in your story?
☐☐	Have you decided how and where you will plant clues or red herrings in the story?
☐☐	Theme—Something the story is trying to tell/teach us. The moral of the story. Can you define the intended theme of your story in one sentence?
☐☐	Plot—The story itself. Everything that takes us from point A to point Z. Do you have a rough outline of each scene and chapter?
☐☐	Characters—Have you made a list of all the characters that will take part in your story?
☐☐	Characterization—Have you made a chart describing the various characteristics of each of your characters?
☐☐	Setting—Have you chosen a location for the story?
☐☐	Time—Have you chosen a time for the story?

☐☐	Conflict—Do you have a specific problem the hero/heroine has to solve?
☐☐	Climax—Have you decided how, when, and where the problem will reach its peak?
☐☐	Resolution—Have you decided how the problem will be solved and by whom?
☐☐	Point of View—Have you decided on a specific point of view from which to tell your story?
☐☐	Flashbacks—Have you decided when and where you might be able to use flashbacks?
☐☐	Foreshadowing—Have you decided when and where you might be able to drop some hints of things to come?
☐☐	Mood—Have you decided on the mood or moods you want to create in your story?
☐☐	Atmosphere—Have you planned the types of atmosphere you will need to use to create the moods you hope to achieve?
☐☐	Dialogue—Have you decided what type of dialogue you will use? Normal? Slang? Dialect? Formal?
☐☐	Action—Have you planned action that will keep your story – fast moving and exciting?
☐☐	Exposition—Have you explained why these characters are here and what they are trying to accomplish?
☐☐	Did you try to involve the five senses?
☐☐	Epiphany—Will any of your characters suddenly realize exactly what's happening and what needs to be done?
☐☐	Symbolism—Have you decided what types of symbols you might use and where?

LITERARY DEVICES

Literary devices can add interest to a story. Have any of the following been included? These are just a few of the simpler devices that could be used.

YN	Question
☐☐	Does the story contain personification? Personification is a figure of speech in which human qualities are attributed to an animal, object, or idea. For example: The leaves danced, the wind whispered.
☐☐	Does the story contain similes? Similes make comparisons by using the words "like" or "as." Her laugh was like fingernails on a chalkboard.
☐☐	Does the story contain metaphors? A metaphor is a figure of speech in which one object is likened to another by speaking as if it were the other: For example: The new basketball player stood tall among his team members, a redwood tree among a forest of spindly pines.
☐☐	Did you use euphemisms in the story? She's a few bricks short of a load.
☐☐	Did you use ironic situations?
☐☐	Did you use sarcasm?
☐☐	Did you use oxymorons?
☐☐	Alliteration: repetition of the same sound beginning several words in sequence. We will watch, wait, and worry.
☐☐	Anadiplosis ("doubling back"), the rhetorical repetition of one or several words. Specifically, repeating a word at the end of one clause and the beginning of the next. Human beings always have a need, a need for bigger, a need for better, a need for more expensive.

☐☐	Anaphora: repeating a word or phrase at the beginning of successive phrases, clauses, or lines. We like to read. We like to dance. We like to play.
☐☐	Antistrophe: repeating the same word or phrase at the end of successive clauses. We went to Hawaii, and got sunburned. We went to Bermuda, and got sunburned. We went to Jamaica, and got sunburned. Then we went to Switzerland, and got frostbite! (Sorry, I couldn't pass up the opportunity to make a joke.)
☐☐	Onomatopoeia: use of words to imitate natural sounds. Eeeaaah, Eeeaaah–equals sound of a siren, Rrrraaarrrhhh–equals a lion's roar.

EDITING YOUR STORY
GENERAL PROBLEMS TO WATCH FOR

YN	Question
☐☐	Are quotation marks used correctly?
☐☐	Are apostrophes used correctly in contractions and possessives?
☐☐	Do all sentences begin with a capital and end with the proper punctuation?
☐☐	Are there unnecessary adjectives?
☐☐	Are there unnecessary adverbs?
☐☐	Did you use the correct words: its/it's, there/their/they're, to/two/too, are/our, would of/would've? For example: could of–instead of could've
☐☐	Are modifiers in the right places?
☐☐	Have the words "up" or "down" been used where they aren't needed?

☐☐	Were the words, "that", "was", "were", "which" and "had" used unnecessarily? Have you eliminated "is" and "are" as much as you can and written actively, not passively?
☐☐	Did you use a lot of words ending in–ing,–ly?
☐☐	Do subjects and verbs agree in number?
☐☐	Did you use your spellchecker?
☐☐	Did you use your grammar checker?
☐☐	Did you use your thesaurus?
☐☐	Did you do a final proofread to catch any mistakes your spellchecker and grammar checker may have missed?
☐☐	Did you check for missing words?
☐☐	Did you check for words that weren't deleted and are just sitting there for no reason?
☐☐	Did you check for unnecessary repetition of words or phrases?
BEWARE THE DREADED 'NYMS	
☐☐	Antonyms—words with opposite meanings. For example: good/bad, black/white, up/down, inside/outside.
☐☐	Synonyms—words that mean the same thing. For example: repair/fix.
☐☐	Homonyms—words that are spelled and pronounced alike but have different meanings such as with the noun quail and the verb quail, or the noun flight and the verb flight, etc.
☐☐	Heteronyms—a word spelled the same as another, but having a different sound and meaning. Bass voice/bass fish.
☐☐	Homograph—a word spelled like another but with a different meaning or pronunciation. For example: read/read, lead/lead.

☐☐	Homophone—a word having the same sound as another but of different meaning, or spelling. For example: to, too, and two; their, there, and they're; pale/pail; sale/sail; red/read; led/lead. Bound—I was bound for Detroit when the train derailed. I was bound and gagged.
YN	General Critique Section
☐☐	Has the work been proofread and made as error free as possible before submitting it for a critique?
☐☐	Has the work at least been checked for spelling errors before submitting it for a critique?
☐☐	Does the story work? Is the story new and interesting? Was the story easy to read?
☐☐	Does the first sentence contain a hook that will grab the reader's interest?
☐☐	What Point of View is used? Is the Point of View consistent? Would the story be better written from a different Point of View?
☐☐	Does the narrator intrude in the story?
☐☐	Does the author introduce a character at the beginning of the story, or keep you wondering who he/she is?
☐☐	Are there places where the author seems to "dump" too much information?
☐☐	Are there missing words, or words that don't seem to belong in a sentence and are just sitting there for no apparent reason?
☐☐	Is the subject appropriate to the age of the intended audience?
☐☐	Does the story flow smoothly and logically?
☐☐	Do chapters begin and end where they should?
☐☐	Does the writer SHOW or TELL the story?

☐☐	Did the author use language that will be easy for all readers to understand?
☐☐	Do many sentences begin with the same word?
☐☐	Does the author continually repeat things?
☐☐	Are there any major grammatical errors?
☐☐	Are there any major punctuation errors?
☐☐	Does the author continually use he/she, or her/him instead of the characters' names?
☐☐	Is there much use of passive wording, such as: there was, there is, there are, it was, it is, and-or he/she was, he/she is, etc.?
☐☐	Are all sentences complete, or do sentence fragments make sense? Are sentences short and choppy? Are there a lot of run on sentences? Are sentences so confusing you must read them several times to understand them? (In scripts, many writers write in fragments and it's okay as long as it's understandable.)
☐☐	Are paragraphs too long and hard to read? (In scripts, no paragraph should be longer than five lines. Dialogue, too, should be short.
☐☐	Does the story contain old, tired clichés? Mad as a hatter, mad as a wet hen, drunk as a skunk, ferocious as a tiger, etc.
☐☐	Are the loose ends tied up at the end of the story?
☐☐	Is the story something that you would like to read more than once?
THEME	
☐☐	Does the story have a definite theme?
☐☐	Can you define the theme in one sentence?
☐☐	Is there a consistent mood to the story?
☐☐	Did the story leave you feeling confused?

DIALOGUE	
☐☐	Is the dialogue realistic/natural/appropriate language level for the age of the intended audience?
☐☐	Does the dialogue move the plot forward?
☐☐	Is there too much dialogue, or too little?
☐☐	Did the author use other dialects, or foreign phrases? Is it easy for readers to understand?
☐☐	Did the author use any unusual or technical terms that many readers would not understand?
☐☐	Did the author use dialogue tags other than said, too many dialogue tags, unnecessary adverbs in dialogue tags?
☐☐	Did the author repeatedly use characters' names when the characters were being spoken to?
☐☐	Did the author include actions in place of dialogue tags?
SETTING	
☐☐	Do you know where and when the story takes place? Does it matter in this story?
☐☐	Does the author show the setting through the actions and/or dialogue of his/her characters?
☐☐	Is there enough description to allow you to picture the setting in your mind?
CHARACTERS	
☐☐	Are the characters believable?
☐☐	Does the author show how his/her characters think and feel?
☐☐	Do you feel as though you know the characters by the end of the story?
☐☐	Do minor characters support the main character, and the development of the story?
☐☐	Is there a villain/antagonist?
☐☐	Does the villain/antagonist take over the story?

☐☐	Do the characters seem stilted and/or undeveloped?
☐☐	Is the story a monologue?
☐☐	Does the main character bring the story to its conclusion?
PLOT	
☐☐	Does the first paragraph draw you into the story?
☐☐	Does the first paragraph leave you wondering what the point of the story is?
☐☐	Does the first page make you feel like you must keep reading?
☐☐	Does each scene move the story forward?
☐☐	Does the author use foreshadowing to create tension?
☐☐	Does the author telegraph the outcome of the story?
☐☐	Does the story come to a believable conclusion?
☐☐	Does the ending leave you wanting to read more?
☐☐	Does the ending leave you frustrated? (Explain)
CONFLICT	
☐☐	Is there any type of conflict in the story? (emotional, physical, etc.)
☐☐	Does the author use conflict to build the tension slowly?
☐☐	Does the author use actions/dialogue to show the conflict?
☐☐	Does every action have a corresponding reaction?
☐☐	Does the dialogue fit the actions and reactions?
☐☐	Can you define the conflict in a few words?
☐☐	Is the conflict resolved at the end of the story?
☐☐	Would you recommend this story to others?
Use this area to explain your personal thoughts and feelings to the author.	

The following story was adapted for a film—luckily it was already in the shape I wanted so I could use chronological method, but that is not always possible. Notice how everything that is written in the script can be seen.

THE UNBORN

By Serita Stevens

Watery warmth surrounded me as I wriggled my toes, my fingers, and allowed my eyelids to flutter open. The gentle motion of the rocking chair combined with the vibratory hum of my mother's singing lulled me into a peaceful mood. I didn't even feel like kicking today.

I think my first awareness was of Mother -- of her heartbeat, her humming, and her happiness. I was glad to be a part of her.

But the blissful existence didn't last long.

I was in my sixth month of uterine life when Eddie stormed into our presence. Even before he yelled, I sensed the anger and heard the heaviness of his footsteps thumping on the wooden floor.

"You whore! Why the hell didn't you tell me the baby wasn't mine?"

Mom jerked her body upright, forcing me into a sitting position. I could hear the shocked surprise in her voice.

"But it is yours, Eddie. I swear it. You're the only one I've slept with. The only one I love."

"Liar!"

He slapped us then. I cringed with the pain almost as much as she did.

It didn't take me long to understand that Eddie was the creep who'd fathered me — and that he wasn't too excited about my existence. But I knew Mom loved me. She'd told me so often and I believed her. I wanted to believe that everything would be okay for the two of us. The trouble was, she loved Eddie. I think it was because she'd been beaten by her father.

Eddie moved in with us and nothing seemed the same after that.

Oh, sure, he could be nice. He'd take us to the park and buy us ice cream. But when he'd drink, he was horrid. He'd get to talking about his folks and how his mother had betrayed his father.

After he beat us, he'd always ask, "You okay, babe? "

Mom would nod and they'd make up. But I felt my tiny heart harden against him.

When she wasn't feeling well, he'd coddle her, but I never felt he really meant it. She would tell him she was okay and smile -- as if she believed him. I loved to feel her smile. She would rub her stomach. I yearned to have her hold me.

"The baby moved today. You want to touch?" Mom asked him one night.

"Can I?" Eddie asked.

He never bothered asking me so I didn't usually oblige him. Sometimes I'd kick — but not often because that hurt Mom too.

"Gonna be a football player that kid." Eddie bragged after one of my more vicious kicks. "Maybe he'll come out with a wrench in his hand."

"Eddie, please," Mom pleaded. "If anything, she'll come out with a book in her hand."

"No kid of mine's a patsy." His snarl startled me. "Sounds like you're trying to prepare me -- so I won't be suspicious, huh. I know damn well my kid's a boy. "He slapped us. I winced feeling my mother's pain. "Well, who the hell was you with before me?"

Mom was crying. "Eddie, I swear. It's you I love. The baby's yours. It can't be anyone else's."

"Yeah, well, you better believe I'm gonna make sure." He stormed out of the house and stayed away for several days. It wasn't nice, but I hoped he'd drink himself to death and get out of our lives. Mom and me needed only each other.

Both Mom and I were glad when he was gone. Then she could play her music. Mozart, she told me -- and would hum to me. It was times like these when I really wanted to be born, to let her cuddle me in her arms.

***

Eddie continued to become more and more irrational in his behavior. I pleaded with Mom to get away from him. Maybe I had a premonition. I tried to tell her that I didn't like him, but she'd talk to me and placate me, saying that she told me lots of other things too. Things she probably wouldn't have said if she knew I really listened to her.

I was reaching the end of my seventh month. Only two more to go and then Mom and I would really be together. But I feared for her and I was afraid of Eddie.

***

"Did you have to look at that guy like that?" he asked, slamming the door as we came home one night from a party.

"Eddie that guy is my doctor!" She paused. "And I wasn't looking at him."

"Don't lie to me!"

He hit her again and again. I felt my own anger growing as I clenched my fist. If I could have cried I would have. But my tear ducts weren't yet formed.

Eddie was beating us almost daily now. I hated him more and more. Now when we were alone, she didn't play her music. She just cried. I wanted to reach up and comfort her. I wanted to tell her how it hurt me when she was sad. But she wouldn't listen to me and she wouldn't leave him.

This man wasn't worthy of being my father. I knew I was going to have to take matters into my own hands.

I was eight and a half months when he hit us again.

"Eddie, please. I love you. The baby loves you."

No, I don't! She knew I didn't. But she was so sacred of him she would lie.

He continued hitting her. I tried covering my head and fending off the blows that were coming to me. I yearned to protect my mother, but I couldn't. I was too helpless.

The punches continued until I could barely breathe — and suddenly there was silence. Not even a heartbeat from above.

I found myself gasping for air.

In the distance I heard him crying, "Oh, Janey! My God, Janey!"

The sound of the ambulance siren was the last thing I heard as I vowed that I would survive and I'd make him pay.

I'm not sure exactly what happened after that. I heard noises again and knew that I hadn't died. Then I saw the brilliant white lights. Rubber gloved hands lifted me out and away from Mom. They cut the cord which had bound us all those months.

"Apgar 5," a voice said. "I think we might have saved her. Get her into the incubator. Start the oxygen. Run a bilirubin."

They righted me and I looked back at the table. My mother lay there -- unmoving. I knew she was dead and I let out a shriek.

The nurse rolled my crib out past two men standing in the hall. I didn't have to ask which one was Eddie. His nervous pacing and blood shot eyes gave him away. God, he looked hideous with his low bushy brows and huge nose. I hoped I hadn't inherited anything from him. Hatred curled my fist, which I stuffed in my mouth, vowing my revenge.

As I was driven past, the guy in the white coat put on a hand on Eddie's shoulder.

"I'm sorry Mr. Hutchins. We tried to save her but—"

"Oh, my God! No! No, Janey isn't dead. I loved her. I swear, I did."

The doctors voice was smooth. "Of course, you did. But we reached her too late." He paused. "However, we did save your baby. You have a wonderful baby girl. Quite a fighter considering her prematurity. Do you want to see her?"

Eddie's mouth dropped open. "Her! You saved the kid and you didn't save Janey!" He grabbed the doctor's collar and began to shake him.

"Please, Mr. -- Hutchins --" The doctor paused, trying to catch his breath. "We performed an emergency c–section. I thought -- you'd be -- pleased."

Eddie released the doctor nearly throwing him against the wall. "Yeah. I'm pleased," he said, scowling. "How d'ya suppose I'm gonna raise a brat by myself. "

"Mr. Hutchins, I realize your situation is difficult, but it's not unique. I'm sure —" He loosened the knot on his tie. "Do you want to see your daughter?"

"Yeah. Sure."

They brought Eddie into the nursery. I knew I must look a sight with all these tubes and things they'd stuck in me, but no matter what it took, I was going to live — and make him pay for murdering my mother.

His mouth gapped open as he stared at me. "My God, she looks like — Janey." As he looked down at the crib, I hated him even more than before. I would have my revenge.

Weak as I was from the delivery and everything that had happened already, I managed to summon all my powers as I stared directly at him and forced my brain to project the message. "YOU KILLED HER. I HATE YOU."

I saw the horror in his eyes and knew he'd heard me. I cooed and smiled as I kicked off my blanket.

"I gotta get me a drink." He turned and left the nursery.

***

It was several days before he came back. I struggled to get stronger and knew he was supposed to take me home today. I didn't want to go with him, but I was still helpless in this new body. I tried to tell the nurses what Eddie really was, but none of them seemed to understand that he'd murdered my mother. But I cared.

It was after five when he came into the nursery to fetch me. I waited until he stood over the crib and I could smell his whiskey breath. ***"I'm gonna kill you, Eddie."***

Once more I saw the reaction as his eyes glazed over. He probably drank too much. I gurgled and gave my cute baby act for the nurses.

"This kid's not normal. She can talk." Eddie's voice cracked.

"Oh, Mr. Hutchins," the older nurse, the one I called Granny, laughed, clucking her tongue. "Of course, she's normal."

"You don't understand. The kid talked to me."

Granny laughed. "Oh, Mr. Hutchins. All new parents think their baby's special. But I assure you, little Jane won't be talking for several month's yet."

"Her name ain't Jane," Eddie looked like he was going to swing at the nurse. "Her name's Jennifer."

Granny shook her head, putting me down as she opened the chart. "You wrote the name yourself." She showed him a copy of my birth certificate.

Eddie blanched.

I cooed and smiled.

Granny picked me up again, wrapping me in the blanket. She handed me to him.

"I'm going to kill you, Eddie. Just like you murdered her." I stared directly at him and knew he -- and only he -- could hear me.

"Jeez! I need a drink."

"Careful, Mr. Hutchins," Granny warned. "You'll drop her." She paused, taking me away from him. "Are you sure you can take care of her."

He picked me up gingerly. I stared without blinking at him and thought how much I hated him.

Weeks turned into months.

Eddie hired a nurse to take care of me so that he wouldn't have to bother. I was happy that he didn't come near me, didn't try to touch me.

Sometimes I'd laugh and smile. Sometimes I'd pretend to be his loving daughter. But other times, when he'd be drinking, I loved speaking my mind to his.

"I'm gonna kill you, Eddie. Just like you killed my mother." He would blanch and then I'd take it a step further, drawing Mommy's voice from memory.

"Eddie, I swear. This baby is yours. I love you, Eddie. I loved you."

Eddie would grow pale and drop whatever was in his hand — usually a drink. He'd flee my room and not return for several days.

As I got older and began to talk, it seemed wisest to bide my time.

Gradually, Eddie forgot about my threat. Probably, he thought it was just the alcohol talking. But I didn't forget.

I waited and waited. One day, my chance would come.

"D'ya always gotta have a book in hand, kid?"

I smiled. I knew it irked him. "But I like to read, Daddy. Didn't Mommy like to read too?"

I'd just shrug. Unnerved, he'd head off for the nearest bar. I wasn't strong enough yet, but the time was coming closer. I would get my revenge. Only I didn't know how.

***

The older I got, the more I looked like my mother. I grew my hair long, like she had.

Eddie never said anything but I knew my resemblance to her unbalanced him.

It was on my sixteenth birthday that I found the trunk of old clothes stuffed in the back closet. I knew they had belonged to my mother.

Other kids had parties for their sixteenth birthdays, but then other kids didn't have a father who'd killed their mother.

It didn't take long for me to find the flowery print dress Mom had worn on the day she died. It billowed out about my waist because of course she'd been pregnant with me then.

I knew Eddie would be home soon. Finding the Mozart record, I sat down on the rocking chair and waited.

Twilight turned to darkness and I continued to sit.

It was after midnight when I heard the sound of his steps in the hall.

Waiting in the bedroom, I let the motion of the rocker soothe me as the outer door opened and closed.

"Where the hell you get that record, kid?"

He was drunk -- just like before. I didn't answer but allowed the spirit of my mother to enter me and then I stood, silhouetted by the moonlight as he opened the door.

"Eddie, I love you. Eddie -- "It was her voice I spoke in, and her face I took on as I walked slowly toward him, pleased with the shocked look on his face.

"Eddie, why'd you have to be so cruel. Why'd you have to kill me? I loved you, Eddie."

With each step I took toward him, he took several back. I don't even think he realized how near the window was to him. The look of horror on his face was worth every moment of my life on this earth plane with him.

He took yet another step backward -- falling through the open window that I had waiting for him.

I walked to the window and looked down five floors below at the twisted remains of the body which had been my father.

The police and doctor who came with my call were as nice as could be. Everyone in town had known about Eddie's drinking problem -- and no one suspected anything.

"I'll report this as an accident, Miss Hutchins," the doctor said.

I looked up at him and realized he was the same one who had delivered me.

"Thank you, doctor." I paused, waiting a moment as the words sunk in. "You knew, he was never the same after my mother died."

The doctor turned to me, startled. I knew he was wondering how I knew my father before.

I merely smiled.

The End

In the following script example, I used a lot of voice over (V. O.), which really is supposed to be kept at a minimum. But if you see the short film, you will see how we changed and shortened it for the short film.

Please see my trailer for *The Unborn* at http://www. internationalmovietrailerfestival. com/all–trailers/unborn15

Please check out the actual short of ***THE UNBORN*** at

https://itunes. apple. com/us/movie/the–unborn/id583046946

There is a small fee of $2. 99 but a % of the profits goes to a Domestic Violence shelter.

THE UNBORN SCRIPT—NOTE THAT THE MARGINS ON THE DIALOGUE ARE OFF.

INT. DARKNESS OF THE WOMB — NIGHT

LUB DUB of a heart beat as the blood WHOOSHES by.

INT. DARKNESS OF A BARELY LIT ROOM — NIGHT

CREAKING OF THE ROCKING CHAIR, back and forth, back and forth as JANE, 23, sweet and fresh faced contented young woman

HUMS a lullaby. Music from Mozart plays in the background.

Light from a passing car illuminates JANE, long dark hair,

slender, pretty and very much pregnant. Jane rubs her stomach gently.

She continues to hum and rock. Puts her hands on her 8 month swollen belly.

JANE

I'm going to make such a good

mother for you. You are so

special. I --

FOOTSTEPS POUND UP STAIRS.

Jane pauses her chair mid stroke.

DOORKNOB TURNS.

Jane stops rocking. Holds her breath. She turns toward the door not knowing what to expect.

DOOR SLAMS open, vibrating against the wall.

She turns in fear.

INT. STUDIO APARTMENT OF EDDIE AND JANE -- DAY

Jane lays in bed. GROANS. Turns on her side. A shiner on

her left eye.

On the bedside stand are flowers.

Jane looks at the flowers and the crude card.

CARD:

Forgive me Sweet Pie.

JANE

smiles.

PHONE RINGS

MARTIN

You okay, Janey?

JANE

He didn't know what he was doing.

MARTIN

He's hurting you. He's . . . he's

DOOR KNOB TURNS.

JANE

No, he . . . I'll talk to you later.

She hangs up quickly as Eddie comes in bearing a breakfast tray.

EDDIE

Hey. You okay, babe?

(sets the tray down)

Here. Let me do that.

(puts ice pack on her eye)

She shrinks back as if afraid of being hit.

EDDIE

If you hadn't . . .

JANE

I shouldn't have talked back to

you.

EDDIE

And you know, you don't do that.

His fingers caress under her chin.

JANE

(nods)

The baby kicked today. You want to

feel?

EDDIE

(touches her belly)

Won't be much longer now. Maybe

he'll come out with a wrench in his

hand.

INT. DARKNESS OF THE WOMB -- CONTINUOUS

Baby is curled in her placenta.

INT. STUDIO APARTMENT OF EDDIE AND JANE -- DAY

Eddie leans over Jane, touching her face with love, feeling a father's pride. He touches her stomach.

EDDIE

Why the hell isn't he kicking for me?

JANE

It's a girl.

(on his reaction)

At least that's what the doctor

said.

The flowers and vase he brought crash to the floor.

Jane breaks out in sobs.

Eddie storms out of the room as Jane looked glazed at the broken vase and the food over the bed.

INT. DARKNESS OF THE WOMB -- CONTINUOUS

Baby curled in her placenta, her eyes open.

INT. STUDIO APARTMENT OF EDDIE AND JANE -- MOMENTS LATER

Jane rubs her stomach.

JANE

It's okay, baby.

Jane crawls from the bed and tries to clean up the mess.

Stripping the dirty bed, and still sobbing, she goes over to the CD player and puts on her Mozart.

INT. BEDROOM AREA -- A FEW HOURS LATER

Jane emerges from the shower, sans make up. She goes to the make up counter where everything has been put neatly in alphabetical order by Eddie. She accidently knocks a jar from its aligned space.

Hastily, she looks around, fearful that Eddie might notice. She nudges it back into place.

She wipes the fog off the mirror.

Her bruises from the day before are clearly visible. She frowns and begins applying make up. It's not covering it up. She puts on more and more. The thick make up is now more obvious than the bruise.

She speaks in a mantra to herself.

JANE

I love my husband. I do love him.

EXT. DARKNESS OF A BARELY LIT ROOM -- LATER

Across the street the night lights of the liquor store go on and off as the hours pass.

Jane sits in the rocking chair, going back and forth as she repeats her mantra. She's lost in thought.

The dinner table is perfectly set. The candles have burned
low. She anxiously watches the street.

INT. STUDIO APARTMENT OF EDDIE AND JANE -- DAYBREAK

Jane has fallen asleep in the rocker. Her face is starting to show black and blue. She wakes and stares across the street.

PHONE RINGS.

JANE

(dulled)

No, he's not here.

MARTIN

You okay?

JANE

Yeah. Sure.

(forces a laugh)

MARTIN

I meant what I said. You're running

out of time --

JANE

(alarmed)

Martin --

MARTIN

You need to leave him.

Listen . . . listen . . .

JANE

And who's going to take care of me.

You?

MARTIN

My mama, she'll . . . I don't know.

Jane, you have to leave --

JANE

And who's going to take care of me?

You?

MARTIN

I . . . you have to get out of there

JANE

I can't. He'd find me if I did.

MARTIN

Jane, the baby --

FOOTSTEPS OUTSIDE THE DOOR.

JANE

He's . . . He's . . . I have to go.

(abruptly hangs up)

The door opens.

Jane turns expectantly and starts to rise as the door opens.

She wears a long flowery skirt and long sleeved blouse. Her
hair is tied back with a bow.

JANE

That was just . . .

EDDIE

I know who it was.

JANE

Martin just called to --

EDDIE

Sit down, Bitch. I'm through with
you and your lies.

He advances toward her.

JANE

Eddie, please. The baby.

He wipes a clean surface and looks at his finger, checking for dust.

Well, you get the idea. Since the formatting of this little script is not correct, I'm not going to continue it here. There are plenty of places for you to read scripts and look at as I've mentioned in the earlier chapters.

PAGE SET UP

THIS UPPER LEFT AREA IS FOR YOUR ADDRESS

CONTACT INFO AND WORD COUNT

This is how a page is set up.

TITLE, (CENTERED)

YOUR NAME (CENTERED UNDER TITLE)

CHAPTER ONE

INDENT FIVE, DOUBLE SPACE, NO EXTRA SPACE BETWEEN PARAGRAPHS.

ALWAYS PUT A HEADER WITH YOUR PAGE NUMBERS AND NAME OR TITLE

"Oh, I most certainly shall." She waved them goodbye as the pair swam toward the opposite shore.

As they neared the rocks in the center of the river, the sound grew louder until it was there . . . in front of them . . . one of the most beautiful waterfalls Lydia had ever seen. "Oh my Lord!"

"Do you think . . . ?" She asked William.

"I'm getting out the map now."

They climbed onto the other side and stared at the white water rushing down. "I've only seen this in my books," William said. "I am sure this is what Papa meant." He unrolled the scroll. "Here. See. There is the rock that we are on now."

"And there is the waterfall. But there must be hundreds like this on an island of this size."

REFERENCES

Here are some of my favorite books for screenwriting. Many can be purchased at The Writer's Store in Burbank (www.writersstore.com). They also have writing supplies like brads and washers, as well as copies of screenplays.

Iglesias, Karl, Writing for Emotional Impact, Wingspan Press, 2005

Iglesias, Karl, The 101 Habits of Highly Successful Screenwriters, Avon, Adams Media Corp, 2001

Wellman, Wendell, A Writer's Roadmap, 2002

Field, Syd, Screenplay: The Foundations of Screenwriting, NY, Dell Publishing, 1994

Cook, Marshall, Freeing Your Creativity: A Writer's Guide, Writer's Digest Press, 1992

Campbell, Joseph and Moyers, Bill, The Power of Myth, NY, Doubleday (1988)

Venis, Linda (ed), Cut To The Chase: UCLA Writer's Program, Gotham Books, 2013

Pyne, Stephen, Voice & Vision: A Guide To Writing History and Other Serious Nonfiction, Harvard University Press, 2011

Edson, Eric, The Story Solution, Michael Wiese Productions, 2011

Vogler, Christopher; McKenna, David, Memo From the Story Department, Michael Wiese Productions, 2011

Riley, Christopher, The Hollywood Standard (2nd ed), Michael Wiese Productions

Egri, Lajos, The Art of Dramatic Writing, NY, Simon & Schuster, Inc (1960)

Alessandra, Pilar, The Coffee Break Screenwriter: Writing Your Script Ten Minutes At A Time, Michael Wiese Productions

Synder, Blake, Save The Cat and Save The Cat Goes To The Movies, Michael Wiese Productions

Brewer, Robert Lee, Writer's Digest Guide to Self-Publishing, Writer's Digest, 2013.

Schmidt, Victoria Lynn, 45 Master Characters, Writer's Digest, 2012

Writing Fiction Series–Plot and Structure, Theme & Strategy Description & Setting, Characters, Emotion and Viewpoint, Revision and Self–editing, etc. Writer's Digest Books, www.writersdigestshop.com/write–great–fiction

Edelstein, Linda, Dr., Writer's Guide to Character Traits, Writer's Digest Books, 2006

Stevens and Banon, The Book of Poisons, Writer's Digest Books. 2011

Other great books can be found at The Writer's Digest Bookstore; The Writer's Store in Burbank , California; and Michael Wiese Productions. All have online access.

Go online and read the Scroggins' Reports, Deadline Hollywood, The Wrap, Hollywood Reporter, Variety (both have online version.)

Check into ISA (International Screenwriters Association.)

If you are in Hollywood, attend events at the Writer's Guild, Breaking Into Hollywood, Hollywood Networking Breakfast, The Zicree Supermentor Table, Women In Film, Alameda Writer's Group, and others.

SELF-PUBLISHING RESOURCES

A few of the companies to investigate if you decide to self–publish

Abbott Press	www.abbottpress.com
Amazon Create Space	www.createspace.com
Book Baby	www.bookbaby.com
Wise Ink, Creative Publishing	www. wiseinkpub.com
Pubslush	www. pubslush.com/
Wave Cloud	www. wavecloud.com
Balboa Press	www. balboapress.com

There are many more out there, but compare and see what you get. Some not only edit your material, but assist with distribution, as well. (The latter is one of the hardest things for writers to do themselves.)

Now that you have read this whole book, I expect you to write wonderful stories. Write what you are passionate about and don't let anyone ever tell you that you cannot succeed. DON'T LET REJECTION GET YOU DOWN, BE PERSISTENT AND CONTINUE TO BE CREATIVE.

If Anyone Tells you that you are not a writer, prove them wrong. Sit down and write! You can do it. Have faith in yourself. If those moments of self doubt overwhelm you, remind yourself that you are a writer.

APPENDIX

TRAITS TO PICK

aberrant
academic
accepted
accepting
accomplished
ace
activist
adamant
aimless
airy
anarchistic
artful
artificial
artistic
authoritative
available
average
adaptive
adroit
adventurous
aesthetic
affected
affectionate
afraid
aggressive
agreeable
alarmed
alcoholic
alert
alienated
allusive
analytical
analytical
ashamed
anarchistic
angelic
angry
animalistic
animated
annoying
affable
antagonistic
antiquated
anxious
asexual
authentic
arrogant
braggart
brainy
breathtaking
Buddha
buff
buffoon
bulky
bored
bouncy
calm
canny
cloddish
clowning
clueless
coarse
civil

chutzpah
Christ–like
chivalrous
cherubic
childlike
chilly
cheerful
cheesecake
chattering
cheesy
charming
chaste
changeable
changeling
charismatic
catty
cavalier
ceremonious
caring
care giver
composed
concentrating
congenial
confused
contradictory
convict
controlled
contrary
approachable
argumentative
aristocratic
ascetic
jovial
joyful
judged
judgmental
junior
junkie
just
kaleidoscope
keen
kid
kidding
kind
king
know nothing
knowing
knucklehead
mortified
motivated
mournful
moved
moving
muddled
muddy
mule
multiple personalities
murmuring
musical
muted
myopic
mysterious
mythic
man of the world
manacled
manageable
manic
maniac
manipulated
many interests
martyr
marginal
masquerader
master
masturbatory
meandering
nonfunctional
nonpartisan

nonplused	neutral	nonbeliever
nonsensical	nice	nonchalant
non sequitur	nice girl	nonconformist
normal	nice guy	nonentity
nosy	nervous	nonexistent
nubile	negligent	nearsighted
notable	neglected	nebbish
notorious	nihilistic	necromancer
nuisance	nimble	natural
numb	nitwit	naughty
numbskull	no good	nautical
nut	noble	narrow
nymphet	noble-minded	narcissistic
needful	nobody	narcotized
needy	nocturnal	nymphomaniac
nervous breakdown	noisy	
neurotic	nonaccepting	

There are many more traits you can use. Make up your own combinations of traits and list them as you recall them.

There are more traits listed in the Writer's Digest Book, Character Traits.

CPSIA information can be obtained at www.ICGtesting.com
Printed in the USA
BVOW11s1949210814

363665BV00007B/126/P